The Classroom Behavior Manual

The Classroom Behavior Manual

How to Build
Relationships with Students,
Share Control, and
Teach Positive Behaviors

Scott Ervin

Alexandria, Virginia USA

1703 N. Beauregard St. • Alexandria, VA 22311-1714 USA
Phone: 800-933-2723 or 703-578-9600 • Fax: 703-575-5400
Website: www.ascd.org • Email: member@ascd.org
Author guidelines: www.ascd.org/write

Ranjit Sidhu, *CEO & Executive Director*; Penny Reinart, *Chief Impact Officer*; Genny Ostertag, *Managing Director, Book Acquisitions & Editing*; Allison Scott, *Senior Acquisitions Editor*; Julie Houtz, *Director, Book Editing*; Megan Doyle, *Editor*; Thomas Lytle, *Creative Director*; Donald Ely, *Art Director*; Masie Chong, *Graphic Designer*; Keith Demmons, *Senior Production Designer*; Kelly Marshall, *Production Manager*; Shajuan Martin, *E-Publishing Specialist*

Copyright © 2022 Scott Ervin. All rights reserved. It is illegal to reproduce copies of this work in print or electronic format (including reproductions displayed on a secure intranet or stored in a retrieval system or other electronic storage device from which copies can be made or displayed) without the prior written permission of the publisher. By purchasing only authorized electronic or print editions and not participating in or encouraging piracy of copyrighted materials, you support the rights of authors and publishers. Readers who wish to reproduce or republish excerpts of this work in print or electronic format may do so for a small fee by contacting the Copyright Clearance Center (CCC), 222 Rosewood Dr., Danvers, MA 01923, USA (phone: 978-750-8400; fax: 978-646-8600; web: www.copyright.com). To inquire about site licensing options or any other reuse, contact ASCD Permissions at www.ascd.org/permissions or permissions@ascd.org. For a list of vendors authorized to license ASCD e-books to institutions, see www.ascd.org/epubs. Send translation inquiries to translations@ascd.org.

ASCD® is a registered trademark of the Association for Supervision and Curriculum Development. All other trademarks contained in this book are the property of, and reserved by, their respective owners, and are used for editorial and informational purposes only. No such use should be construed to imply sponsorship or endorsement of the book by the respective owners.

All web links in this book are correct as of the publication date below but may have become inactive or otherwise modified since that time. If you notice a deactivated or changed link, please email books@ascd.org with the words "Link Update" in the subject line. In your message, please specify the web link, the book title, and the page number on which the link appears.

PAPERBACK ISBN: 978-1-4166-3078-4   ASCD product #122033   n2/22
PDF E-BOOK ISBN: 978-1-4166-3079-1; see Books in Print for other formats.
Quantity discounts are available: email programteam@ascd.org or call 800-933-2723, ext. 5773, or 703-575-5773. For desk copies, go to www.ascd.org/deskcopy.

Library of Congress Cataloging-in-Publication Data
Name: Ervin, Scott, author.
Title: The classroom behavior manual : how to build relationships with students, share control, and teach positive behaviors / Scott Ervin.
Description: Alexandria, Virginia USA : ASCD, [2021] | Includes bibliographical references and index.
Identifiers: LCCN 2021042031 (print) | LCCN 2021042032 (ebook) | ISBN 9781416630784 (Paperback) | ISBN 9781416630791 (PDF)
Subjects: LCSH: Classroom management--United States--Handbooks, manuals, etc. | School discipline--United States--Handbooks, manuals, etc.
Classification: LCC LB3013 .E72 2021 (print) | LCC LB3013 (ebook) | DDC 371.102/40973--dc23
LC record available at https://lccn.loc.gov/2021042031
LC ebook record available at https://lccn.loc.gov/2021042032

30 29 28 27 26 25 24 23 22 21   1 2 3 4 5 6 7 8 9 10 11 12

To Jessica
God only knows what I'd be without you.

The Classroom Behavior Manual

1

A Dramatic Proposition

Fifteen minutes into my first day of teaching, blood splattered across my face.

The day had started peacefully enough. I arrived to substitute in a 5th grade classroom. School started at 7 a.m., and my students for the day appeared to be sleeping. I began teaching, even though no one was listening. Things were going better than I had anticipated.

Then it happened.

While standing, chalk in hand, next to what we called a "blackboard," I heard a commotion somewhere outside the room. I turned quizzically toward my newly acquired students, and one boy in the front row rolled his eyes, exasperated with my slow comprehension, and explained the situation: "It's a fight."

I sprang into action, sprinting full speed out of the classroom and leaving 25 5th graders to educate themselves. Following the noise, I ran into a small, smelly room. I, a male substitute teacher on his first day, had just run into the girls' bathroom. So far, so good.

I immediately came upon two 6th graders. One girl was fully on her back, her legs furiously attempting to pedal-kick a long-limbed girl who had maneuvered around the kicking action and was enthusiastically beating the snot out of the first girl's face. Blood was flying everywhere, and as I grabbed Punching Girl's shoulders to pull her off Kicking Girl, an inexplicably large amount of blood flew from the fist of Punching Girl, landing on my face and neck.

Once I had separated Punching Girl from Kicking Girl, a female staff member walked into the room and yelled, "What the hell are you doing?!" Looking back, I think she might have been talking to me.

As I remember it, the staff member walked with the girls to the office and I went back to the classroom. I wiped the blood off myself with a dry paper towel and attempted to teach. I was never asked about the incident.

As it turned out, my adventure in the bathroom went only slightly better than the rest of the day. Strangely, my heroics in the girls' restroom did little to impress my newfound class. Mostly asleep before the fight, once I returned from my adventure, they had all woken up. A majority of the students refused to sit in their desks, or work, or be quiet, or be pleasant to each other, or not swear at me. Breaking up another fight in the classroom immediately before dismissal bookended the day nicely.

When I received the 4:30 a.m. robocall for a kindergarten substitute position the next morning, I gladly accepted. Fifth and 6th grade bathroom fight club officiating would have to wait, at least for a day. Kindergarten: how hard could it possibly be? Kindergartners were what, 5 years old?

My second day was going to be so much better than my first.

Like the previous posting, the school for day number two was in a rough part of town. Dilapidated homes and boarded-up storefronts surrounded a sturdy but aging school building. I checked in with an unenthused school secretary.

While the neighborhood and school office staff were less than welcoming, the kindergarten room, my home for the day, was like a scene from a Candy Land board game. It was fantastically colorful and well decorated. The space was perfectly clean and nicely organized. Exhaustive, detailed lesson plans were laid out neatly. They expressly described each moment of the day: how to turn in work, where to sit, how to line up for lunch. The day's materials were arranged at right angles on the teacher's desk and reading tables. Most important, there were clearly stated rules on the board next to a color-coded, card-based behavior chart, with each student's name printed neatly on a transparent plastic pocket holding three cards.

I had hit the substitute teacher jackpot. This was going to be a piece of cake! They had tested me the previous day, but the Gods of Education were smiling down upon me now. With every possible angle and loose end already taken care of by what appeared to be the best teacher in the history of the world, I casually perused the day's lesson plans before confidently leaning back in my chair and waiting for the day to begin.

Things began as I had hoped they would. Three rather timid small souls wandered through the door, wondering who I was and what I was doing there. This was a welcome, healthy reaction to seeing a substitute teacher in the classroom.

It was also the last normal event of the day.

A guttural yell worthy of a battlefield charge rang out as a child with an angry, furrowed brow barreled into Candyland. The complete lack of a reaction from the other students to this feral lunatic should have tipped me off as to what I was dealing with, but I immediately walked into the hallway and asked a teacher, whom I had not yet met, what had happened in the hallway to have triggered this student into exhibiting such rage. The teacher, looking confused, peered into my room and said, "Oh, that's just Robert."

I stared at the teacher, stunned.

"He's always like that."

It felt like the wind had been kicked out of my chest. And it was about to get worse.

"Just wait until you meet David."

You've got to be kidding me.

I didn't meet David right away. We started without him, which was a great relief, since Robert was walking around the room punching people, grabbing things out of their hands and throwing them. At one point, he and another student squared off, prizefighter style, in the corner of the room. I separated them. Keep in mind, I had not yet had time to introduce myself to anyone. I was too busy running around stopping kids from injuring each other or destroying the room. Robert's entry into the room seemed to have caused a switch to be flipped in the minds of the previously inert students. I had heard horror stories about teachers having to run around "putting out fires." I wasn't putting out fires. I was in the middle of a fire . . . and burning.

One boy kept yelling that he was about to "lose his mind up in here." One girl was crying hysterically for a reason that I could not begin to understand. It is possible that she had been punched in the face. There is a very good chance that I would not have noticed. There was too much going on to be able to know what happened. One boy acted as Robert's sidekick, walking next to him as he whispered excitedly in his ear. Robert was still yelling at the top of his lungs and still throwing things and punches. The well-crafted lesson plans lay neglected as I ran around the room and dove across desks to prevent child-on-child violence and property destruction. The secretary came over the loudspeaker to ask for the attendance that I had "forgotten" to send. I remember thinking, "If I turn to find the attendance paper, one of these kids is going to be killed."

Then David walked in.

Fantastic.

I will never forget how he walked into the room with a bizarre smile on his face, looked at me, then, like a moth to flame, still smiling broadly, went immediately to the only person doing her morning work in the room, took her paper, crumpled it up, and threw it in the garbage.

I began using both of my behavior management skills: screaming and yelling. Neither had any effect. David and Robert wandered around the room. Robert hurt people, and David took their stuff. Kids continued to cry, threaten, bait each other, and run out of the room. I tried pulling kids' cards. No one cared, except for one boy who, when I pulled his final card, quickly evacuated the classroom. Thank goodness, David was kind enough to go looking for him, even though I asked him to please, please God, not do that.

I called the principal to remove students four separate times that day. I could have called 30 times. By the third removal, she was not pleased. Each student would come back a half-hour after they left, and immediately go back to doing whatever it was that got them sent to the office in the first place.

I didn't get to more than 30 minutes of the beautifully crafted lesson plans that had been left by the teacher—a teacher for whom I now had a lot of questions. I believe that 15 of those minutes of instruction occurred during the brief period of time when both Robert and David were in the principal's office.

After seven of the worst hours of my life, the children were gone. I cannot fully express the amount of helplessness that one feels after attempting a job they always wanted to do and failing completely. The profound defeat was overwhelming—and was somehow made worse by the fact that the people who just defeated me were 3 feet tall.

I slowly shuffled out of the classroom and down the hallway. Tired, dehydrated, and done, I turned the corner into the office as the school secretary spoke. "Here's your sub now," she said to a woman with her back to me.

The leader of the class that had just ripped through my soul turned around. My first thought was that she looked like I felt. She was a young, tired-looking woman. I guessed that she was around my age. Her eyes looked sad and anxious as she clutched a water bottle while saying words that I didn't expect: "I'm so sorry."

She wasn't trying to be funny or flippant. She was expressing sincere empathy for what she knew I had just endured.

"What in the world just happened to me?" I exhaled. I put my hands on the counter between myself and the school secretary and slowly collapsed on top of the linoleum, extending my outreached arms across the counter. If I had not still been in shock, I think I might have started crying. "They were completely out of control. How in the world do you control those kids?" I asked.

She laughed a slow, sad laugh. "Who said I can control those kids? Your guess is as good as mine. I took today off for a mental health day. I'm just here for an Intervention Assistance Team meeting."

"How do you stay sane? Is it really like that every day?"

"I wasn't in there with you, but I am guessing it is pretty much the same. I'm sorry you had to deal with them today. I just needed a break. And I don't stay sane. This is my last year teaching. I'm quitting. I'm done. It's my second year. I have no idea how I'm going to make it to the end of the year. I taught 5th grade last year and it was horrible. I thought kindergarten would be easier, but it's not."

I was stunned.

"But your room, it's so perfect . . . you've got the rules up . . . and the cards . . . doesn't that stuff help?"

"It worked great for the first morning on the first day, and then all hell broke loose in the afternoon. I've been in hell ever since."

"What happened? What happened at the end of the morning that made them act like that?"

I got the idea that this question would have offended her if she had any kind of respect for me or my opinion. She let out what could be described as a cross between a sigh and an exasperated chuckle.

"You mean, what did I do to mess them up in my first three hours with them? Look, what you saw today—they came in like that. A lot happens to these kids before they show up on the first day of kindergarten."

I felt bad for asking the question, but I pressed on. I needed help. I wanted answers. "Can you tell me anything that actually works in getting these kids to do what they're supposed to do?"

She picked up a box of files and started walking toward the door as she spoke. "Look, I really am sorry to put you through what you went through today, and I don't want to be this negative. This isn't the person I want to be, which is why I'm getting out. But I have to be honest with you: nothing works."

"Nothing Works"

Those words haunted me, and with every day of the several months that I continued to work as a substitute teacher, they proved to be more and more correct. Every day,

I failed to get students to be cooperative, no matter how much or how loudly I yelled. Every day, I saw the teachers and principals around me failing in very much the same way. Even the most experienced educators were often no better off than I was. Even those who were doing all of the right things to elicit positive behaviors—clearly stating rules, using consequences, having good lesson plans, praising positive behaviors, and having routines set up for how to manage the room—even those teachers had rooms that were out of control. It seemed that nothing was working for anyone.

During my master's program observations of different kinds of schools, suburban, rural, and private, I saw a similar dynamic. Students may not have been as difficult to control, but in every class, there always seemed to be at least one, but usually a few, "tougher" students for whom traditional discipline strategies were ineffective, and they often seemed to make the class's general behavior worse. These few students appeared to be able to take over most classrooms, leaving their teachers at a loss as to what to do.

"Nothing works." Even in the face of the mounting affirming evidence, I still wondered, how could this be true? After all, students had been around forever, teachers had been around forever, teachers who teach teachers to teach had been around forever, and the problem of having to get students to use positive, prosocial behaviors had been around forever. How could educators not know *exactly* how to get students to act in a way that made the classroom better, schools better, society better, and the students themselves better?

During the several months I spent in perhaps 20 different school buildings as a substitute teacher, and then the two years I taught in my own classrooms, I was determined to figure out what worked. To be clear, my open-minded curiosity had no impact on my own behavior management deficits. I continued to yell and attempt to intimidate my students, and every day I drove home defeated, exhausted, and distraught.

"These Kids . . ."

What made the situation more frustrating was that, almost every day, I was asking for advice for how to manage behaviors, just like I did on that second day of my teaching career. And when actual advice was given—something beyond "nothing works"—it was almost always the same, and it often started with the same two words:

"*These kids . . .*"

I was searching for how to manage the behaviors of all kids, but the answers I received to my questions were answers for how to manage a *certain kind* of student.

As I was in a district that served a very high percentage of students who were poor and members of minority groups, what was being communicated was clear, and the advice was almost always similar: *"These kids need to be dealt with sternly. . . . They don't get a lot of love at home, so they won't respond to it well at school. . . . Show them who is boss. . . . Get up in their faces. . . . Don't give them an inch. . . . They won't take you seriously unless you yell. . . . They only respect strength. . . . You have to be tough, or they'll run all over you."*

In my interviews for teaching jobs, two years in a row, I was told by two different principals to "never smile in front of students." It was made clear to me that this was a condition of my employment.

Even then, I knew that these instructions on how to deal with "these kids" went directly against what we know about how human brains work. The human brain cannot effectively work, learn, and function when faced with fear and threats. The human brain cannot function until the organism in which it is vested has been able to establish a functional environment whereby the organism can have all safety, control, and love needs met.

Even then, I knew that this advice about "these kids" was classist and racist. I think we all did.

But we took the advice anyway. We took this advice for the same reason someone wandering for days in the desert will eventually drink the sand: there was no alternative. Behavior management advice given in college either didn't exist or was wholly inadequate to the point of being insulting. Write good lesson plans and there won't be any misbehavior? Really? Have consequences for misbehavior? Great. What do those look like? Praise students? Huh. Why do the most difficult students act worse when I praise them? Have routines for classroom tasks and clearly define rules? Great. What do I do when students refuse to follow rules and procedures? What then?

The terrible trick that is played on educators is that this ineffective behavior management advice is not only ineffective with all kids, it is particularly ineffective with "these kids." It is so unsophisticated, and so dismissive of the effects of trauma, that it is least effective with the students who need it the most! Tragically, this often leads educators to feel hopeless about their ability to help "these kids."

The ugly truth is that when this advice causes you to crash and burn over and over and over, most people, in their desperation to do the job that most of us have been dreaming of doing since we were kids—will take any advice offered, especially when everyone around us has that advice reinforced by principals and fellow teachers every day.

The truth is that we were all really good people doing very bad things to students. We had all voluntarily chosen to work in that district, where a very high percentage of our families dealt with high rates of generational poverty and our students experienced much higher than average rates of trauma. We wanted to help the students who needed us the most. Why were we yelling at them all day long? Why were we working ourselves to death in an attempt to scare and intimidate students into submission? Why? Because we did not know what else to do.

This horrifying way of working with students was able to exist in the vacuum caused by not having quality ways to manage behaviors available to us. Cumulatively, it turned the schools that I saw into machines that accidentally reinforced negative, antisocial behaviors. In this vacuum, these schools, through no fault of their own, systematically trained students to get what they wanted (attention, avoidance, or control) through negative behaviors. Of course, this is not the fault of the students, who depend on educators knowing how to manage behaviors. It is also not the fault of the educators, who depend on universities to teach them how to manage behaviors.

As I was working through my master's degree program, I knew and socialized with teachers who taught in every kind of school with every kind of student. We often discussed a similar trend: the "these kids" phenomenon also enveloped schools that only had a small number of "these kids." To be fair, students who grow up in generational poverty do tend to have more adverse childhood experiences (ACEs). These traumatic experiences give students a higher chance of having attention problems and a higher tendency toward behaviors that many consider "impulsive," among a tragically long list of other negative effects (American Academy of Pediatrics, 2014). Many of these behaviors have been reinforced at home, often before the child's first day of kindergarten. What I noticed (and what I continue to notice now, years later, as a behavioral consultant) in these schools is that many teachers will subscribe to the "these kids" fallacy with students whom they know to have had multiple ACEs: "Johnny is just different, and I need to treat him differently. I need to intimidate Johnny into learning and listening to me."

The irony is that this reaction to a student being perceived as more difficult is the exact *opposite* of what Johnny needs, and will be *especially ineffective* with Johnny *because* he has experienced more trauma than the average student. Students who have had several ACEs, no matter how much money their parents make or what color they are, need to have measures taken to make them feel *more* safe and *less* threatened, not *less* safe and *more* threatened.

The use of intimidation and fear as a means of getting students to be cooperative works the least with "these kids," the ones who are in most need. This is yet another terrible trick played on educators who, once again, may see their own failures as a sign that there is no hope for their most vulnerable students.

What I and other teachers accidentally took part in was a tragic one-two punch: many of these students had an acute sensitivity to these assaults due to their level of trauma, and we assaulted their brains with intimidation and fear. This misstep is a major contributor to the school-to-prison pipeline. Educators are not taught how to manage behaviors, so many accept the "these kids" fallacy out of pure desperation. They internalize the fallacy and attempt to scare and intimidate students into working hard and behaving. When such tactics predictably backfire, educators suspend the students. Tragically, this reinforces the negative behavior, because students who are intimidated and scared every day understandably enjoy getting a break from the intimidation and fear of school. Finally, to get more breaks from intimidation and fear, they use more and more negative behaviors, successfully getting suspended until they are expelled or they drop out. This is the essential motor that runs schools often called "dropout factories."

There are surely other factors contributing to the school-to-prison pipeline, such as the conditions that cause traumas outside school in the first place, but this ubiquitous dynamic is a significant one. The data are clear:

- Half of all students who enter 9th grade with three or more suspensions on their record will drop out of high school (Balfanz, Byrnes, & Fox, 2014).

- *One out of* 11 high school dropouts is currently in prison. For African Americans, the ratio is *one out of four* (Eley, 2009).

- *One out of* 131 *people* in this country is currently sitting in a prison cell (Public Safety Performance Projects, 2009).

- *One out of* 31 *adults* in this country is in jail or prison, on parole, or on probation (Public Safety Performance Projects, 2009).

Students with high ACE scores are failed by ineffective, incomplete, or nonexistent behavior management techniques. These techniques accidentally encourage negative behaviors, causing vulnerable students to repeat, explore, and heighten their behaviors, which leads to suspensions. Suspensions often lead to expulsions or dropping out. Dropping out often leads to prison.

I believe I knew all of this at the time. Still, I continued in my ways for lack of any other ideas. Hurting the students that I wanted to help was destroying me, not to mention destroying them. I knew something had to change.

Approaching a Breaking Point, and Then, a Breakthrough

After having my own classrooms for two successive years, teaching 5th and 1st grades, I knew I was reaching my physical and emotional limit for hurting kids no matter how badly I wanted to help them. As I prepared for another year, this time at a different school with the same set of challenges, I knew one of three things was going to happen. Either I was going to quit after a nervous breakdown, or I was going to get fired for having a nervous breakdown in class and hurting a student, or I was going to learn how to do my job. Since no one had helped me in the first two years of my teaching career, I was skeptical about my chances of avoiding possibilities numbers one or two.

The next year, I began teaching at a school that had just been founded. As a brand-new school, it had a highly advantageous student-to-teacher ratio and a school culture that was carefully and thoughtfully curated. Even though it served a neighborhood that actually had a slightly higher rate of generational poverty than the school in which I had served before, I was able to just barely find my footing as someone who could be successful in getting students to cooperate. Through careful trial and error, as well as some conceptual professional development, I started to notice and act upon new insights: students used slightly more positive behaviors when I was able to build relationships with them, were nicer to me when I was able to share control with them, and decreased the frequency of negative behaviors when I stopped them from getting what they wanted using such behaviors. I started to be able to handle students better than other teachers. Still, what I was doing was sloppy and only somewhat effective: I was having to think too much about "behavior management" while I was teaching. I started to dabble in creating procedures that did the relationship building and control sharing for me, *while I was teaching*, and I started to create strategies that I would later use habitually, without thinking, that would do the same. I felt like I had the necessary foothold now to be able to someday become the teacher I always hoped I could be—though I still had a long way to go.

✢ ✢ ✢ ✢ ✢ ✢ ✢ ✢ ✢ ✢ ✢ ✢

Up until now, I have given you very few, if any, reasons for why you should be reading this book. After all, at this point, all you know about me is that I was very aware that no one had the ability to manage behaviors very well, that I wanted to figure out how to do it, and that I asked a lot of questions about that while suffering through the worst two years of my life.

Here are a couple of other things to know about me that may also discourage you from continuing to read this book:

- *I am not patient, and I have a bad temper.* This may seem like a strange thing for an author to admit in a book that is supposed to teach teachers how to be nice to students.

- *I was not a "good teacher."* My lesson plans were weak. I couldn't write student learning objectives (SLOs) or reading improvement monitoring plans (RIMPs) to save my life, and I couldn't map out curricula. I was disorganized, forgetful, and unable to effectively enter grades into the database on time, monitor progress, or be a good school employee in general.

But here is why you should keep reading: I look at life through a certain kind of lens. I respond to problems by thinking, "This is terrible; I have to make it better." This comes from my innate hardwiring. I was born this way. It's who I am, and it is very annoying to be around—or at least, that's what my wife keeps telling me.

The benefit for you, the reader, is that *every single day* of my teaching career, I have thought, "This is terrible; I have to make it better" while looking at every aspect of my teaching. The reason I was so hopelessly bad at the aforementioned activities was because I knew that there was no way I could even *begin* to teach until I could get students to be cooperative and hard-working, let alone have the time and mental bandwidth to be able to do the mountains of work that educators have to do. I knew, almost instinctively, that I couldn't come close to being able to do everything I needed to do to be a "good teacher" if I couldn't create a positive classroom environment where my students could learn, I could teach, and students would consistently use positive behaviors.

With every day, no matter how successful I was, I thought, just like during the initial dark days, "This is terrible; I have to make it better."

So I did. Every day, I would work at making something that would improve the situation: effective strategies and procedures for building relationships, sharing control, and holding students accountable. And every day, I reviewed what I had made and thought, "This is terrible; I have to make it better," and so those strategies and procedures became more tested, durable, and effective every time I used them.

As a result, I became better than any teacher I had yet seen at building relationships, sharing control, and holding students accountable. I went from relying on prayer as a behavior management tool ("Please, God, don't let Angela be in my class next year") to actually requesting that all of my grade's most difficult students be put on my roster. I was asking for "these kids" be put in my class. Over the decade that I used these strategies and procedures, I did not have to appeal to an administrator for discipline one single time. Not one office referral. Not one suspension. Not one expulsion. The school-to-prison pipeline encountered a serious disruption when it attempted to run through Mr. Ervin's classroom.

As my procedures and strategies became more and more effective, and I became more and more fluent in my use of them, I noticed something amazing: not only did my students use positive behaviors at an incredibly high level, but they were also learning! Both my behavioral *and* academic outcomes were excellent! Even though I was and remain naturally bad at all of the elements of teaching, like writing lesson plans and learning goals, I was able to pay more attention to them because I was no longer drowning in a sea of negative behaviors!

I now have the honor of traveling the country teaching educators these strategies and procedures. I get to hear how the use of these procedures and strategies has saved educators' careers. I get to coach teachers in their classrooms and show them how, the more effectively they use their strategies and procedures, the fewer negative behaviors they have. I get to save educators from having to endure experiences like my first two years of teaching, asking but never getting the necessary means to do my job.

I get to tell them what I learned: that behavior *management* is impossible. It implies that you can *manage* behaviors that are out of control (you can't). What is possible is *behavioral leadership*: the ability, through systematic use of strategy and procedural instruction, to *change* negative behaviors while simultaneously managing all behaviors. A leader creates function *and* oversees the management of it.

A leader must be able to model the behaviors they want to see in the people around them. Without behavioral leadership, it is difficult or impossible to act like the person you want your students to emulate, because you will have to deal with so many negative behaviors that you will not be calm enough to model the positive behaviors you want your students to use. Behavioral leadership allows educators to be the leaders that their students need them to be.

This is why behavioral leadership is a foundational necessity for successful classrooms and instruction. Without behavioral leadership, you can't come close to doing everything you need to do and being the person you need to be in order to be the most effective educator you can be for your students.

Without behavioral leadership, students won't be able to efficiently and sufficiently learn positive behaviors and responsibility. Without behavioral leadership, the school-to-prison pipeline will continue unabated. Without behavioral leadership, students will be spending their days in classrooms that are not as healthy, safe, engaged, supporting, and challenging as they could be. Without behavioral leadership, equal access to education will continue to be impossible. We will continue to use unsophisticated and hurtful behavior management strategies that trigger students with high ACE scores into using negative behaviors that will disrupt learning and lead to suspensions and expulsions. Entrance into the school-to-prison pipeline will continue to be the result.

It is not enough to disrupt the school-to-prison pipeline; it must be destroyed. It is not enough that some students have access to behavioral leadership educators. All students in all schools deserve access to classrooms where the educators know exactly how to build relationships, share control, and hold students accountable for their actions and inactions without anger or haste. Educators who are trained in behavioral leadership can create classrooms where students feel safe and loved, and experience the healthy control they need to be able to function and learn. In these classrooms, students can learn the behaviors and habits necessary to be successful and happy in life.

We can't control or know everything about what happens in the lives of our students when they are not at school. We don't even know what will happen to them after they leave us in the afternoon and before we see them again the next morning. Therefore, we should treat all of our students as if, during that time, they were abused or neglected. Why? Because some of them were. We should treat all students, every day, with the care and love necessary to make sure their school days are as calm, engaging, and educational as they possibly can be.

Did you figure out the trick of behavioral leadership? While behavior management fails all kids—and fails "these kids" more than anyone—behavioral leadership is not only effective with "these kids"; it is effective with all kids! All kids benefit from a calm, kind teacher who builds relationships, shares control, and teaches positive behaviors.

All students—no matter who they are, what has happened to them in their lives, or what they experienced that morning—if treated this way, every day, will feel safe enough, cared for enough, and loved enough to be ready to learn and thrive while they are in your classroom.

All students belong. All students can succeed. The book you are holding is the manual for how to do this.

Let's get started.

2

Before You Begin

Understand the why and the how of this manual.

Several months after I started substitute teaching, I achieved the unthinkable: for the first time, the 5th grade class that I had been teaching for weeks was quiet. I had done it. I had their attention. They looked at me, their eyes wide, their attention rapt, their bodies still, their voices silent.

For 10 seconds.

Then, one snicker chorused and escalated into a classroom filled with belly laughs. Across the room, the desk I had just thrown lay in silent testament to my behavior management skills.

Oops.

Everyone has a breaking point. That day, I hit mine.

I can describe all the events and conditions that led up to my abrupt outburst, but really, I had just one reason for picking up that desk, flinging it into a wall, and proceeding to yell incoherently at an 11-year-old boy: I had no idea what I was doing.

Nothing had changed since the first day that I had arrived to substitute. Nothing worked. I was educated. I was hardheaded. I was committed. I was where I wanted to be.

But nothing worked.

I was broken in. I knew the kids. I knew the school and the community. I recognized the challenging conditions that trailed them into my classroom.

But nothing worked.

I listened. I cared. I tried. I kept showing up.

But nothing worked!

No class I had taken, no degree I had earned, no book I had read had trained me to elicit positive behaviors from students who had been trained to exhibit negative behaviors long before they walked through my door.

I spent the rest of that year and the next year doing the same things I had been doing—minus throwing desks. I tried everything I had been taught: I kept behavior charts, called kids' homes, sent students to the principal's office, issued warnings, posted rules, established routines, praised good behavior, and imposed punishments for bad behavior. I experimented with other methods: I threatened and cajoled, yelled and lectured, begged and bribed, took away lunch time and recess, and kept kids after school.

It was exhausting, debilitating, and entirely ineffective. I was not teaching. Instead, I was simply reinforcing every negative behavior the students had already learned. Something had to change—and that "something" needed to be me.

That's why I wrote this manual.

Why

Fast-forward about 15 years.

It was my favorite time of day. I had just finished my read-aloud—Michael Buckley's *The Unusual Suspects*, from his *Sisters Grimm* series. My students, the toughest in the building, had seamlessly begun their Silent Work procedure. The students had transitioned using the Lock-It-In procedure, one team at a time: first the Butterfly Marines, then the Vikings, the Fireballs, the Sharks, and finally, the Tigers. The students immediately went to work completing their leveled reading group assignment from the previous day.

While they worked—yes, *worked*—I took a few minutes for myself. I sank into my desk chair, rested my chin in my hand, and stared out my open window. It was one of those rare days in May when my classroom was comfortable despite the school's lack of air conditioning. I looked at my students. Some were still working on their assignments, while others had moved on to books of interest that they read silently while sitting at their desks or lying on the carpet.

I thought back to those first years of teaching. I remembered the anger, frustration, and helplessness I had felt. I remembered the lectures, warnings, and threats I had used. I thought about how such tactics had nearly destroyed me. Then, I observed the peaceful, calm environment that I now got to enjoy every day.

The kids hadn't changed. The students with whom I was working were probably even more difficult than the student whose desk I had thrown, so many years before. But I had changed.

I knew what I was doing.

Now, instead of counting down the minutes until the end of the school day like I did during my early years in the classroom, I spent time with my students outside school. I took them to basketball games. I had them dropped off at my house at 5 o'clock in the morning when their parents couldn't arrange other transportation. Each year, I took my class on a field trip to Ohio University, located two hours away.

Now, instead of counting down the days until the end of the year, I cried every June at the thought that I wouldn't be seeing my students again until August—and often, never again. On the last day of school each year, my students huddled in the middle of our classroom with their arms around one another's shoulders. In the middle of the circle, I knelt on the floor and tearfully expressed what I felt about their potential, how much I loved them, and how I would always remember them. Big, tough kids cried with me.

That day, relaxing in my desk chair, I thought about how grateful I was to have saved my career—to have saved my soul—by learning *how* to work with kids, no matter how difficult they were.

It sounds like a Hollywood movie, but it isn't. In movies, teachers have near-magical powers whereby caring is enough. Just by caring about kids, they transform their lives. The caring spills forth in a montage of well-written lines and heart-wrenching scenes—none of which address a single effective way to train students to exhibit positive behavior. The fairy godteacher somehow just reaches them—by caring, by listening, by connecting, by understanding, by standing up for them, by bending the rules, by shaking some sense into them, by confronting their dangerous realities, by using so-called "tough love," by POOF! Hollywood magic.

In real life, it doesn't matter how much you care for kids if you don't know how to get them to use positive behaviors. It just doesn't. It's not that the tens of thousands of teachers who quit every year don't care about kids. It's not that they don't want to be there and do better. They just don't know what they're doing. They can't train students to be people whom they want to be around because they haven't been trained themselves.

But I had learned how to train students.

It was a bittersweet feeling to watch my students that day. That June would be my last June huddling in a circle in the classroom. I had resigned my position as a teacher at Fairborn Primary School. The demands of politicians and bureaucrats who couldn't do my job in a million years had worn me down in a way that even the toughest of my students in those early years had not.

Besides, I had a book to write.

I had learned how to elicit positive behavior from even the most challenging students, and I could—I would—teach those procedures and strategies to other teachers.

Here is the exciting part: if I can do this, *anyone* can do it. I am not an organized person. My lesson plans were weak. I have a temper and I am easily frazzled. But I got my real-life Hollywood ending with my kids. If I can attain this fantastic level of success, you can, too.

That's *why* you need to read this manual.

How

Over the past 20-plus years, I have been a teacher, principal, discipline specialist, superintendent, and behavioral consultant. I have never been a teacher or administrator at a school where the poverty rate was lower than 60 percent. I spent the first decade of my career in the city of Dayton, Ohio, in schools with at least a 90 percent poverty rate. For the last 10 years of my teaching career, I requested to have the most difficult students in my room. The poverty rate of the students in my classroom during that time was never lower than 90 percent. For the last six years of my teaching career, I worked in one of the largest primary schools in the United States, with nearly 450 students in each grade. During that time, I continued to request the most difficult students. One of the years I taught 3rd grade, I had a 95 percent poverty rate in my room, and yet, 95 percent of my students passed the Ohio Third Grade Reading Guarantee. Those numbers are nearly unheard of, especially for a teacher like me who isn't good at writing lesson plans, isn't tremendously organized, and can't do curriculum mapping or write a student learning objective to save his life.

How did I do it? I used specific and explicit procedures and strategies to elicit positive behaviors from students in a calm, assertive way. These prosocial behaviors included (but were not limited to) hard work, treating others with kindness, being courteous, and using an appropriate voice level. After creating these procedures and strategies, 99 percent of students' time in my classroom was spent on task. Students loved being in my classroom, and I loved being with my students, no matter what kind of behaviors they came in exhibiting on the first day. For the last six years of my teaching career, I had students whose combined office referrals for behavioral infractions the previous year numbered in the hundreds. Yet not one time in the last decade of my teaching career did I use an administrator for a disciplinary situation—not one referral, suspension, or expulsion.

This manual details how I accomplished these goals. The following chapters explicitly and systematically teach how to use specific procedures and strategies to create a functional, prosocial classroom environment. The aim of this book is to help schools produce healthy, successful people who work hard, treat others well, and make the world a better place.

A copious amount of research shows that to create a functional, prosocial classroom, students need quality interactions with calm yet assertive teachers who build relationships, develop empathy, share control in healthy ways, hold students accountable through appropriate consequences, and have consistent classroom procedures. Researchers have written extensively on this subject. They are experts at understanding why: *why* do students need empathy? *Why* are relationships important? *Why* do students need a healthy amount of control? But this is not just another *why* book.

This book is a manual. It is a *how* book. It contains procedures and strategies that enable teachers to gain control of their classrooms. A strategy is a plan of action designed to achieve a major or overall aim. Using Learning Opportunities and the Calm Signal fall under this category. Procedures are simply an established way of doing something. Procedures included in this book include the Lock-It-In procedure for effective transitions, the Student Nickname procedure, and the Class Rule procedure, just to name a few.

Through the implementation of these procedures and strategies, this manual teaches how to build relationships, develop empathy, give away control in a healthy way, and hold students accountable through appropriate consequences. Using these tools allows students to think and work in a relaxed environment with the highest standards of behavior, free from anger, threats, punishments, suspensions, and expulsion, and as a consequence, teachers are able to guide their students to become successful, prosocial children who will grow into successful, prosocial adults.

The procedures and strategies taught in this book are organized into two skill sets: building positive relationships with students and sharing control with students in healthy ways.

Building Positive Relationships with Students

I had been taught that building relationships with students was a great way to gain control in the classroom; however, I wasn't specifically taught procedures to build those relationships. I decided to create these procedures myself and developed a way to establish them as routines within the first three weeks of the school year. After those three weeks, I never had to think about them again, because the students themselves maintained them.

The procedures and established routines allowed me to create a classroom where my students loved to be. They knew that no one was going to hurt them. They felt like their classroom was their turf. They knew that we were all on the same team, that we were family.

To be clear, I built relationships by using procedures—not just by "being nice." Being nice to difficult students, by itself, is nearly worthless. Difficult kids will act out more when you go out of your way to be nice. Challenging students usually have trust and self-esteem issues, and they will test you by exhibiting negative behaviors to see if you truly like them and if you are able to place limits on them—something that they desperately need and want.

I have found that it is impossible to build relationships with 25 to 35 students in a classroom just by "winging it." That is, it's impossible to build relationships just by being nice enough in any given situation that you don't damage relationships. My difficult students had experienced too much success getting what they wanted through argument, aggression, and manipulation for me to be able to build a positive relationship while tolerating these negative behaviors.

That's why this manual describes how to build relationships through procedures that train students to exhibit positive behaviors. Establishing these procedures as routines creates an environment where all students feel the safety and ownership necessary for them to be prosocial members of their classroom who are ready to learn.

This manual also explicitly details strategies for building relationships that can be used under specific circumstances. For example, particularly difficult students in functional classrooms may find themselves in the middle of an emotionally positive Bizarro Lecture when they do something particularly wonderful. Effective teachers can use Strategic Noticing to reinforce positive behaviors by noticing them (see Chapter 4), as well as Extreme Respect strategies to model the exemplary behaviors that are expected in a functional classroom.

Used cumulatively, these Relationship-Building Procedures and Strategies are half of the necessary tools for creating a safe, loving, calm, and nurturing environment.

Sharing Control in a Healthy Way

Well-meaning teacher education professors often advise their pre-service teachers to share control with their students. This is good advice, and you'll find that you can either give control to students on your terms, or they will take it on theirs. This is a well-researched dynamic (McCombs, 2010). However, explicit and systematic instruction as to *how* to do this in a classroom has been difficult to find—until now.

When I first started teaching, I had no idea how to share control, or what control I was supposed to share, or when I was supposed to share it. So I ended up doing what most teachers do: I hoarded the control. This is what teachers typically do when they have a large number of difficult students provoking power struggles. With no training, and with no procedures in place, I felt that I had to hold on to as much control as I could because I felt so out of control. Very quickly, I found myself barking orders in a desperate attempt to gain or maintain that control: "Sit down! Be quiet! Stand up! Line up! Work harder! Pay attention!"

It was exhausting at the time, and it is exhausting to think about now.

Every time I took control away from a challenging student, the student tried to get it back; hence, the term "power struggle." Sometimes, students would try to regain control through overt aggression (e.g., swearing at me, throwing a chair). Sometimes, they would use passive aggression (e.g., pretending not to hear me, not turning in assignments). Either way, trying to take control away from my students trapped me in power struggles that I was destined to lose—because you never win a power struggle with a child. That's a fundamental concept we'll come back to in later chapters.

The Control-Sharing Strategies in this manual, such as Gentle Guidance Interventions and Delayed Learning Opportunities (DLOs), are highly effective and allow you to share control in appropriate ways. They are supported and maintained through explicit, systematic procedures through which you elicit the positive behaviors you want by giving away the control you don't need.

This manual teaches you how to establish Control-Sharing Procedures as routines, alongside the Relationship-Building Procedures, in the first three weeks of the school year. After that time, implementation of the procedures will require little effort on your part because, again, the students themselves will maintain the routines. Students take ownership over a classroom environment in which they feel safe and trusted enough to learn.

Consequences Within Procedures

Building relationships and sharing control makes it very likely that even the most difficult students will be cooperative most of the time. However, even the best-behaved students have bad days. When students slip up and forget to follow the procedures, or in the first weeks, when students are more likely to deliberately challenge the procedures, you must deliver appropriate consequences with empathy.

To make it as easy as possible to be calm but assertive, consequences are woven into the procedures themselves. These consequences within the procedures are called Procedural Learning Opportunities or PLOs. By holding students accountable through appropriate consequences, students will learn that, although we love them and will grant them their fair share of control, we are in charge. Consequences for not being cooperative and not following classroom procedures are systematically and explicitly taught throughout this book.

A Realistic Book for Real-World Classrooms

I wrote this book because it was the book that I needed but did not have when I started teaching. I knew that my students needed to work hard, treat me well, and treat one another well. I think I even knew that my students would never behave any better than I did. The conundrum for me was the same problem that other teachers, particularly those working with difficult students, face: you cannot be the teacher you want to be if you do not know how to get your students to exhibit prosocial behaviors in the classroom. Teachers who spend every day dealing with antisocial behaviors cannot themselves sustain the positive behaviors that they want to model for their students. Rather, they end up exhibiting the same negative behaviors that they want to stop, thus perpetuating the cycle of dysfunctional, antisocial behavior.

To gain students' cooperation in the classroom, teachers must create an environment where prosocial, positive, and functional behaviors are consistently used and modeled by both teachers and students. To do so, we need to understand two facts. First, children have a strong need for quality relationships in general and with an authority figure specifically. Second, children, like all people, have a strong need for control and will rebel or resist when their control needs aren't met. I needed a realistic book that taught me how to use Relationship-Building and Control-Sharing Procedures and Strategies in real-world classrooms with real-life students.

So I wrote it.

The Classroom Behavior Manual

Note that the title of this book does not involve the terms "student behavior," "behavior management," or even "behavioral leadership." This manual is not primarily about student behavior. Positive student behaviors are desired outcomes. This manual does not concentrate on outcomes; it concentrates on inputs. The inputs are the educator behaviors: what exactly do educators do to create a prosocial classroom? When you use the strategies and procedures as explicitly taught in this book, student behaviors will be more positive so that educators can be calm and regulated enough to behave in such a way that creates a high "behavioral ceiling," or the behavioral level of the classroom's teachers: students can only aspire to attain the behavioral level of the adults around them. The procedures and strategies in this book will help educators behave like the people they would like their students to become. This is the manual for creating a fully functional environment where everyone's behavior is prosocial, and no one's behavior is antisocial.

Only within this environment can teachers succeed. And only within this environment can students achieve and thrive.

Don't Just Read This Book

Please don't just read this book. It's a manual: use it. Use it to put into place procedures and strategies that allow you to be calm and assertive with even the most difficult students.

Procedures: Go at the Prescribed Pace—or Slower

You may be tempted to try to consume this book's content rapidly and implement every single procedure and strategy immediately. Don't. The best way to use this material is to implement the procedures according to the "First Three Weeks of School" schedule (see page 100). Do not try to go faster than prescribed. You may, however, need or want to go more slowly, because either you are uncomfortable following the schedule, or your school requires more academic accountability during this time. Go at the pace with which you are comfortable. Don't openly defy your administration just to be faithful to the suggestions in this book.

Strategies: Pick and Choose

In contrast to procedures, the strategies outlined in this book can be used as needed or as opportunities arise. I recommend experimenting with one or two strategies per day rather than trying to memorize all of them and deciding which to use on the fly. As a teacher, you already juggle too much information at any given moment.

Here's my advice on how to learn and use the strategies:

1. Read the book.
2. Ignore all strategies you don't want to use. Never use them.
3. Write down each strategy that you like on a sticky note or sheet of paper.
4. For the first two weeks, before you start your school day, choose two strategies to use.
5. Each day, place a note listing the day's strategies on your desk or table.
6. After the first two weeks, start incorporating more strategies each day—or continue to only use two per day, if that's what you're comfortable with.

By the end of the first three weeks, you should have a good command of all the strategies that you want to use so that you can deploy them as needed.

Again, I cannot emphasize enough that you should ignore any strategies and procedures that you don't like or that you feel don't fit your personality, teaching style, students, or class environment. Pick the ones that feel and work best for you.

Keep Doing What You Have Been Doing

This may seem like a strange suggestion for a behavior manual to make. If you have teaching experience, keep using any and all systems and techniques that you feel are effective. Methods and processes that have worked for you in the past may continue to work for you in the future. After all, the entire reason I'm writing this manual is because I have found methods that work. Perhaps you have, too. You may even want to continue to use methods that don't work (and you have plenty of these, or else you would not be reading this book) as a security blanket. Your stress level is an important variable in being able to be empathetic while holding kids accountable. As your confidence in the procedures and strategies grows, and as you see that the consequences within the procedures are far more effective than any other system, you will be able to abandon the less than effective methods that you have been using in an attempt to elicit positive behaviors.

The Behavior Chart: How and When to Throw It Away

One of the most common ineffective means of eliciting positive behaviors is a behavior chart. For most teachers, behavior charts fall squarely in the category of "things I do that I know do not work but that make me feel slightly less out of control."

You can keep using this tactic, if you feel you need it, but as you learn and deploy the procedures and strategies taught in this book, you will eventually find that you can set it aside.

For those who hold on to the behavior chart after the start of a new school year, I offer a particularly effective way to discard it (when you're ready) that will support relationship building with your students:

1.   Wait for a moment when behavior in the room is perfect. A completely silent moment during quiet work time, such as the Silent Work procedure (see Chapter 8), is an optimal moment.

2.   With emotion and volume, say something like this: "Team Awesome [see Class Nickname procedure, Chapter 5], I'm sorry to interrupt you. I'm looking around, and I must tell you that I owe you an apology. Not one of you is causing a problem for anyone. You are being fantastic and taking care of business. I feel like this behavior chart that I have been using is silly. I think that it's for people who can't manage their own behavior, and I see that you can. I'm so sorry that I have been insulting your intelligence by using this thing. It is unnecessary. You all obviously don't need it."

3.   Choose the most difficult student who has been exhibiting the most positive behaviors lately and continue: "Dontonio, would you please rip that thing off the wall?"

4.   Allow each student to throw away any clips or cards that you have been using. Feel free to let them break or tear the cards, clips, or assorted doodads first.

This Book Is Not Another "Thing"

Any teacher who has been around for more than a few years has seen "things" (e.g., curriculum, methods, ideologies, processes) come and go. Many of us have been around long enough to see "things" come, go, and come back again (often with different names). Eventually, many educators (myself included) have stopped trying to learn new "things."

Why have we stopped trying?

- We can't possibly add another "thing" to what we're already required to do.
- We don't have any more room in our brains.
- We know that if we ignore the latest "thing" for long enough, it will go away.

What makes this manual different? "Things" take time and energy away from you. They're distractions that produce few, if any, positive results. They are easily discarded and replaced. This manual is not a "thing" because it does not take time and energy away from you, it does produce positive results, and it cannot be easily discarded by your administrators.

For every minute you spend reading this book and using its procedures and strategies, you will get hours back by training your students to exhibit positive, prosocial behaviors so you can teach and they can learn.

I Promise

Over the past two decades serving in the field of education, I have worked in and visited hundreds of schools. During that time, I have learned a universally true lesson: there is nothing more valuable than the time and energy of an educator. Demands are put on educators that are unfair and unrealistic. These demands make it difficult to manage the daily business of the classroom—business that extends well beyond the classroom walls.

I promise that this book will not be another demand. It will not make your life more difficult.

I promise that you will get back the valuable time and energy you spend reading this book many times over.

I promise that by adopting these procedures and strategies, you will expend minimal effort to train students to be hard-working, prosocial people.

I promise that this book will help you experience the empowerment and joy that come with being successful at teaching students.

I promise that creating this positive classroom environment will dramatically improve your life and the lives of your students.

Let's get to it.

3

Before They Arrive

Set up the classroom for optimal behavioral leadership.

Many years ago, I accepted a position teaching my own 1st grade classroom—two days before school started. I spent 16 hours each of those days decorating and setting up a pretty awesome-looking classroom, especially for a male teacher. Desks were lined up just so; name tags were created; book bins and reading areas were arranged perfectly. Colorful bulletin boards (oh, what bulletin boards!) were posted in both the room and the hallway with encouraging words and room to display the quality, wonderful work that was sure to come from my students.

I had timed, to the minute, when we would be transitioning from one well-planned activity to another. Nothing was left to chance. Every moment had been played over and over in my mind. I knew exactly how I would take attendance. I knew where my hallway passes and nurse's passes were and, by golly, I knew how and when to use them. I had a class roster and a bus list. Everything was in place. I was ready. My room was ready.

Then the day began.

In the first hour, a kid pulled down my behavior chart while his new friends laughed hysterically. My plans for timely and organized transitions were a joke: several students would do what they wanted when they wanted to do it, wandering aimlessly around the room in the meantime.

As the day wore on, the challenges continued to accumulate. Three boys whom I had seated next to one another in orderly rows acted anything but orderly the entire day. One student refused to do any work. He appeared to be taking 1st grade as an elective. One literally tried to strangle his friend during dismissal. The day was an utter disaster. As we reached its merciful conclusion, I developed the sinking feeling that all of my preparation was a waste of time. As my students were *finally* getting on the bus, all I could think was "I really thought I was prepared. *Now what?!*"

It's Not About Classroom Management

As it turns out, I had successfully set up my room for proper classroom management, at least as well as I could as an inexperienced teacher: the desks were in rows, and things were neat, orderly, and generally appealing. I had processes, procedures, and tools in place for the classroom's academic and administrative needs. I had even meticulously planned for how to avoid student traffic jams, and I had done sufficient planning to avoid general confusion in the classroom.

These aspects of running the classroom are so important, but they are not the focus of this book. There are already two fantastic books written on this subject: *The First Days of School* by Harry K. Wong and *The Classroom Management* Book by Harry K. Wong and Rosemary T. Wong.

While this book will help with classroom management, it is about behavioral leadership. This chapter will not show you how to manage your classroom because the books above already have. Instead, this chapter will show you how to set up your room to be optimally effective for *changing and managing students' behavior*.

Here's what you will learn:

- How to place students on teams according to their academic levels and behavioral issues for optimal behavioral leadership
- How to position the students and yourself within the classroom so that you can properly monitor students and effectively use Gentle Guidance Interventions
- How to explain your methods to parents and administrators

This chapter is relatively short. There are no instructions on how to set up systems, charts, or forms, because this manual does not call for any of these instruments. Rather, it shows you how to set the stage for an optimal environment in which you can elicit positive behaviors from your students using the absolute minimum amount of time and energy. Notice the wording: this chapter only *sets the stage* for that optimal environment. Subsequent chapters will teach you how to create and maintain it.

Creating Teams

If you don't organize your students into teams before the year starts, you are missing a golden opportunity for them to build ownership, teamwork, and functionality in the classroom. Set aside some time to work on this before the start of the year. It may take a couple of hours, but it will be time well spent that saves time later.

Why teams?

- Belonging to smaller team units (compared to the larger classroom) gives students a greater sense of ownership and provides for more group accountability.
- Creating and correctly using teams allows you to more easily manage the classroom while also enabling students to more effectively self-manage.
- Team interaction provides students more real-life opportunities for struggle and growth (more on that throughout the book).

The teams you create will sit together all year long. Although the entire team can be moved to a different location, individual students will not be moved to another team for any reason (see Chapter 5).

The following is a specific process that you can apply to any grade level to create balanced, functional teams. Whenever possible, have teams created before the first day of school; however, for middle and high school classes, you might want to wait until the second week. This will let you get a handle on individual students' behavior levels and give you more time to prepare, since you will have several different classes with many students.

So what does the process for creating teams look like?

1. Determine the number of teams that you will have based on the total number of students. For our purposes, I will use a roster of 25 students. I will create five teams and assign five different academic and behavioral rankings. You want to keep the groups small—no fewer than four students and no more than six. A class of 24 students might have six teams of four, while a class of 26 might have four teams of five students and one with six.

2. Obtain two colors of large note or index cards. I work with orange and blue. Write the name of each female student on the first color card and the name of each male student on the second color card. (These cards are designed to make it easier for you to access information and arrange your students; they do not reflect gender-fluid or transgender identifications. Feel free to use any colors you like.)

3. Use whatever data you have about each student's academic ability to rank your students from A to E. Assign the five top academic performers an "A," the next five most proficient students a "B," and so on. If you find that you need more information, seek it out. It will be time well spent. This includes researching students who are new to the district, even if all you can find are parents' comments offering a general sense of past academic performance. Write academic ranks on students' cards. You might also add clarifying information on a students' academic performance. (Note: Adjust the number of rankings you assign based on the number of students on teams: A to D for teams of four students, A to F for teams of six students.)

4. Use whatever information you have about each student's behavior to rank your students from 1 to 5. Assign the five students who have a record of exhibiting the most positive behaviors a "1." Assign the five students who have a history of exhibiting the most negative behaviors "5." Rank the remaining students in groups from 2 to 4 based on their general behavior history. Again, if you need to, seek out information from former teachers and administrators. (Note: Approach parents only as a last resort, as they are often ineffective reporters in this area.) When determining a behavioral rank, consider each student's level of cooperation, treatment of other students, treatment of educators, self-treatment, willingness to work, and general attitude. Write behavioral ranks on students' cards. You might also add clarifying information on a student's behavioral history. (Note: Adjust the number of rankings you assign based on the number of students on teams: 1 to 4 for teams of four students, 1 to 6 for teams of six students.)

5. Sit in a comfortable place with a large flat surface in front of you; a kitchen table can be ideal. Arrange your teams using your completed student cards. Put an equal number of students (or as close to an equal number as you can) on each team. Make sure that each team has a balance of academic and behavioral ranks. For example, each of our sample teams should have at least one A, B, C, D, and E as well as a 1, 2, 3, 4, and 5. Any number of combinations is possible. For example, one team may have A1, B3, C2, D5, E4, but another might end up with A1, B4, C3, D2, E5. Try to balance the number of girls and boys on each team and to do what is necessary to create diverse teams within your classroom. Consider all known factors including, but not limited to, race/ethnicity, gender identification, physical disabilities, and so on. Perfect distribution is not as important as simply making an effort to not have homogeneous teams.

6. Review your initial team plan and make any adjustments needed—before school starts. Some considerations before you finalize your arrangements:

- **Do not** put students who have had major problems with each other in the past on the same team.
- **Do not** put the "class bully" on the same team as the "class victim."
- **Do** assign "Blue-Collar Bullies" and "White-Collar Bullies" to the same team (see sidebar).

Bullies and Where to Put Them

Although hybrids exist, bullies tend to come in one of two forms. Where to put the bullies in your classroom depends on how you identify them.

- *Threatening Bully (TB)*. This bully is your rough-and-tough "give me your lunch money" type. TBs use the blunt instruments of physical threats and violence to intimidate students that they perceive as smaller and weaker. Oftentimes, these students are not subtle about their bullying.
- *Sneaky Bully (SB)*. This bully uses insults, backstabbing, and gossip to bully other students. SBs tend to be subtler than their TB counterparts. They know how to manipulate teachers and others by presenting appropriate, prosocial behavior, so they can be more difficult to spot.

When creating teams (and seating charts), keep in mind that TBs often neutralize SBs. SBs might be weaker (physically and emotionally). Particularly among younger students, SBs are often physically intimidated by the mere presence of TBs. An SB will usually avoid a TB as well as those students who are friendly with the TB. In this way, friends or supporters of the TB often fall under the TB's protective umbrella. In addition, the TB is less likely to intimidate other students when positioned to protect other students against an SB. The TB feels a relatively healthy sense of control in this instance.

Positioning Students in the Classroom

Once you have put your students on teams, you need to decide where they will be sitting. This involves two considerations: first, where teammates will sit relative to one another, and second, where teams will be positioned within the room.

Team Configurations

You want to start by arranging students in their team configurations. This means you need to group tables or desks together. For elementary school, desks that face each other or tables are optimal for true teamwork as well as for holding one another accountable. I also recommend this arrangement for older students if it fits with your educational plan. Figures 3.1 and 3.2 show clustered teams and teams grouped in rows. Notice that the arrangement of tables and desks creates distinct team areas, with space separating each team from the others.

Begin by arranging your team clusters or rows on paper and in your physical space. Figure 3.1 shows team clusters using tables. You can also arrange clusters by having individual desks face each other. Figure 3.2 shows team rows using desks. You can also arrange rows using long tables.

Figure 3.1

Team Clusters

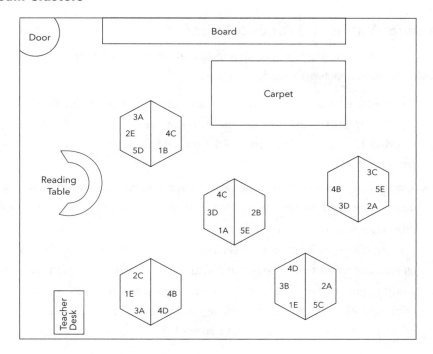

Figure 3.2
Team Rows

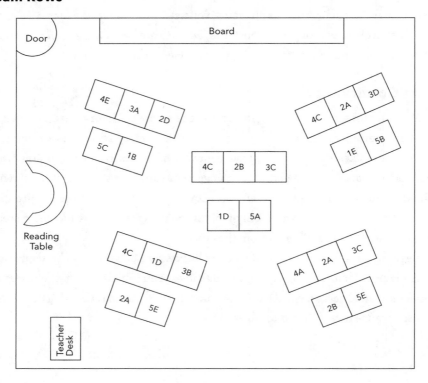

Seating Within and Among Teams

To be optimally effective, you should also arrange seating within your teams, keeping these parameters in mind:

- *Surround 5s with 1s and 2s.* You want to sandwich 5s between 1s and 2s. However, as you arrange the team spaces, be aware of the 5s' placement with respect to other teams. You don't want a 5 from one team backing up against a 5 from another.

- *Surround Es with As and Bs.* Again, try to keep in mind the arrangement of students with regards to other teams, too. Prioritize placement by behavioral rank.

- *Place the 5 who has a history of the most severe behavior close to the area where you will most often be during independent work time.* For instance, if you are an elementary school teacher who works with small groups during silent sustained reading, put your most difficult 5 on a team near the spot where you will be working with small groups. Make sure you are behind that student's ear and, if possible, positioned at the vertex of a Power V (see pages 34–35). Do not separate the 5 from the rest of the team or the class. Similarly, if you are a middle or high school teacher who works at a desk or board near the front of the class, then you probably want to place the most severe 5 close to the front of the room, but be sure not to put all of the 5s in the front row of the class.

Testing Your Configuration

Once you have your teams arranged, it can be helpful to physically place students' cards on the desks or tables where students will be sitting to test your configuration. Spend some time navigating the room as you might during different activities (e.g., instruction, individual work, group work). This lets you visualize where problems might occur. You might notice that you put a 4 or 5 from one team a little too close to a 4 or 5 from another. Maybe you separated two students into different teams because they have a history, but you put their teams right next to each other. This activity will help you foresee problems that you might miss if you just sketch out your plan or arrange cards on a table. If you decide to adjust your original configuration, be sure to test it out, too!

Positioning Yourself in the Classroom

A Power Position (PP) is a place from which the teacher can see every student. There is a specific process to find these positions. Although you are likely to move around your classroom frequently, teachers often spend a lot of their time delivering instruction from certain optimal locations. For example, teachers of all age groups tend to address their class while at the board at the front of the room. Those who teach younger students may spend several hours a day at a reading table. Middle and high school teachers likely spend time at their desks or at a projector. Whatever grade you teach, think about the locations from which you deliver instruction at different times of the day. Write those places down, either as a list or on your classroom diagram.

Now arrange students' cards on the desks or tables where they will be sitting. Using your list or diagram, go to the places where you spend time giving instruction. Ask yourself the following questions to determine whether these spots are PPs:

- Can you see students while they are seated at their desks or tables?
- Can you see students at common areas and workstations?
- Can you see students at the pencil sharpener and the trash can?
- Can you see students at a lab table, sink, or other special utility space?

If yes, congratulations! Your instructional spots are PPs. If an instructional spot is not a PP, then you need to rearrange your room.

Identifying Secondary Power Positions

In addition to instructional PPs, you should have at least two other Secondary Power Positions (SPPs). An SPP is a place from which you can see every student when you are not giving direct instruction. Study Figure 3.3. Notice the central locations of the instructional PPs, and then contrast them with the peripheral SPPs, where you could position yourself when not teaching to observe the classroom.

Figure 3.3

Instructional Power Positions and Secondary Power Positions

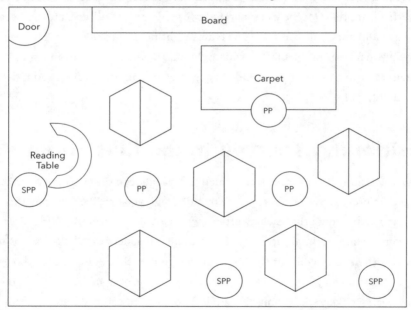

Having PPs and SPPs will optimize your effectiveness as the classroom's Friendly, Loving Alpha (FLA). An FLA is a teacher who is confident, assertive, and loving, and who establishes themselves as the kind boss of the classroom.

Setting Up Your Class to Use the Power V

The best position to monitor a student is from a 45-degree angle behind the student's ear. From here, you can observe what a student is doing and where a student is looking without the student being able to see you making these observations.

The students you most need to monitor are the 5s, the students with the history of using the most negative behaviors the most often. Place your 5s in positions where you can be behind the ears of at least two of them when you're in a PP. This positioning forms the Power V (see Figure 3.4). If your classroom has two "super 5s" (i.e., two students who have significantly worse behavior than everyone else), you should seat them where you can create a Power V with them. Whenever possible, if you can arrange students so that you can be behind three 5s' ears from one PP, then you have established an especially effective PP—the Power E (see Figure 3.5). Make sure you have arranged your classroom in a way that you can take advantage of more than one Power V or perhaps one Power E.

Figure 3.4
Power V

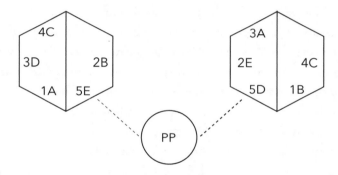

Figure 3.5
Power E

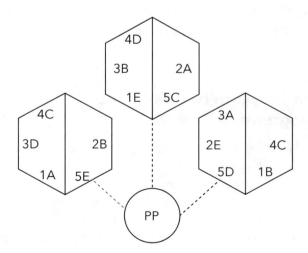

Addressing Team and Seat Changes

When parents ask if their child can move seats, the short answer is "There will be no team or seat changes."

No matter how well you arrange your students, difficulties between them will arise throughout the year. Students who don't like each other will have issues; students who like each other will have issues. This is normal, healthy, and expected. From time to time, students will become frustrated or upset, and they will want to move. Likewise, parents might become aggravated that their student is having trouble with another student on their team. They will want you to move their student or the other student. At some point, even you might be exasperated and think that you can fix a problem by moving someone. Fight the urge to attempt to solve the problem this way.

Why? Because students need to figure out how to deal with different, difficult, and otherwise disagreeable people. The price tag for doing so while still in school is as low as it will ever be. The costs of learning to navigate social challenges go up as students age and venture forth into the world as adults. It is better that students learn strategies for dealing with people they dislike or with whom they have differences in the safer environment of school, as minors, rather than later, in a less protected environment at an age when they are held to greater account for their actions.

Also, as you will learn in Chapter 7, you will be monitoring students and gently guiding them toward positive behaviors. You will also be using consequences to teach prosocial behaviors so that students will *not* cause problems for others, regardless of where they are sitting. In short, your classroom will be the safest, most well-monitored place for students to learn how to deal with difficult people.

How to Respond to Concerned and Disgruntled Parents

To begin with, as you make your plans at the beginning of the school year, I urge you not to send out a position paper on your permanent seating policy. You want to avoid organizing your own mob of angry parents. Later, if parents complain that it's "not fair" that their student must sit next to the class bully, or daydreamer, or kid who eats her snot, then you can explain that life is not fair. Gently add that you care too much for their student to trick the student into thinking that life is always fair and accommodating.

Keep in mind that no student—no person—is entitled to a place in life where they feel completely comfortable with their surroundings at all times. That's not how life works.

Here's a sample longer answer that you can give parents who contest the seating or team arrangement. You can modify this response for the students themselves as well as for administrators who might be asked to intervene.

I care too much for Joseph to steal this opportunity for growth from him. For Joseph to be successful in life, he will need to deal with all kinds of people. Now is the easiest and best time to learn these hard lessons. I properly monitor all students and will help guide Joseph through this tough time.

Using Team Color-Coding

During the first few weeks and throughout the year, every individual on every team will have the opportunity to decorate and adorn their team area, bins, books, and journals. This creates a tremendous sense of ownership among students over their teams and their classroom. You can help set the stage for this process before the school year begins by color-coding student workspaces, areas, and materials.

How much or how little color-coding you do will depend on the age of your students, your resources, and your personal preference. I recommend using strong, solid colors. In my classroom, I had five teams. I assigned each team a bold color: red, blue, orange, green, or purple. I decorated with these colors wherever and however I could before my students arrived for the first day.

I bought colored bins (one for materials, one for hanging folders). I used colored tape to adorn book bins, spelling list holders, and locker numbers. I placed colored stickers on books and journals. I prepared and handed out color-coded math journals. Finally, in my 1st and 3rd grade classrooms, I used a carpet with matching colors for students to sit for direct instruction. The carpet had six rectangles of each color; students could only sit on their team color. You will be amazed at how creating cohesion in this way truly generates a feeling of belonging in the classroom!

If you've followed the instructions of this chapter, you have now set yourself up for success. If you've never made these types of preparations before, you've never given yourself much of a chance to optimally lead behaviors. Once the students show up, it's going to get harder before it gets easier. But now—perhaps for the first time— you are ready for the challenge.

Part I

Relationship-Building Strategies

Make your students fall in love with and take care of you.

I was 9 years old, and I hated my life.

I was a 3rd grade student in Mrs. Johnson's room. I felt as though my entire life was school, and I hated, hated school. Suffering from what I now understand to be a clinical level of anxiety, I experienced every day as torture from the moment I woke up to the moment I went to sleep. I was either at school or worrying about school. I was either working on schoolwork or dreading schoolwork.

Mrs. Johnson was, by far, the meanest person I had ever encountered. She was unforgiving of any mistakes. I worked excruciatingly slowly (and still do to this day), and she thought it would help me to work faster and harder if she barked at me to work faster and harder. It did not.

Under these conditions, being able to work diligently and effectively at school went from difficult to impossible. Although school had been stressful the previous year (I still remember fretting about having to memorize and recite a poem called

"The Black Cat"), I was considered a smart, extremely capable student, and the report given to Mrs. Johnson by my 2nd grade teacher was glowing. When academic expectations increased dramatically in 3rd grade, however, I fell behind, and my anxiety about my failures—compounded by Mrs. Johnson's reactions to those failures—overwhelmed me. The teacher calling me "a real disappointment" in front of all my classmates did not help.

Even during brief moments of success, Mrs. Johnson was there to snuff out any positive feelings that flickered within me about my class, my teacher, and myself. Once, by the sheer accident of happening to know my 7s times tables because they corresponded with the scoring of touchdowns and extra points in football, I had, for the very first time, done well on a dreaded multiplication quiz. Having earned a perfect score instead of my usual F, I wanted to show my accomplishment to my family.

"Can I take this home and show my mom?" I asked Mrs. Johnson, holding out my perfect quiz. To this day, I remember her exact words. I remember where I was standing and what she was wearing.

"Since when are you so interested in math?!" She snatched the quiz out of my hand and ripped it up in front of me, throwing the scraps of quiz on the ground. She then told me to pick the pieces up and throw them away. In full view of my entire class, I cried quietly, on my knees, as I did as I was told.

✣ ✣ ✣ ✣ ✣ ✣ ✣ ✣ ✣ ✣ ✣

I hated Mrs. Johnson for a long time. She was the reason I became a teacher: I didn't want students to have to go through what I went through. I thought that, as a good person who cared about kids and their well-being, I could help students, even ones who had struggles and challenges.

Of course, I found out that I was wrong. It's so easy for people to read that story and think about how they would never do what she did. It's easy for people to say that they would never ride students to the point where the students felt so trapped and stressed that they hated their very existence. Not only is it easy to say, but it makes people feel good about themselves to think that they are good, that others are bad, and that if only more people were good (like they are), then schools, communities, and our world would be good, too.

I found out the truth during my first few days of teaching. The truth is that all of us are capable of both good and evil. The amount and kind of good or evil that we are capable of varies depending on many factors, not the least of which is the amount of stress we are under. The truth is that teaching, even under the best of circumstances, is stressful.

Looking back now, I can see that the truth in Mrs. Johnson's class was that she had had no training in behavior management and had taught for a very long time without encountering students as challenging as we were. That particular year, she had the unprecedented challenge of dealing with multiple extremely difficult students. Her understandable stress manifested itself in poor teaching, constant frustration, yelling, and some evil, horrible teacher behaviors. The fact that four students were expelled from our class the next year bore witness to our status as a class that tore through our school like a wrecking ball.

Without the support of specific and explicitly taught strategies for staying calm and encouraging positive behaviors when dealing with difficult students, the job of a teacher becomes impossible to do effectively. Traditional behavior management makes these behaviors worse, compounding the problem. When teachers attempt to do the impossible, in a high-stress situation, without the knowledge of strategies and procedures to make behaviors better instead of worse, they become capable of doing great evil, as Mrs. Johnson did. And as I did.

Staying calm is the result of the effective use of a specific strategy. You will learn it in this section of the book. Encouraging positive behaviors is a strategy, and you will learn how to do that, too. Being able to bond with students and guide them to act the way you want them to act is not something that results from simply "being a good person." You have to master the following specific strategies in order to build the relationships you need so that you can act like the teacher you want to be.

4

Relationship-Building Strategies

The Calm Signal

Particularly honest educators, when learning these behavioral leadership strategies, often say something like "All of these strategies for building relationships and sharing control are well and good, but what if I'm not calm enough to use them? What if, instead of modeling positive behaviors or using Gentle Guidance Interventions (see Chapter 9), I get too mad too quickly and just yell at kids before I can remember to do these positive things?"

The first and most important answer to this absolutely excellent and essential question is that educators must create, train themselves to use, and then use a Calm Signal in order to separate a stressful stimulus (students' negative behaviors) from their response. The Calm Signal acts as a pause button: the teacher will breathe, say the response, and remain in a thinking state in order to calmly react with helpful, positive strategies instead of a negative response like yelling or tearing up an A+ math quiz.

That is the reason the Calm Signal is the first strategy taught in this book: without it, many educators will have trouble using the other strategies taught subsequently. While the techniques in Chapters 4 and 5 are set into place in the first three to six weeks, and then more or less run themselves as part of a set plan, teachers need to be in the right state of mind to be able to remember and then actually use the strategies. (Notice that within these procedures, I use my own Calm Signal as a place-holder; feel free to use mine, or create your own and plug it in.)

The Calm Signal is a Pavlovian cue to the brain of the teacher and the brain of the student, indicating it is time to be calm, to relax, and to think. Over time, the use of the Calm Signal can keep both teachers and students in their prefrontal cortex, where they are still able to think. The expert educator will use the Calm Signal almost constantly in the beginning of the year in an effort to remain calm and encourage students to remain calm as well.

The "Bad Kid" Cycle and How to Stop It

Students who consistently use negative behaviors to get what they want use negative behaviors as a matter of habit. This bad habit usually starts at home: children notice that when they use a negative behavior (perhaps arguing or screaming about not getting a wanted toy), they may get the tangible thing that they want (the toy). Of course, when this scenario repeats, the child may create a bad habit of negative behavior because they consistently get the desired "thing."

Additionally, if the adult does not give the child the toy, but they do get angry, they are also giving the child what they want: the feeling that they can control an adult. Many children would rather have that feeling of control than a toy.

Parents will only rarely react to this shifting power dynamic by consistently giving in to demands of their small children (giving the toy). What does often happen is that, as children see their negative behaviors becoming more and more successful at getting more and more control over their parents' emotions, they start using more and worse negative behaviors to get even more control, creating a power struggle that reinforces the child's negative behavior as long as the parent continues to get angry. This is the Bad Kid Cycle.

Unfortunately for teachers, this cycle continues when the child begins school. The student has developed a habit of getting what they want (think "toy" or "control of an adult"). Predictably, they attempt to continue the Bad Kid Cycle at school.

That's where educators come in.

For the sake of the teacher, the school, and the student, the educator must stop these students from continuing the Bad Kid Cycle. This is done by not giving in and not getting angry.

Of course, telling a teacher not to get angry in response to an out-of-control classroom would be worse than worthless advice. Any teacher with a functional limbic system trying to "grin and bear" an onslaught of negative behaviors will eventually become very angry indeed. Furthermore, human beings cannot effectively train themselves to not do something (in this case, to not get angry). Brains don't work like that. The human brain needs to be trained to *do* things, not to *not do* them.

This strategy is what you actually do to break the "Bad Kid" Cycle.

Choose a Calm Signal

You will need to choose or create a sound, word, or very short phrase that you will use as your Calm Signal. Create or choose carefully; if you use it correctly, you will be saying this phrase thousands of times per year until the end of your career.

Choose a Calm Signal that sounds like something you would say or is something you already say. Here is a list of suggestions:

Oh, man.	*Huh.*
Oh, boy.	*Oh.*
Yikes.	*Whoa.*
Yeesh.	*Blerg.*
Ugh.	*(The sound of a slow exhale)*

To create your own, follow these guidelines:

- Pick a Calm Signal that you cannot make sound sarcastic, no matter how hard you try. "Really?" and "Seriously?" are not acceptable. If you find yourself to be the kind of person who can make *any* words sarcastic, choose or create a sound instead of a word.
- Your Calm Signal should be no more than three (short) words long.
- Your Calm Signal must be something that won't annoy you if you have to say it 100 times in a day—because some days, you might.

Once you have picked a signal that works for you, you are ready to begin your Calm Signal training.

Train Yourself to Use the Calm Signal at Home

If you sleep in the same bed with someone, alert them to the fact that you are going to do the following: as you are falling asleep, inhale deeply. On the exhale, say your Calm Signal. Say it calmly, softly, and slowly. (See why you had to warn your significant other?) Do this until you are asleep. Do it every night for two weeks. Even if you can't quite fall asleep while doing this routine, it will file your Calm Signal in a part of your brain where it will be easier to retrieve than if you never did this at all.

During these two weeks, when you are calm (perhaps doing things around your house or while reading a book), inhale, then exhale saying your Calm Signal, just like you did in bed. Continue to use your Calm Signal when some small thing doesn't go your way: you can't find your car keys, you get put on hold by your health care provider, or you realize you forgot to pay a bill.

Train Yourself to Use the Calm Signal at School

During or after these initial two weeks, start using your Calm Signal at school when the kids aren't there yet. Optimally, you could use it while preparing for the first day. Just like at home, when something doesn't go your way (your class list isn't in your mailbox, you're running late to a meeting, or the copier is broken again), use your Calm Signal before reacting in any other way. Practice using your pause button over and over and over again.

Next, use it when your students are in the room. Don't wait until things get rough! Start by using your Calm Signal when something mildly annoying happens: you didn't make enough copies, you realize that you taught the wrong lesson, you sent the wrong students to reading groups. Then, when a student uses an annoying behavior that may have previously caused you to react with something not appropriate, not helpful, and not in this manual, inhale and use your Calm Signal. Later, you will learn to follow up with one of the Gentle Guidance Interventions (GGIs; Chapter 9) or Delayed Learning Opportunities (DLOs; Chapter 11), which will be accessible because you have a working pause button that allows you to remain calm enough to do positive things!

Notice that the use of a Calm Signal is *responsive*: it is prompted by some type of potential stress. Most commonly, this will be a negative behavior from a student. The rest of the Relationship-Building Strategies—the Argument Shield, Strategic Noticing, Modeling, and Bonding—are *preventive*. They will prevent negative behaviors so that the use of the Calm Signal and subsequent interventions will be less necessary. When used cumulatively, each strategy makes the other strategies more effective!

The Argument Shield

A student may become frustrated when a teacher uses the Calm Signal and remains calm and relaxed throughout its use. After all, if the student is trying to gain control of the teacher's emotions through negative behavior, the teacher's lack of agitation can be annoying, and therefore the Calm Signal may actually increase some students' frustration in the short term. The most common method that students may use to attempt to gain or regain control is to try to argue with the adult. While a student trying to argue with a teacher may be triggered by the use of the Calm Signal, the Argument Shield strategy can be used whenever a student attempts to argue. It will be 100 percent effective in stopping you from being controlled by a student's attempt to argue.

Savvy students know, at least subconsciously, why they can win every argument with a teacher: students don't have to win the argument logically. They only have to control the emotions and the time of the teacher. Therefore, the goal of the Argument Shield is to train the students not to argue by giving away the least amount of control over your time and emotions as possible. Doing this involves a simple, two- to three-line script, the first of which is the use of your personal Calm Signal, which you have already selected. The key is to use *exactly* this script and to never deviate from it if a student is attempting to argue. Say these lines lightly, quickly, and without stopping instruction or whatever you are doing. Only use the final question if the argument attempts continue after the second line:

(Student tries to argue)

Teacher: (Calm Signal)

(Student tries to argue)

Teacher: I don't argue.

(Student tries to argue)

Teacher: . . . And what did I say?

Repeat the last question as long as the student continues to argue, until you decide to delay a Learning Opportunity, when and if necessary.

Each of these three lines has a specific purpose:

- The Calm Signal stops the teacher from becoming angry and giving the student their desired control, while at the same time it does not exacerbate the problem with extra words and/or emotion.

- Saying, "I don't argue," simply sets the limit.

- ". . . And what did I say?" uses the power of questions to make the student think instead of making a demand. Simply repeating the limit will likely engender more resistance.

By using this simple strategy and never deviating from it, the teacher shows the student that they will not get what they want through argument, and they will learn, with each argument attempt, not to argue.

If a student becomes so disruptive that thinking and teaching become impossible, the teacher simply uses their DLO script (see pages 227–229) and gives the Learning Opportunity later.

Remember, it takes at least two people to have an argument. If you use this strategy, you are guaranteed to never be one of those people!

Strategic Noticing

Human beings repeat behaviors that are noticed. Noticing a student's behavior makes them more likely to repeat that behavior. This is true of both positive and negative behaviors. Not only are noticed behaviors repeated, but they are often explored and heightened; students who see that a behavior elicited attention are likely to experiment with using that same behavior in a slightly different or enhanced way.

The 11th grade student who is noticed saying "thank you" by the principal will be more likely not only to say "thank you" to a teacher later that day, but also to explore using similar polite behaviors, such as saying "please" when asking the lunch server for extra mashed potatoes. The student will also be more likely to heighten these polite behaviors by calling a teacher "ma'am" or even writing an unsolicited thank-you email.

Conversely, a 1st grade student who is noticed poking a classmate under the table is more likely to do it again. Furthermore, the student will be more likely to explore similar behaviors in the "violence" genre, perhaps pushing another student in line. The student is also more likely to heighten the level of violence; perhaps being noticed will lead the student to experiment with punching another student in the face.

Educators need to systematically notice positive behaviors in order to encourage them, while simultaneously ignoring (when possible) or giving minimal attention to negative behaviors. Unfortunately, in nearly all schools, negative behaviors are noticed more than positive behaviors. This is why behaviors tend to get worse in every classroom every year, from fall to spring. It is why the worst-behaved students in any school are often the oldest students: they have had negative behaviors noticed for the longest amount of time, so they use the most negative behaviors. Teachers are accidentally and systematically training kids to be worse every day by noticing negative behaviors but not positive behaviors.

In practice, many of us fail to pay attention to positive behaviors because, by definition, those behaviors do not cause a problem, so they do not *need* to be addressed. The result is that nearly all teachers ignore most positive behaviors while encouraging negative behaviors. This dynamic causes more dysfunction than any other factor in education. Without "flipping" this dynamic—without systematically practicing the Strategic Noticing of positive behaviors and minimizing the attention given to negative behaviors—the average student behaviors will get worse month by month and year by year.

The "Good Kid" Cycle and How to Perpetuate It

The "Good Kid" Cycle works exactly like the "Bad Kid" Cycle. Some of the students in your classroom have found, through experience, that they get the things that they want through using positive behaviors such as being polite and pleasant, solving problems without violence, and working hard. They have learned that they get good grades, special privileges, and academic and athletic success through using positive behaviors. They have also learned, often through considerable experience, that they get loads of attention when they use positive behaviors. That attention, as well as the positive trappings of using positive behavior, helps students develop a habit of positive, prosocial, "good" behaviors. This is the "Good Kid" Cycle.

The adults in the lives of these students have done you a great service: they have set you up for success by training the students to use positive behaviors. Still, in order to perpetuate the "Good Kid" Cycle, we must consciously and systematically use Strategic Noticing to reinforce the positive behaviors that these prosocial students are using to get what they want. Every teacher who has ever worked with difficult students has felt the angst that comes from realizing that they have been giving attention to negative behaviors from antisocial students all day and more or less ignoring the prosocial students. Strategic Noticing solves this dynamic.

Flipping the "Bad Kid" Cycle

By engaging your Calm Signal and not getting angry, you break the Bad Kid's habit of using negative behavior to get what they want. This is essential, but it is only half of the equation. By merely not giving the student what they wanted (no tangible "thing" and no anger), you have stopped the negative behavior from being functional. Now, you must systematically reinforce positive behaviors.

You should systematically give properly communicated attention to all of your students by noticing them *only when they are using positive behaviors!* Keep in mind that none of this means that kids who have been conditioned to use negative behaviors will just cease and desist using negative behaviors right away. After all, those behaviors have been getting them what they want for a long time! But when you notice the positive behaviors of their classmates, you are providing a simple instruction booklet for how to get attention in your classroom. They will receive this instruction booklet on the first day that you start using these strategies, and sometime after that, they will use it.

The way you *perpetuate the "Good Kid" Cycle* will be the exact same way that you *flip the "Bad Kid" Cycle*, and you will do both simultaneously and without having to think about which one you are doing! It will be fantastically simple and will be the number one tool in eliciting positive behaviors that you will ever use.

The How

To use Strategic Noticing in response to positive behaviors, simply say the following:

I noticed [enter positive behavior here].

That's it. There's nothing else. If there is anything else, you did it wrong.

The list of positive behaviors that you can notice is literally endless. Here are some that you can use in your classroom:

I noticed that you are listening.

I noticed that you are working hard.

I noticed that you treat people well.

I noticed that you play fair.

I noticed that you sat down and got right to work.

I noticed that you waited patiently for me.

I noticed that you waited silently in line.

I noticed that you washed your hands thoroughly.

I noticed that you are silent.

I noticed that you all are silent.

I noticed that you all are staying to the right of the hallway.

I noticed that you all are working cooperatively.

I noticed that you raised your hand.

You can also notice when students accomplish things academically.

I noticed that you indented your paragraph.

I noticed that you balanced the equation before solving for x.

I noticed that you followed through when passing the ball.

I noticed that you all are using the word wall to spell your words correctly.

Praise Is Not Effective Enough

Note that the strategy involved noticing, not praise. Praise can be somewhat effective with healthy students. It will not be effective with difficult students. Even so, "somewhat effective" is not good enough. "Somewhat effective" means that the teacher has to do too much thinking and that the strategy only works sometimes with some students.

Many difficult students have self-esteem issues and trust issues. If you say, "You are great!" those students will say to themselves, "No, I'm not! What are you up to and what do you want from me?" They will often use even more negative behaviors in order to get you to stop praising them. Why? Praise involves a value judgment. "You are great" means "I have judged you to be great." Difficult students hate value judgments.

Fight the urge to notice and then praise:

> I noticed that you are working hard . . . and that's great!

Praise isn't effective enough to be included in this manual. Stick to Strategic Noticing.

"Liking" What Students Do Is Not Effective Enough

Many untrained teachers, particularly teachers of younger students, will say aloud that they like certain behaviors: "I like the way Tyreke is sitting." This may be somewhat effective with easier, younger kids, but it will backfire horribly with everyone else. Here's why: difficult kids don't want you to "like" what they do, and they *really* don't want you to like what they do in front of their friends! Again, "somewhat effective" strategies are not good enough to be included in this manual. Don't like what students do—*notice* what they do.

A Behavior Management Paradigm Shift

Before reading this manual, most teachers will have some semblance of the following philosophy about teaching and behavior management: *When everything is going well with behavior, I will teach. When things go poorly, I will react to those behaviors, stop them, and then go back to teaching.* As we have discussed, this paradigm leads to ignoring positive behaviors, encouraging negative behaviors, failing to perpetuate the "Good Kid" Cycle, and reinforcing the "Bad Kid" Cycle.

Instead, with Strategic Noticing being our primary means of preventing negative behaviors, our new philosophy is the following: *I will immediately notice positive behaviors before I teach and while I am teaching, over and over again. This will prevent a vast majority of negative behaviors. When things go poorly, I will gently guide students back to using positive behaviors with minimal attention. If that doesn't work, I will use other strategies learned from this book.*

Instead of reacting to and reinforcing negative behaviors, effective teachers systematically put a vast majority of their energy toward prevention. Ashley Owen, a 3rd grade teacher and behavioral leadership coach, created a very effective rule of thumb that we now call the 70-20-10 Rule: 70 percent of all energy and time you put toward behavioral leadership should go toward the use of Strategic Noticing, while 20 percent should go toward Gentle Guidance Interventions and only 10 percent to the use of Delayed and Procedural Learning Opportunities (described in the latter section of this book).

While implementing Strategic Noticing is incredibly simple, remembering to do it often enough is more challenging. However, prioritizing this technique will improve your life more than any other change that you could possibly make to your teaching.

All teachers should use Strategic Noticing every 90 seconds, all day long. Another way to put it: for every 30 minutes you are with students, you need to notice 20 times.

A common reaction—one that you are probably having right now—is that Strategic Noticing will take too much time. It won't. Strategic Noticing takes no more than three seconds. Over the course of any half-hour period, 20 instances of Strategic Noticing will take no more than 60 seconds. Remember that noticing positive behaviors frequently will prevent a vast majority of negative behaviors that take days, sometimes weeks or even months, away from your instructional time every year.

Strategic Noticing is a preventive strategy. Putting time and energy toward prevention is more effective than putting energy toward responsive action. Keep in mind that the procedures already outlined also act as preventive measures. The cumulative effect of implementing Relationship-Building and Control-Sharing Procedures is that you will unleash a tidal wave of negative behavior prevention every single day without even thinking about it!

Accountability: How to Make Sure You Notice Every 90 Seconds

Again, this is the hard part. Nothing prompts you to do Strategic Noticing: you need to do it even when all is well. Therefore, you may need some help from someone else to make sure your Strategic Noticing frequency is high enough for optimal negative behavior prevention.

Ideally, your school will hire a Behavioral Leadership Classroom coach to help you with this and the use of every other procedure and strategy in this book. If not, you can simply ask another person to tally the number of times you use Strategic Noticing. That person does not need to have any training other than you telling them to tally how many times you say "I noticed that you _____" without following it up with praise. Of course, schools are busy places, so anyone helping won't have a lot of time. But if they can spare five minutes, that can be enough to spot-check you to make sure you are noticing enough. Here are your frequency goals for optimal prevention, depending upon the amount of time being observed:

- 30 minutes: 20 Strategic Noticings
- 20 minutes: 14 Strategic Noticings
- 10 minutes: 7 Strategic Noticings
- 5 minutes: 4 Strategic Noticings
- One 50-minute period (high or middle school): 34 Strategic Noticings

These numbers denote the minimum amount of Strategic Noticing necessary. Having someone holding you accountable will allow you to better remember to keep up your frequency in order to prevent negative behaviors. Only by thoughtfully attending to Strategic Noticing can you be successful in this area.

Hints for Optimal Strategic Noticing

Bombard your students with Strategic Noticing in the first five minutes of the day and the first five minutes after lunch or recess. There are two reasons for this. First, it is easier to remember to use the technique immediately after a break from students and for just five minutes, especially when you are just starting the practice. Second, overwhelming students with Strategic Noticing when they enter the classroom for the first time in the morning and in the afternoon reminds them about what kind of behaviors (positive ones) get attention in your classroom. This is especially important for students who get attention for negative behaviors at home or during lunch or recess. Noticing in this way sets the tone of a classroom.

Middle and high school teachers can concentrate on getting 20 Strategic Noticings done in the first 10 minutes of every class period, for all of the reasons above. This is especially important for students coming from classes that have teachers at the helm who have not had Behavioral Leadership Classroom training or have not read this book. This is not to say that you should stop noticing after doing 20 Strategic Noticings in the first 10 minutes. Note that in a 50-minute period, you will still have to notice 14 more times for minimally sufficient frequency.

It is helpful to use the Strategic Noticing Strategy in age-appropriate ways. For all age groups, preK–12, public group noticing (e.g., "I noticed that you all are working very hard") is always effective.

As students get older, starting around 5th grade, you may want to start experimenting with private noticings. This kind of Strategic Noticing involves using a soft voice or whisper, or noticing when no other students are present. However, you should consider the needs or your particular students. Many tough, even difficult high school students never get tired of being publicly noticed for their positive behaviors. Just experiment. Keep in mind that many students will remark on how odd it is that you are doing so much noticing, even when you move from public to private statements, but students pointing out the noticing does not constitute a reason to stop. If a student reacts to a Noticing with "SO?!" simply respond with "I just happened to notice" while walking away.

Strategic Noticing Will Change You

When you don't consciously focus on noticing positive behaviors—students walking, working, and being kind—you will often focus on negative behaviors. When you focus on negative behaviors and notice them more, you can perpetuate even more negative behaviors. It creates a downward spiral that destroys teachers by turning formerly positive people into negative people who encourage more and more negative behaviors throughout their careers.

Conversely, if you continually make a conscious effort to notice positive behaviors, especially if you do so hundreds of times per day, it will not only make positive behaviors more and more common throughout the rest of your career, it will make you more positive.

We become what we continually focus on.

Preventive Movement

As a teacher, you should move around the room as much as possible. Preventive Movement (PM) involves walking around the classroom even when all is well. This should happen as much as possible. Once you begin to use Strategic Noticing as a matter of habit, and once you are able to use the other strategies and procedures in this manual, you will become a powerful force for constantly reinforcing positive behavior while gently guiding students back to using positive behaviors if they start experimenting with negative behaviors. Moving throughout the room enables that force to seem ubiquitous to students. You want your students to feel as though that force is everywhere!

For times when it is difficult to implement Preventive Movement, you can engage in one of two specialized forms of Preventive Movement: Preventive Sweeps and Preventive Charges.

Preventive Sweep

A Preventive Sweep can be useful for a high school math teacher tethered to a projector or a 2nd grade teacher located behind a reading table teaching small groups. In either case, find short breaks in the instruction to wander around the room for proximity to your students. You can even stop briefly near an individual student who might be on your radar, whether or not you notice that student experimenting with a negative behavior.

Preventive Charge

Use a Preventive Charge not only to forestall negative behaviors but to have a little extra fun. While most Preventive Movement involves slow, calm walking around the room, this strategy is done with all of the running speed you can muster. With no warning and for seemingly no reason, try sprinting from wherever you are in the room to a Power Position and teaching with greatly increased volume and emotion. This works best when you find yourself having to be at the board or anchored in one position and you feel like you are behind on your Preventive Movement. Your antics will surely prevent negative behaviors, as well as refocus anyone whose attention may have been wandering.

Of course, combining Strategic Noticing with Preventive Movement is essential. Moving around the room is the cornerstone of effective behavioral leadership, and stopping and putting your hand on a student's shoulder or chair can make for super-charged, highly effective noticing. Teachers who neglect the use of these strategies cannot be optimally effective.

Modeling

Establish a High "Behavioral Ceiling"

The Behavioral Ceiling is the concept that your students will never behave any better than you do. You set the Behavioral Ceiling with your own personal conduct. The behaviors that you model should be the exemplary behaviors that you want your students to use. If you want students to be polite, you must be polite. If you want your students to be peaceful, you must be peaceful.

This advice, by itself, is not very useful. In fact, the three modeling strategies that follow are not very effective by themselves. The truth is that if a teacher does not know how to use the procedures and strategies contained in this manual, there will be so many negative behaviors present in the classroom that it will be very difficult to act like a person you would want your students to emulate. Without ensuring that they are able to employ the strategies and procedures, admonishing teachers to "behave well" is a useless, insulting, and frustrating demand.

For some of your students, you may be one of many positive role models in their lives: they have parents, relatives, and coaches who model positive behaviors for them. For others, you may be the first adult they have ever encountered who behaves in the way you would like them to behave. These students have no chance of using excellent behavior if you aren't modeling it for them. One cannot aspire to be what one has never seen.

Extreme Respect

Respect—the concept that people should treat others the way that they would like to be treated—is the cornerstone of positive, prosocial human conduct. When respect is present, families, communities, and societies can be healthy. When it is absent, these same institutions crumble. One of your many jobs as a teacher is to concentrate on modeling respect as thoroughly as possible so that your students will be given a sterling example of how a respectful person behaves.

To be clear, when working with difficult students, it is, for most people, impossible to be perfectly respectful unless you use the procedures and other strategies. Extreme Respect is only one of the many pieces of the puzzle, but it is essential. Even when using most or all of the other pieces, implementing this strategy is a challenge simply because teaching is very, very difficult!

There are three different ways to use *Extreme Respect*:

- *Extreme Respect ESPNs.* The first and easiest way to model Extreme Respect is to practice it while doing ESPN Greetings and ESPN Goodbyes (further explained in Chapter 5). These are the least demanding circumstances to use the Extreme Respect method. First of all, first thing in the morning, no students have pushed any of your buttons! You have yet to make any of the 1,500 educational decisions required of you every day. You only need to do one thing at a time: greet students. In short, when you are ESPN Greeting students at your door, you are still in your right mind! Similarly, when you are giving ESPN Goodbyes, you know that you no longer have to see students anymore that day, which could, potentially, be a very happy time for you, especially early in the year before your students have been effectively trained to use positive behaviors that don't drive you crazy!

  With these advantageous logistics in mind, make sure you bask in, and take advantage of, these relatively low-stress moments as the optimal time to model Extreme Respect. Take the time to concentrate on your ESPN: make real *eye contact*; give a real *smile*; use authentic, FLA *physical contact*; and say their *name* (and eventually their nickname). Take time with both the Goodbye and the Greeting to interact with students while perhaps using a more formal register.

- *Using "sir" and "ma'am."* The second way to show Extreme Respect is to call students "sir" and "ma'am," instead of demanding that students call us these words. Model the use of these culturally acknowledged words of respect every day. Again, the easiest times to do this are when you are using the ESPN Greeting and Goodbye procedures.

  Calling students "sir" and "ma'am" is especially important for the time before you have given students their nicknames (further detailed in Chapter 5). In fact, before I gave students nicknames, whenever possible, I only called students "sir" or "ma'am." These words simultaneously model manners and build relationships—and addressed the needs of students for whom the use of their real names hurt relationships.

- *Extreme Manners.* From the moment students arrive to the moment that they leave, you want to be the Shining Light of Manners. Take a moment to think of the most polite and well-mannered person you have ever met. Try to be that person. Again, this might involve a more formal register than your students or even you are used to. When students are speaking, look them directly in the eye and smile, nodding your head when appropriate. The following words and phrases should be used as much as possible:

  > *Please.*
  > *Thank you.*
  > *Would you mind doing me a favor?*
  > *It is great to see you!*
  > *I am so honored to have you in this class.*
  > *My friend, I am so ready for this day!*
  > *I am glad to have you here today.*
  > *I look forward to seeing you tomorrow.*
  > *You make our class a better place to be.*
  > *Take care of yourself tonight.*
  > *Be careful going to the game tonight.*
  > *Pardon me. After you, sir [ma'am].*

All of these examples are appropriate for all grade levels. Do not shy away from the use of these phrases because they may be different in tone and register compared with what your students hear in their homes and communities. That is, in actuality, part of the point: you are purposely using these expressions in order to model an extremely respectful way of communicating.

Again, using Extreme Manners during the ESPN Greeting and ESPN Goodbye procedures is incredibly important and also exceptionally easy. It creates a gateway that gives each student the cue that they are entering and leaving a place where the level of respect is at an incredibly high plateau—one that they may or may not have experienced in the past, and one that they may or may not be experiencing at home.

Act Like a Butler

You want your students to take care of their responsibilities. The best, most effective, and easiest way to do this is for you to model taking care of your responsibilities by creating a safe, functional learning environment in which you deliver excellent, organized instruction. In this way (and in no other way) you are employed to *serve* your students. Do that. Be excellent. Be organized. Have everything at right angles. Make sure your tech is set up in advance. Have your read-aloud in the right place. Think about how a butler is in charge of making sure that everything is *just so*. Be fastidious—in full view of your students.

Again, some of your students will have seen this level of responsibility from adults, but some of your students may not have. Setting such an example could be transformational for these students.

When you have failed to live up to your responsibilities—when things are not *just so*—act like a butler who has spilled the tea, or forgotten to put out the cookies, or failed to clean the hardwood floors: apologize profusely. Apologize if your technology doesn't work. Apologize if you can't find your read-aloud. Apologize for accidentally leaving windows open and making students in the back of the room cold. Apologize for not having enough copies, and apologize for teaching something the wrong way. This says to your students that you respect them and want to serve them by instructing them, and that you take these responsibilities seriously.

Apologize

Apologizing to students is critical to building relationships with them. It models respect, shows your students that you care, and demonstrates that you are strong enough to ask for forgiveness. Finally, apologizing models the use of an apology so that students will eventually use this important life skill themselves!

Besides apologizing for failing to live up to your responsibilities of creating and maintaining a functional learning environment, there are other great opportunities to apologize to your students:

- *When something outside your control causes a problem.* This models the über-responsibility of highly successful people and is an opportunity to model taking responsibility for more than the casual observer would deem to truly be your responsibility. It says to your students "I love you, I care for you, I am in charge of making sure you have an opportunity to have an excellent school experience, and the buck stops with me." A grade-level trip being unexpectedly cancelled, a school pizza party being postponed, and even an unexpected power outage are all good reasons to apologize to your students. This is the level of responsibility that excellent leaders take for their companies (CEOs), cities (mayors), or schools (principals). Perhaps your modeling will lead some of your students to assume this level of responsibility in their lives when they become a CEO, mayor, or principal.

- *When another adult is unkind.* If another teacher or adult is unkind to your students, your silence will be interpreted as tacit approval. This is not acceptable. You are under no obligation to support a teacher who walks into your class and yells at your students or to remain silent when a recess monitor belittles your student. Besides taking any other steps necessary to defend your student, it is imperative that you apologize if and when these things happen. Many of the reasons for this kind of apology are the same as above, but an additional one is that your students will understand that you care about them and their feelings *and* that you feel responsible for making them feel safe when they are at school.

- *When you cause a problem.* Remember the rules for the classroom? You are not allowed to cause a problem, just as your students are not allowed to cause a problem. When you do, just like your students, you need to solve it. For instance, if you accidentally bump into a student as you are doing your Preventive Movement, saying you are sorry and making sure the student is all right models both apologizing and solving the problem that you caused. If you accidentally have a student do the wrong math problems, apologizing profusely and personally erasing the erroneous work will go a very long way to model responsibility, care, and problem solving, thus building your relationship with the student.

Bonding

These Bonding strategies will lead students to fall in love with you, supercharge the effectiveness of the Modeling strategies, and make them remember you forever.

Go Out of Your Way for Your Class (Without Conditions)

I still remember the first thing I did right in my teaching career. (Unfortunately for me and my students, it didn't occur until six months into my first year of teaching.) Our staff had organized a potluck for lunch. Someone had brought in some absolutely amazing chicken wings, and by the end of our lunchtime, there were still perhaps 60 wings left. I stopped a fellow teacher from throwing them in the garbage, which would have been a crime against humanity. I took the wings to my classroom, along with plates and napkins. When my 5th grade students came back from recess, I offered them a chicken wing snack. I still remember the silence and stunned looks on every one of the students' faces. "What did we do?" Jacquata asked, wondering what this was a reward for. I just smiled (this was rare) and said that they didn't do anything and that I got these wings, that they were delicious, and that I just thought that they might want some wings.

My students, still stunned, suspiciously and slowly formed a line, picked up some wings, napkins, and plates, and sat down to eat their wings in a mild state of shock. Most of the students even said, "Thank you." This was perhaps the first time those words had been spoken in that classroom by them or by me!

When you can, you should do things for your students. Never do them as a reward. Never do them with conditions. Just do them because you like to. The simpler and easier to do, the better, as you have so little time. Here are some things you can do to go out of your way for your students, with parental consent, if necessary:

- Get a giant bag of candy and give the candy to your students.
- Buy pizza for your students for lunch.
- Set up a waffle bar for your homeroom.
- Set up an ice cream bar for your last period class.
- Hold class outside.
- Host video game parties at lunchtime.
- Take students down the street to an ice cream shop and buy them ice cream.

Again, none of these things should be done as a reward, and they should be done for everyone, without conditions. Going out of your way for your students builds relationships; "reward parties" only for those who are cooperative with teachers can destroy them.

The only exception to withholding these events from students is when not taking part in them is part of a logical DLO. A student who has been acting dangerously should not go to an ice cream shop. A student who has been running out of the room during instruction should not be allowed to attend class outside with everyone else. When cases like this occur, notify the students and make alternative plans. However, you should *never* tell a student that they "need to behave" if they want to have the reward party/fun thing. For more on logical DLOs, see Chapter 11.

Go Out of Your Way for Your Individual Students (Without Conditions)

Do things for your students that relate to what they need or want. Go out of your way to do things and purchase things for your students. Again, this should *never* be a reward for behavior; you should *never* say something like "Don't interrupt me all week, and I'll get you a comic book." You *can* say, however, "I heard you talking about how you like *The Incredible Hulk*, so I got you this comic book."

Here are a few other ways to go out of your way for individual students:

- Check out books from the library the student would like.
- Help the student register for an outside-of-school activity (with parental consent).
- Go online to research an interest or concern of the student and share what you found.

Most difficult students have had very few adults do nice things for them for no other reason than to be nice. This can include parents and relatives as well as teachers in schools where tangible rewards are often dangled in front of students (reward parties/dances or prizes from the treasure chest). The fewer times in a child's life that adults have been nice to them for no reason, the more effective these strategies will be.

Authentically Finding Common Ground and Sharing Your Life Authentically

It is a well-worn and conventionally accepted practice to try to find common ground with your students as a means of building relationships. This can be effective when done authentically, but it can backfire when done in a contrived way.

Trying to connect with students by finding common ground should only be attempted when there truly is common ground. Students have an amazing ability to sniff out a teacher who pretends to have a mutual interest with them. If you do not like Cardi B, don't pretend that you do. They will know, and your pretense will cause damage to your relationship. If you do not actually like basketball, or the L.A. Lakers, or ballet, or shopping, or Instagram, don't try to fake it.

The honest reality is that if you are a 65-year-old middle-class woman who was raised on a farm in Minnesota, you may not have a lot in common with a 9-year-old boy born in Mexico and living in inner-city Houston. The good news in this situation is that you can still share your own life authentically, and this can be more effective, easier, and sometimes more rewarding even than finding common ground. Sharing how you were raised can be endlessly fascinating to students, especially if it is different from how they are growing up. It will greatly increase students' ability to see you as a person with feelings, hopes, and dreams if they know more about who you were as a child, who your parents are or were, and what type of lifestyle you had as a child.

Who you are now is also important to share. Sharing the area in which you live, how you live, and with whom you live allows students to relate to you as a human and not just a teacher. Bringing in pictures, talking about their families, and, as much as possible, talking about your family and even having your family visit with your students are all authentic ways of building relationships.

Allow Yourself to Be Silly

Being able to be silly in front of other people takes and demonstrates strength. It is an FLA (Friendly, Loving Alpha) move. Students want to bond with FLAs. It makes them feel safe and fulfills a control need to know that they are protected by and friendly with an FLA. This is an alpha strategy. In addition, the older students are, the more effective being silly in front of them becomes, because middle and high school students often do everything they can to *not* look silly in front of their peers. These students tend to see intentionally looking silly in front of people as a monumental feat, and they respect it.

Incorporate silliness into your lesson plans. Plan out a time where you know you will be goofy. Many of the procedures that follow already include times to do this in a scripted way (the Nickname Ceremony in Chapter 5 or Shake It Out in Chapter 8, for example). Look for opportunities throughout the day to be weird. When middle and high school students roll their eyes (they will), that means it's working. *Make it weirder!* The goal is not for students to think that you are cool; it is to make them realize that you are the FLA. You are not their friend; you are their weird boss who loves them.

Allow Yourself to Not Know Things

One of the hardest parts of being a child is that children barely know anything yet. So many unknowns make the world a scary place. Admitting that you don't know things shows your students that everyone is, more or less, in the same boat: everyone has plenty of things to learn. Handling not knowing things correctly is so important. Here's how to do it in a helpful, realistic way that builds relationships with students, models for students how to have a growth mindset, and allows for optimal student growth. This can be done whether discussing something within a lesson or something wholly nonacademic.

Step 1: Admit ignorance. Don't do this immediately. First model the behavior by pausing and thinking, perhaps with a confused look. Then say the magic words: "I don't know."

Step 2: Ask someone in the class for an answer. Do not skip this step. It gives you the opportunity to let your students know that you respect their intelligence level. You can ask the entire class if they know the answer. Or you can show specific students that you respect their superior knowledge on a subject by asking them the question instead of or before asking the entire class.

Step 3: Go find the answer. If it is an academic unknown and there is time to do so, model finding the answers to problems by using whatever resources are appropriate or convenient. Whenever possible, use the academic resources available in the form of textbooks, glossaries, and so on, but also feel free to simply use the internet. The lesson is in the doing: not knowing things is fine; just go find the answer!

Listening

Telling teachers who work in a chaotic classroom environment to calmly and thoughtfully listen when students are talking is perhaps the most ignorant, useless, tone-deaf advice that someone can give a teacher. As all teachers who have been in this situation know, this kind of listening is impossible when chaos is happening all around you. That is why the use of this skill when working with difficult students is really only possible in the context of using the procedures and other strategies contained in this book. Once you are using them and have cured most or all of the chaos, *then* you can listen in such a way that will help build relationships. It doesn't work the other way around; you can't build relationships with students quickly and strongly enough and thereby get order just by listening to them.

While this may seem obvious, some of your students will never have been listened to in this way by anyone, or at least not by an authority figure. Students who are only listened to by friends in this way will only listen to their friends. Think about the friends of your most difficult students. Doesn't it seem important for your students to be listened to by someone besides their friends?

This is how to listen to your students effectively, whether they are coming to you for advice or asking an academic question.

1.   Look at your student. Take your eyes off the computer screen or teachers' edition textbook and make eye contact with your student.

2. Use your Calm Signal to calm you and your student down enough to be in an optimal state of mind.
3. Listen without interrupting.
4. Pause before responding.

If you don't have time in the moment, let them know that they deserve more attention than you can give in the moment, make a note, and make an appointment to talk to them later. This listening strategy shows your students that you care about them and about what they have to say, and that you are truly there for them.

Physical Contact

When and how you have physical contact with your students may be dictated by school policy, personal comfort, the needs of individual students, and a host of other issues, and should be done within the parameters set by your administrators and at your own risk. Nevertheless, safe physical contact with students is an essential element of bonding with them. The minimal essential amount of physical contact with students has already been woven into the fabric of your classroom if you are using the ESPN Greeting and Goodbye procedures (Chapter 5). As a teacher, I very often would have physical contact with students as a means of encouragement, of celebration, and to show calm.

A pat on the back can be great when a student is working but needs some encouragement to persist at something that is difficult. A hand on the shoulder while leaning into the student may help get a student over an emotional hump, perhaps when working on something that is a bit dry (e.g., a test prep exercise, a vocabulary quiz). For younger students, leaning on them while waiting at the head of the line or even resting your arm on top of a student's head can both build relationships and communicate calm "alpha-ness."

Giving Your Time Outside School

In addition to going out of your way at school, going out of your way for your students outside school hours has a profoundly positive bonding effect with students. Taking time for students when we are not contractually obligated to shows them that we *want* to be around them even when we don't *have* to. The problem, of course, is how to do this while living our own lives. The answer is to use your time outside school to maximum effect by building strong relationships efficiently in short bursts of time. Here is how:

- *Do home visits before school starts for 3 to 10 of your most difficult students.* The moment you pet your student's dog, you will immediately have a better relationship with your student's parents. People often hold their first impression of others forever. A parent's positive first impression of their child's teacher as an actual human being in their home may become permanent. There are other environmental and biological issues at play here as well. Many parents, particularly parents of difficult students, had bad experiences in school, and schools make them horribly uncomfortable or even scared. To have your first interaction with a parent under these conditions is a recipe for disaster. It is far better to have your first interaction with parents in their home, where they are usually more comfortable.

  The *only* goal of this home visit is to have a healthy interaction with the family. Do not bring *any paperwork or materials of any kind.* For many families, someone holding papers at their door will appear to be an unwanted bill collector. Besides, bringing materials makes you look like someone with an agenda. This will erode trust. The goal here is to build trust. No materials, no agenda.

  Do not call in advance or arrange a meeting. It is not worth the time and effort necessary to coordinate a meeting and meeting time, especially when some families will go through great lengths to avoid interacting with you. You also don't want to set too formal a tone for the casual interaction you're trying to set up.

  Do not enter your student's home or request to do so unless invited. As we all can attest, homes are not always "visitor ready." Be ready for a conversation on the porch or in the hallway.

  Just have a conversation. Get to know the family. Pet a dog. Remark about a cat. Just be a person. Be safe. Take a friend with you, if that feels appropriate. If you feel uncomfortable in any situation, politely excuse yourself and leave immediately.

- *Make five positive calls home each week for three weeks.* A vast majority of these calls should be to the homes of your most difficult students. The goal is to build relationships with these students and their families. Invariably, parents of difficult children have dealt with negative calls from school for years, in the case of students above kindergarten or 1st grade. Positive calls home may help "flip the script." Students from these families have learned to get attention not only from their teachers but also from their families through negative behaviors. A positive call home gives the family an opportunity to give attention to a report of positive behaviors. In turn, this gives students a taste—perhaps for the first time—of what happens in life when they use positive behaviors, which increases the likelihood that they might continue to use those behaviors.

When you make these calls, have something specific and positive to share about the child. Make it authentic and real. If it is in any way true, remark that you like their child. Keep in mind that many of these families have been through and continue to go through a world of worry, hurt, and pain because of their child's behavior. They might be tremendously anxious, angry, or defensive about their child.

I tend to mention actions that the student took that were positive that relate to something that I like about them. Here are some things I have called parents about:

Hi, Mr. Jacobs. This is Mr. Ervin. I'm calling about Derrick. I wanted to let you know that he had a fantastic first day in improv class with me. He learned and followed the rules of improv right out of the gate, and the other kids followed suit. His display of leadership as an 8th grader in a class with students in 5th through 8th grade really helped me out today!

Hi, Mrs. Allen. This is Mr. Ervin. I'm calling about Tyrell. He had an awesome day. I really noticed how the other kids respect him and follow his lead. I think that even though they would follow him no matter what he does, he has been setting a really positive example by following rules and being kind to other students. I'm glad I get to have him in my fourth period class.

Hello, Ms. Stremanos. It's Mr. Ervin. I'm calling about Jenae. She's hilarious. You must get a kick out of her every day. You probably know, but she gave her introductory speech about herself, and she was so funny and very confident in front of the group. I wanted to let you know how much I appreciate the fact that even though she has this amazing sense of humor, she never tries to cut up when it's not appropriate, and she waits for the right times to be funny. I just really like her and appreciate her for that. You've got to be very proud of her.

Hello, Mr. Boykins. It's Mr. Ervin, Brian's teacher. I wanted to tell you that I saw your kid playing football on the playground today. Wow! Now

I understand what I had heard about him. He's just an amazing athlete. I wanted to let you know that I really appreciate the way he carries himself, and I know you have a lot to do with that. I know that he's not a big fan of school, but I want to work with you guys on getting him what he needs in bite-sized pieces so he can avoid getting frustrated, and so we can get him to do well enough to stay eligible for sports. He has such athletic and leadership gifts that he could become an amazingly successful person, and I want to help with that.

Perhaps just for fun, or perhaps because I am a bit mischievous at heart, I always like to pause immediately after saying who I am and that I am calling about their child. Very often, I will get some form of "OK, what did he do now?" or worse. Then I can tell them that I am calling for a completely positive reason. I have found that this sometimes breaks a kind of spell. It seems to allow the parent to reassess their child and think that perhaps things might be different this year, that perhaps their child isn't incorrigible, that perhaps there is hope.

If a student, particularly an extremely difficult student, does something positive, don't wait to call home. You or another teacher or an administrator may have to deliver some bad news about their child at some point, so try to have the "good call" before you or someone else is forced to have the bad one.

After the first three weeks, make a point to make a positive call to a student's home every week. Don't forget: schedule time to make the call and put it on the calendar. If a student does something you want to call home about, do so as soon as it is convenient and ignore your scheduled time, but make sure you take the time to make that call every week.

- *Attend two sporting events per season.* Showing up at sporting events so that students know that you care is an old idea. It isn't necessary to show up to every game; you can make efficient use of your time by going to two sporting events per season during the year: two in spring, two in winter, and two in fall. Take summer off.

    If you are lucky enough that multiple students are on the same team (this is more common with older students), this becomes very efficient. There might be cheerleaders involved as well. Bring as many of your own friends and family as possible. Be loud and conspicuous. Reinforce positive behaviors that you see from your students by loudly affirming them. Grit, determination, and toughness can be enthusiastically reinforced. Have your friends and family do the same. Tell the cheering section the name(s) of students that you are there to see, and have them use their names when cheering. If your student has a nickname and is comfortable with you using it in this context, you can yell that name (ask about this before game time). Make it very clear that you care about the outcome of the game or match. Make sure everyone on and off the field of play notices that you are there.

- Eat lunch with your students at least one time per week until February. Showing your students that you want to spend time with them even when you don't have to is invaluable. Do so at least once a week, making sure to take time for yourself and that you have enough time to make your copies, set up your lessons, and so on. Of course, secondary teachers usually have schedules that only allow them to eat with certain lunch periods. Still, word will travel that you are a teacher who likes spending free time with students, and this can go a long way toward building relationships with all of your students, not just the ones you can eat with.

    Keep in mind that you can take just five minutes to be with your students and then go do what you need to do during the rest of the lunch period. Relationship building can be done during this time, and lunch monitors generally appreciate teachers being with students in the cafeteria. However, this time should *never* be spent cleaning up after students or opening packages and containers. This time is for relaxing with students.

- Sit on a parked bus with a student at least once per month. After you have used the ESPN Goodbye procedure to usher bus students from classrooms, hop onto a bus. Greet the confusion of the bus driver with a smile and sit with one of your students for a few minutes. Talk about anything. This may be a chance to do some private individual Strategic Noticing or just to shoot the breeze. It is, again, just showing students that you want to be around them even when you are not being paid to do so. Older students may act like they are annoyed or confused by your presence, but that is irrelevant.

Part II

Relationship-Building Procedures

*Make your students fall in love with and
take care of their classroom.*

Someone had tricked me into becoming a principal.

Having been hired as a teacher four years prior, I was now the head of a school with a 98 percent poverty rate. One morning, as I was monitoring our students at breakfast in our Commons area, a group of 2nd graders stood to go to their classroom. At the back of the line, three students each jumped on one foot while kicking one another's feet playfully. To get their attention over the low rumble of the other students, I raised my voice just slightly and asked the rhetorical, one-word question: "Guys?" I then used the Confused Eye Intervention (see Chapter 9: eyes convey a perplexed look; head tilts; hands face the ceiling). This move says, "You are so smart and great; why are you doing this?"

One of the kickers, Travis, had just joined our school. This was his first day. I had met him the previous month when he registered and had greeted him at the door earlier that morning. I had had no other interaction with him. Travis got one last kick in before muttering something under his breath and slowly joining the line.

The second Rockette, Ronika, had been in my 1st grade class the year before. I had looked her in the eye, smiled, shaken her hand or hugged her, and said her name hundreds of times. Her class team had been the Bulldogs. I had given her a personal nickname: Sparkles. She was an excellent writer, and I had told her so emphatically. We had built a fantastic relationship the year before. Ronika immediately stopped kicking and looked as if a tragedy had occurred as she walked quickly to the line.

The third culprit was Jason. Jason had also been in my class the prior year. I had built a strong relationship with him the same way I had with Ronika. In fact, just two months before the start of the school year, he had been the ring bearer in my wedding. We were buds. After my tiny intervention, the blood drained out of Jason's face, and he rushed to get into line as well.

Travis looked at Jason like he was crazy.

Ten minutes later, Jason's teacher called my office and requested that I come to her room. When I walked through her door, I saw Jason in the corner, sitting on the floor crying as hard as I have ever seen a child cry. Believe it or not, Jason was a tough kid. But there he was, losing it in a puddle of tears on the first day of 2nd grade. To be clear, I had not yelled. I had just said, "Guys?" as loudly as was necessary for the trio of kickers to hear me. Yet here we were. I ended up taking Jason to my office and giving him a cot where he could lie down. I felt terrible that I had upset Jason so profoundly. It was not my intention.

With that one intervention, I elicited three totally different results, related to the depths of my relationships with the students.

Most people do not take care of things they do not feel ownership over. Students must feel ownership of their classrooms in order to take care of that space, one another, and you, the teacher. Students' relationships with their teachers are inexorably linked with their relationships to their classrooms. A student who feels like a visitor in a classroom is less likely to cherish and take care of that space and the people in it than the student who feels like a citizen of the classroom. Just as any society depends, in part, on its environment to thrive, so too does your classroom. To build strong, effective, positive relationships, you need a class environment that fosters a shared sense of ownership. So how can you guide students to develop that sense of ownership so they will build positive relationships with you and with one another?

Every student who comes through your door has a unique set of expectations, quirks, interests, and goals. Some of those goals will be antithetical to your own. You, as the teacher, have a task to do: your job description says that you must teach all of those students. The fine print between the lines demands a great deal more of you, because your students must first be open to learning. In your classroom, you can't just make it up as you go. You must lay the groundwork for your class's society by creating an environment in which students are open to and able to learn whatever you have to teach. With all of the other responsibilities you have as a teacher, you can't do this on the fly.

Teachers cannot instill a sense of ownership in their students or build effective relationships with them simply by taking advantage of momentary opportunities when (or if) they arise. This is particularly true with challenging or difficult students, which includes those who come into the class with antisocial goals. Teachers are far too busy to conjure up relationship-building magic on the spot, and students know how to exploit busyness.

Chapter 5 explicitly teaches Relationship-Building Procedures that can be woven into the fabric of the classroom. These procedures provide a structure through which students develop ownership and build relationships every day. You should introduce them in the first three weeks, and then use them with the students every single day. As the procedures become part of the classroom, students will begin to feel like part of the classroom, too. Moreover, the procedures are designed to put students in charge of their own behavior, which in turn, helps them feel in charge of their classroom and reduces the time and energy required of you. Students come to see the classroom as *their* classroom—not a classroom owned by the teacher to which they have been arbitrarily assigned. And when students feel ownership of their classroom, it is easier for you to teach.

5

Relationship-Building Procedures

ESPN Greeting

ESPN is an acronym that stands for four things that you, the teacher, must do with every single student who walks into your room every single day: make *eye contact*, *smile*, engage in *physical contact*, and use the student's *name*.

As a principal, I used the ESPN Greeting procedure with every student who walked through the front door of my school. I consider it to be the single most important Relationship-Building Procedure and behavioral intervention known to humankind. Humans are hardwired to want and need this interaction from others, and they are hardwired to bond, often permanently, with those who share it with them. The systematic use of this procedure alone will significantly improve the culture of your classroom or school. The more difficult and dysfunctional the student population, the more significant the change will be. If you do nothing else, *do this*.

The Procedure

1. Initiate meaningful eye contact. Human beings have a biological need to connect with other human beings. There is no better way to do so than by looking students in the eye. It is a sign of respect, kindness, and affection. In addition, when an educator initiates meaningful eye contact, it signifies appropriate dominance. This is the first building block in creating an effective, healthy student–educator relationship, with the teacher as the Friendly, Loving Alpha

(FLA). Students know that FLAs love them, will take care of them, and are in charge.

2. Offer a genuine smile. A smile sets the tone for the day and lets each student know that they are welcome and liked. A smile also lets everyone know that the FLA is calm, assertive, in control, and ready to go.

3. Initiate friendly, safe physical contact. Again, students have a biological need for appropriate physical contact. This is a wonderful opportunity to model a proper handshake—firm, respectful, welcoming, and genuine. This kind of handshake establishes the adult as the FLA while forging a connection with the student. The teacher should hold each handshake until done greeting the child, which includes the greeting itself (e.g., "Good morning!"), the student's name, and time permitting, some personalized small talk (e.g., "How was your game last night?").

4. Use each student's name. Most people love to hear their names. Saying a student's name or, even better, nickname (see the Student Nicknames procedure) personalizes the greeting. It lets the student know that you aren't just going through the motions. This is particularly important for your most at-risk students, who tend to have trust issues, usually for very good reasons. In addition, those students who are most at risk might have developed a negative association with their name being used by an adult (e.g., teacher, parent, or principal). For these students, their name is often said in anger as part of a punitive power struggle, and the use of their name by an adult might trigger them to flight, fight, or freeze. As an educator, you have a wonderful opportunity to change this association. With all students, but especially with at-risk ones, putting positive emotion behind their name can be a game-changer. Use each student's name throughout the day, too. Pause in the hallway to call out a greeting to another student. You'll be amazed at the difference it makes.

Additional Considerations

Combining meaningful eye contact, a genuine smile, safe physical contact, and the student's name begins the relationship-building process and establishes appropriate dominance. It is always possible to execute the ESPN Greeting. If you think you don't have time to make this happen, then you need to adjust something in your routine or schedule. The most important thing you can do each day, for each class, is to be ready to give this greeting to every single student.

To make sure that you are ready, consider and troubleshoot the following logistical concerns:

- *Preparation.* Of course, teachers must already be 100 percent prepared *before* students arrive. You can't arrange materials and use the ESPN Greeting with students at the same time. Part of this preparation should include a "fast start" activity that students can do independently when they arrive while you continue to greet students.

- *Where to stand.* You should position yourself outside the classroom to greet the first student. Walk briskly toward the first arrival, deliver your ESPN Greeting, and accompany the student toward the empty classroom. As students begin to populate the room, stand with one shoulder blade in the room and one outside of the room to monitor both the hallway and the classroom.

- *How to stand.* Do *not* attempt to "get down on the student's level." For those of you who are vertically challenged or teaching in middle or high school, this may be a moot point, but you should stand the same way that you would stand to meet a colleague. You and the child are not equals. The aforementioned exceptions notwithstanding, you are bigger, stronger, and wiser than your students. Don't suggest otherwise with your body language.

- *When to sit/start teaching.* At some point, you must leave the door and begin to engage in other duties, like taking attendance (or teaching!). For teachers of younger students, signing agendas and checking homework might also be necessary. Some classrooms, particularly in secondary schools, might require that teaching begin at the bell. Once you have begun these activities, you must make sure that students come to you for the ESPN Greeting from wherever they are in the classroom. Yes, for middle and high school teachers, this includes coming to you for an ESPN Greeting while you are instructing, even if the student is late. Don't deal with tardy issues right away. Just greet the student and deal with tardy issues at a time that is convenient for you (see Delayed Learning Opportunities in Chapter 11).

- *Abbreviated physical contact for secondary students.* If you have 40 students coming into your room seven or eight times a day, a firm handshake for each student might not be practical. A fist bump, high five, or pat on the back might be easier. For first period (generally, homeroom or advisory), students should be arriving at a slower pace. This is a great time for a handshake. If the entire school adopts the ESPN Greeting, each student will still learn and benefit from this firm, respectful, welcoming, and genuine handshake.

- *Handshaking protocol.* It is important to both model proper technique and use the handshake to establish yourself as an FLA. You want to make contact with the webbing between the student's thumb and forefinger and the same webbing on your hand. Be the first to grip and apply pressure. This will allow you to control the grip of the handshake, establishing friendly, loving dominance. Apply enough pressure to be firm, but don't overdo it and injure your students—it's an assertion of dominance, not a power struggle! Teachers should teach this protocol once during the first week of school. To ensure that you don't lose face if the student walks by without shaking your hand, hold your hand just six to eight inches away from your midsection when greeting your students. Whenever possible, partially block the doorway so that students can't just walk by you. That way you can at least offer the greeting. If a student squeezes too hard, simply say, "Ouch! Too hard!" If the student does not relent or continues to use this negative behavior, use these words as well as your personalized script for "getting to later" to deliver a Delayed Learning Opportunity (see Chapter 11).

- *Encouragement without force.* Initiate eye contact and physical contact, but don't force them. You can offer a greeting and use each student's name without compelling eye contact and physical contact. Students might be reticent to give proper eye contact or physical contact at first. Hold your position and offer. Encourage the eye contact by subtly moving your eyes toward the student's field of vision, but do not aggressively follow their eyes, and never do so while blocking the student's path. As always, smile. For shier students, not squaring your shoulders and sometimes briefly slumping over to make yourself appear smaller can also be helpful. Likewise, don't force the handshake. Remember, you will have 180 chances to modify the behavior of students avoiding contact, so there's no hurry.

Class Nickname

It is difficult to give your students ownership of their classroom while constantly referring to the class as *your* class. No matter the age of your students, you will sometimes need to refer to the group as a whole. When you do so, you can either build ownership by using a name that the students chose or take away ownership by referring to them as "Mr. Johnson's Class." I suggest the former.

The Procedure

On the first day of school, ask your students whose class they are in. Most will probably say, "Yours." Older students might respond with an eye roll and a yawn. Younger students might not pay attention or care about the verbiage. Nevertheless, it is important to let them know that this is actually their classroom and that you are only there to facilitate learning. They will be the ones who manage and lead the room.

After you tell students that the room is theirs, act on it. Explain that to call the class "[Your Name]'s Room" doesn't make any sense, so you are going to give them the chance to name themselves. Inform them that they will be voting to determine a name for the class, then follow these steps:

1. Brainstorm names. Adjourn to team desks/tables (which you created in Chapter 3). Have each team discuss and debate names for the class. Often, especially with older students, this degenerates into "What would be funny/ inappropriate for our teacher to call us all year?" That's fine, for now. Encourage all students to offer ideas but don't force the issue. Allow teams around five minutes to discuss.

2. Identify potential names. Regroup as a class. Call on each student to offer one name. Students who don't want to suggest a name can pass their nomination to another student of their choice. This is strategic. Students who have low control needs will almost always pass to kids who have higher control needs, such as the class clowns who like to be funny. They often get many nominations passed to them and tend to come up with the best names. In turn, the class is likely to choose one of these names, thereby giving this high–control need student a feeling of tremendous ownership each time the name is used for the rest of the year. Write potential names on the board. If any names are totally inappropriate in your view, you can reject them, but accept border-line nicknames for now. A borderline nickname is one that you feel slightly uncomfortable with; let your students know that if one of the borderline names is voted through, then you will need to get permission from the principal to use that name. Often, these names will be sports teams, sayings, and with older students, somewhat inappropriate slang terms often taken from rap songs, *Saturday Night Live*, and so on.

3. Take a vote. Allow students to vote on their favorite names. Give each student two votes. Call out each name and take a show of hands. The top vote getter is the class name for the year. In the case of a tie, hold a runoff vote using just the tied names.

4. Address borderline names. In the event a borderline name wins the vote, let your giggling students know that you will have to go to your administrator and ask if the name is acceptable. If you are too uncomfortable with the name to ask your administrator about it, then the name should not have been considered in the first place. If the administrator approves the name, great! Proceed. If the

administrator nixes the name (but lets you keep your job), you get to go back and tell your students that even though you were cool enough to ask your boss about a name you're barely allowed to say in school, it got rejected. This, in and of itself, is a great way to build a relationship with your class. Repeat the vote using all other potential names. If another borderline name is picked, repeat the process. The best-case scenario is that your students send you back to your administrator several times. Each time you go to your administrator, you show your students that you will go out of your way for them. It can be a fun bonding experience for you to keep coming back empty-handed. When you or your principal tire of this (whichever comes first), you can just come back to your classroom and tell your students that the principal isn't as hip as you are and that you need to give up on the borderline names. Then, erase any question-able names and vote on the remaining ones. No matter what happens, you are giving your students ownership of their room and building positive relation-ships with them.

5. Use the name. Once you have an approved name, congratulations! Your students, especially the most difficult ones, might start thinking differently about this year and their class than they have about previous years and other classes; they may think, "Maybe this year will be different" or "Maybe this is my classroom." Have students make a large banner or sign (or several) with the class nickname for display in doorways and other prominent places in the classroom. From the moment that the name is decided upon, only refer to your class by their chosen name.

Team Nicknames

By the first day of school, you have carefully divided your class into teams and your students have voted for a Class Nickname. Now have your students work with their teams to choose a Team Nickname. You should introduce the procedure for creating Team Nicknames with the Control-Sharing Procedure Real-World Workshop (see Chapter 8). However, it is not necessary for you or your students to understand all the ins and outs of the procedure on the first day of school. Again, for our hypothetical classroom, we will assume 25 students, with five teams of five students.

The Procedure

1. **Prepare.** Create a "Nows and Laters Board" to use during the procedure.

Nows

Unanimously decide on a team nickname

Laters

Create team tags

Read

?

2. **Introduce teams and colors.** Let students know that they are permanently assigned to their teams and their seats. Point out that each team has been assigned a color and that many of their materials have been color-coded accordingly.

3. **Introduce the Team Nicknames concept.** Explain that each team will select a team nickname. Tell students that their nicknames can be any appropriate name that is not the same as the class name or the school mascot. (If needed, apply the same borderline appropriate name practices that you used when choosing the class name.) Let students know that when their team has agreed on a name, it will be their moniker for the entire year. Add that teams must reach a unanimous decision.

4. **Point out the Nows and Laters Board.** Explain how the board works: first, students must complete the items under "Nows"; then, they can move onto the items under "Laters." Point out that, in this case, they have one item listed under Nows. That means, they must choose a team name. Then, they can move on to their Laters. Emphasize that students *must* complete the Nows before they can do the Laters. However, when ready, they can choose which Laters they want to do during Real-World Workshop. They do not need to do all the Laters listed; these are options. (Note: The question mark in the figure represents a Mystery Later; more on this below.)

5. **Let teams work**. Allow teams to take as much time as needed to choose a name. Completion of this task will be the responsibility of each team, not the teacher. "Unanimously decide on a team nickname" will remain as a Now activity until each team has chosen a name or the school year ends—whichever happens first. Do not warn or lecture students about the importance of "getting done" with picking a name. This initial team activity is important in establishing that students bear the responsibility for getting their work done.

6. **Greet new teams.** When a team agrees unanimously, greet them by their nickname and remind them that they are done with their Nows, so they can move on to their Laters. In this case, students can either read a book or make a team tag. (We're not ready for the Mystery Later yet. Hang in there.) Team

tags can be made however you would like, but make sure you have materials (e.g., colored sentence strip paper for each team color) ready for students to use. Encourage each team to incorporate their team nickname and team color in their tags, and allow students to make as many tags as they would like, working cooperatively. How and when tags are used is entirely up to the teacher. They can be attached to the team desks or table; put on team bins, shelves, and lockers; or hung above team areas. Using team tags helps build students' sense of ownership and helps team members start building relationships with one another.

7. **Allow the procedure to motivate struggling teams.** Some teams will have a harder time working together and agreeing on names than others. They will need more motivation. Please note that "motivation" does not mean warnings, threats, or reminders. Instead, when you feel that your students have had ample time to come up with a team nickname, reveal your Mystery Later. Erase the question mark and write something appealing like "recess," "relax outside," or "play in gym," depending on what's feasible given the weather, the school, and the schedule. At this point, relocate your students outside or wherever the fun activity will take place. Teams who have completed their "Now" can enjoy themselves or just take a break. Teams who have not yet unanimously chosen a nickname must sit together, where they will either succeed or fail at agreeing upon a nickname. Either way, their success or failure is their problem—not yours. (If you have more than one adult in your room, teams that are still working can stay in the classroom with the adult.) You are likely to see more motivation from students to finish their Now once the Mystery Later is revealed. When these teams have unanimously agreed on their nickname, allow them to join the fun.

8. **Hold firm.** If a team is unable to agree on a team nickname before the class must move on to other work, keep that Now on the board the next time you have a Real-World Workshop (see sidebar). That team will still need to complete that "Now" in addition to the other "Nows" that will be assigned at that time.

Tying in the Real-World Workshop

This chapter is dedicated to Relationship-Building Procedures; however, keep in mind that you will also be introducing and using Control-Sharing

Procedures on the first day of school and throughout the first three weeks. In fact, the method you used to choose team names is one of those procedures: Real-World Workshop. (You'll learn more about this in Chapter 8. Feel free to skip to page 146 if you would like to understand the rationale and details of this procedure now.)

The Team Nickname procedure serves as a good vehicle for teaching Real-World Workshop because every workshop will use a Nows and Laters Board. As one or more teams is likely to have trouble agreeing on a name, students will learn several facts of life about their classroom through this opening activity:

- A student's problems are not the teacher's problems.
- Conflicts among students create problems that must be solved by the students.
- Getting work done is the student's problem, not the teacher's.
- Consequences can befall entire teams or the entire class at any time, without warning.
- When students finish their work, they get to do things that are more fun than work.

Student Nicknames

Class Nickname? Check. Team Nicknames? Check. That brings us to Student Nicknames. Whenever we go out of our way to give attention to a student in a positive way, it boosts their feeling of classroom ownership and enhances their relationship with their teacher. Giving a special nickname to a student shows that the teacher has taken the time to think of a good, meaningful name. It shows that the teacher likes the student. The chances of students liking the teacher go up considerably when students feel that the teacher likes them.

In addition, many students—especially those who demonstrate negative behaviors—have a negative association with their own names. This results from other adults in their lives using their names in a negative way. Consider how often students who are consistently "in trouble" must hear their name yelled while being corrected or punished. Students who have had traumatic experiences can even go into fight, flight, or freeze mode just by hearing an adult say their name! Some students might associate their names with negative thoughts, feelings, and emotions, which means that a teacher can damage the relationship just by saying their names.

Using a nickname enables the teacher to circumvent and even counter these dynamics. Just as some students might equate "bad behavior" with their name, they might equate a new nickname with a new, better-behaved self. In addition, every time you call students by their nicknames, it improves your relationship with them and increases their feelings of ownership of the classroom and school.

The Procedure

To maximize the relationship-building and ownership process, you should give nicknames in a fun, meaningful way that treats the nickname as an honor. Choosing nicknames and bestowing them on students with a special ceremony are accomplished through specific procedures.

1. **Try to give one student a nickname before the end of your first week, even if it is an abbreviated week.** Why? Nicknames and ceremonies are fun, students love them, and they set a positive tone in your classroom.

2. **Whenever possible, do a Nickname Ceremony at the end of the day on the last day of the school week for elementary students and at the end of your class period with your older students on the last day of the week.** This may cause students to think, as they are leaving for the weekend, "That was awesome! I can't wait to come back here Monday! Wait, what am I saying?!"

3. **Give the first nickname to the student for whom a nickname first pops into your head.** Nicknames should come naturally. You shouldn't force them, and you don't need to first choose a student who has behavior issues just to build a relationship quickly. In fact, you should avoid giving the most difficult students nicknames first. There are two reasons for this. First, some students might think that you are giving preferential treatment to students who exhibit negative behaviors, and this may encourage students to exhibit those behaviors. Second, the tough students to whom you are giving the nicknames may "get wise" to what you are doing and see this as a manipulation, which will increase their resentment. However, you should try to nickname your more difficult students within the first few months. Also, if you have students with the same real name, you might want to pick one of them as an early nickname recipient in order to decrease name confusion in the classroom.

4. **Choose an appropriate nickname that does not embarrass the student.** You want to select a name that is specific to the student, but it doesn't have to be the most original, unique, awesome nickname ever. The process should not add stress to you or your students. Keep in mind that you can use humor. The best nicknames lightheartedly refer to something that is notable about that student.

5. **Approach the student for their approval.** The easiest way to make sure a student likes a nickname is to ask the student! Do this *before* the ceremony. If a student doesn't like the name (or appears doubtful or uncertain), let them know that you won't use the name and you need more time to think of a better name. You can go on to other students while you are contemplating a new nickname for that student, but don't wait too long (no more than a month or so) before getting back to the student with a new nickname.

Alternatively, you can work cooperatively with each student on a nickname, or do both. Choose it yourself when you have a strong feeling about a nickname, or work with the student when you need some help or when you think a particularly clever student may come up with a better nickname than you would.

A Student by Any Other Name . . .

Over the years, I have taught or served as principal to thousands of young people. These are just a few nicknames that I have bestowed along the way. Each one was approved by the student:

- "Red" for a boy with—you got it—red hair
- "Princess Giggles" for one particularly bubbly girl
- "Big Bear" and "Little Bear" for two best friends who were both rather cuddly-looking: one big, one more diminutive
- "Flash" for a student who was super-fast and on the football team
- "Flips" for a gymnast
- "Hoops" for a basketball player

The Nickname Ceremony

Once you have picked a nickname and received approval, you are ready to hold your first Nickname Ceremony. Nickname Ceremonies should occur at the end of a school day during your Afternoon Meeting (see Chapter 8 for more about the Afternoon Meeting procedure). As soon as you have finished the rest of the Afternoon Meeting, you can begin the Nickname Ceremony.

Tailor your Nickname Ceremony to your own sense of fun, humor, and comfort level with silliness. I've outlined some general guidelines below, followed by a walk-through of one of my ceremonies. You can adopt my methods, but it will be more fun to create your own using the guidelines.

The Nickname Ceremony will become a class ritual. As such, it must be something strange, unusual, and, above all, fun. You should make the ceremony an odd, theatrical experience in which you look at least a little silly. For example, it should include some type of faux emotion (e.g., yelling, jumping around with excitement) as well as some special costume or prop. This inspires students to look forward to the ceremony. Looking silly actually helps teachers appear more dominant, because students respect people who "put themselves out there." Being strong enough to purposely let yourself look foolish will help elevate you to FLA status.

Whatever process you adopt, make sure that you use the same one every time. This allows the ceremony to become a ritual, a repeated rite of passage that adds predictability and consistency to the lives of students who may not have either at home.

How my Nickname Ceremony works:

1. Before the Afternoon Meeting, I make sure the nickname recipient not only approves the nickname but also knows the ceremony is happening. I tell the student that when I announce the nickname, the student should ask, "Why?"

2. At the end of the Afternoon Meeting, I have the person who led the meeting—or the Comfort Keeper—turn off the lights (see Chapter 6). I ask the team of the day to pull down the blinds or close the curtains, making sure that enough light comes from the hallway or through the window that everyone can see.

3. I pull out my "Boogada, Boogada" hat (a straw hat with flowers) and staff (a piece of an old bulletin board), and stand before the students, who are seated on the carpet. I silently stare them down for a few seconds, then say, "[Student's first and last name], come forward."

4. When the student stands, I crouch down and stare at the student for a moment. Then, I slam the staff into the ground near the student's feet and loudly proclaim these words: "Boogada, boogada, boogada!"

5. I pause for effect, then declare, "Ladies and gentlemen, I present to you [student's first and last name]. Boogada, boogada, boogada!" I punctuate each "boogada" by knocking the end of the staff on the ground.

6. I continue: "[Student's first name], from now on, your [the class name] nickname shall be . . . [student's new nickname]!" The nicknamed student asks, "Why?" Then, I reach into my pocket, pull out confetti (shredded paper), and throw it toward the top of the student's head. I demand, "WHY NOT?!"

7. I allow laughter to subside, then conclude: "Ladies and gentlemen, I now present to you . . . [student's nickname]!"

8. We use the Class Applause procedure, which you will learn later in this chapter, to conclude the ceremony.

Remember: Keep It Silly, Keep It Strange

My way is just one way to perform the Nickname Ceremony. I encourage you to adopt your own creative approach. Just remember to include these four elements:

- Make it strange and entertaining.
- Incorporate faux emotion (the louder the better) and props or costumes.
- Make yourself look at least a little silly.
- Use the same structure every time. I mean it.

For Secondary Grades: Set It Up Properly and Get Out of the Way (While Monitoring)

Secondary students love to create their own ceremony for this procedure and will very much look forward to it if, while planning and performing it, they both feel emotionally safe and are given appropriate (in this case, a lot of) control. All you must do with secondary students is privately get approval from an individual student on the nickname, as described above, and monitor students as they create and implement the ritual that they will use for the rest of the year. Use previously described procedures for borderline appropriate ritual suggestions. The ritual may be something intricately silly, or it may be something basic and boring. It doesn't matter what it is—it just matters that it is *theirs*.

Have the students be the ones to perform the ceremony with each other, using nicknames created by the teacher and approved by the student. Allow any sharing of the performance of the ritual that is in line with your sense of fairness. You can have a "class clown" lead the ritual every time or have teams of the day perform it. This can depend on how your students want to divide these responsibilities.

Monitor the ceremony planning and performances to make sure students are not being hurtful or mean. Use Delayed Learning Opportunities if and when appropriate (see Chapter 11). As much as possible, stay out of this procedure! This is an excellent chance to sit at your desk with your feet up.

Note that for secondary school, if multiple or all teachers are creating student nicknames, some intraclass communication is in order. Often, homeroom classes will produce nicknames (this is optimal if these rooms do not teach academic content), or the last class will produce the names. For intermediate grades that switch rooms and teachers at lunch, one teacher can create nicknames for one class, and another teacher can create nicknames for the other.

After the Ceremony

From that day onward, use only the student's nickname. Do not use the student's real name. Once a student has a nickname, you will strengthen your relationship with that student *every time you say their name!*

The day after the ceremony, give the newly christened student blank adhesive nametags. Explain that the student now has a personal "Later" (see Chapter 8): they can write the nickname on the tags, decorate them, and place them wherever you indicate. In my room, the nametags go on a student's locker and workbook bin. For younger students, you might want to place the tags after the student has completed them.

Additional Considerations

Teachers should keep in mind these additional guidelines:

- Allow *students to write their nicknames on their work, with a few exceptions.* During standardized testing, you must remind students to put their real names on high-stakes tests, as the test grader will not know who "Princess Giggles" is. At the pre-K, kindergarten, and 1st grade levels, permit students to write their nicknames on their work only after they have mastered writing their real names. This serves as a great incentive for younger students to learn to spell and write their names.

- Do not spend *time trying to get administrators or specials teachers to learn students' nicknames.* They have enough to worry about. As the only adult who knows all your students' nicknames, you will further secure your status as a Friendly, Loving Alpha.

- Begin and continue *the ceremony only when everyone is quiet to a level of your satisfaction (I prefer silent).* To get students to the desired level, you can use the procedures for giving activity choices at the end of Afternoon Meeting (see page 173), and list "Nickname Ceremony" as one of the choices.

- Conduct ceremonies *at the end of the day (elementary) and at the end of the class period (secondary).* Don't feel like a ceremony must be held the day that you decide on a nickname. If you end up short on time (e.g., perhaps a fire drill or other event disrupted the schedule, or you just got behind), or students are not able to get ready in time, then apologize to the nickname candidate and let them know that you will perform the ceremony as soon as you can.

- *Make sure that everyone has a nickname by the end of January (for schools with a traditional calendar), but don't do too many ceremonies too quickly.* The longer a student waits to get a nickname, the more the student will appreciate it once it is given! Don't hold ceremonies for multiple students at the same time—unless they have complementary nicknames like Big Bear and Little Bear.

- *Never use the giving of a nickname as a reward or the withholding of a nickname as a threat or a punishment.* This will damage rather than strengthen your relationships.

- *When you get a new student in the middle of the year, don't choose a nickname right away.* This allows new students to feel like real members of the class once they receive a nickname instead of feeling like they are just getting a nickname by default. If students question why a new student has not yet received a nickname, simply let them know that you have not yet gotten to know the new student well enough to pick an awesome nickname.

Class Applause

Teachers of all grades often struggle to get their students to applaud and show appreciation for the work or presentations of their fellow classmates. One way to solve that problem, while also allowing students to build ownership of their classroom, is to create a new and different way to applaud in your classroom. Giving students ownership of the *way* they express appreciation makes it more likely that they will *show* appreciation. In turn, the more appreciation shown by your students, the more positive your class environment will become.

In addition, the students least likely to show appreciation through applause generally are the ones most likely to "applaud" in an alternative way chosen by the class. These more challenging students also tend to be better at coming up with funny ways of showing appreciation. If the class adopts a method of applause suggested by a more challenging student, that student will likely lead the charge to use the applause all year long rather than rolling their eyes while listlessly slapping their hands together.

The Procedure

1. **Introduce the concept.** During a Morning Meeting (see Chapter 8) for younger students and at the end of a class period for older students, inform

them that you are bored with the normal way of applauding. Tell students that you are giving them an opportunity to create their own type of applause.

2. **Explain the guidelines (not more than once):**
   - The Class Applause must involve a physical motion (like clapping does).
   - The Class Applause must involve a sound (produced verbally or manually).
   - The Class Applause must be appropriate for school.

3. **Schedule a vote.** Let younger students know that you will lead a vote for the new applause after the Afternoon Meeting that day. Tell older students that their vote will take place at the end of class the next school day. Encourage students to talk about possible ideas with one another when they have a chance, such as during lunch or at recess.

4. **Collect nominations.** At the end of the Afternoon Meeting, tell younger students that you will give them a chance to create their Class Applause when they are all seated silently. Call on each student to nominate an applause. Ask for the name of the applause method, explaining that students will be able to demonstrate the method in a moment, and write the name on the board. As with previous nomination procedures, allow students to donate their nomination to another student. For older students, follow the same procedure, but let them nominate regular clapping as a method, if they choose.

5. **Go through the list.** Call on each student to demonstrate the proposed applause. Take a vote after all demonstrations have been made, allowing everyone to vote once. (With older students, you might let them design and lead the voting process.)

6. **Celebrate the choosing of the Class Applause with the Class Applause!**

Regarding older students and clapping: Some middle and high school students might think that a special method of applause is beneath them, because they are the Most Mature People in the Universe. These same students are almost always the ones whom you would otherwise need to cajole to applaud in the traditional way. If you let them nominate and even choose traditional applause over more creative methods, then they will be more likely to actually use traditional applause throughout the year because they had some control over the matter.

Whether younger or older, by creating their own applause, students are creating their own positive, supportive learning environment.

Sample Class Applause: Elementary

One of my 3rd grade classes named themselves the "Bobcats." For their Class Applause, they chose to pose their hands like claws and yell, "Bobcats! Bobcats! Bobcats!" Each time they yelled the team name, they jabbed their "claws" into the air. As time went on, their applause evolved to extend their claws toward the person being "Bobcatted."

Sample Class Applause: Secondary

Secondary students tend to go in one of two directions: totally ridiculous as a means of protesting how utterly stupid this ritual is, or very boring as a means of protesting how utterly stupid this ritual is. It doesn't matter how they feel or what they choose; it just matters that they make a choice so that they own the ritual. I have seen classes choose to make crazy monkey noises (ridiculous), and I have seen classes choose traditional applause (boring). Either way, they ended up feeling more ownership of the room.

Class Handshake

This procedure works much like Class Applause in terms of when and how the class decides on a method. As with Class Applause, you can permit students to run the procedure with appropriate guidance.

The Procedure

1. **Introduce the concept.** Tell students that today they will have the chance to come up with a Class Handshake.

2. **Explain these guidelines (once):**
   - For elementary students, the Class Handshake must take three seconds or less. For middle and high school students who change classes multiple times per day, it must take one second or less.
   - Everyone must be physically able to do the Class Handshake, or it should include modifications for students with physical challenges. This encourages students to be mindful and inclusive.
   - The Class Handshake must be appropriate for school.

3.   **Follow a similar voting procedure as used for the Class Applause.** Remind students to discuss their ideas with one another as they are able.

4.   **After the vote, encourage everyone to celebrate by practicing the handshake with a team member.**

The Class Handshake is a good opportunity to come up with an abbreviated form of safe physical contact. You can use this contact with each student entering and leaving your classroom every day. Some classes choose a fist bump, forearm tap, or high five. Classes can add a verbal element, as well.

The process of voting and choosing the physical contact reinforces students' sense of ownership and helps you build your relationship with them. This applies even to the "too cool for school" students who roll their eyes and look bored while not voting. If students have the opportunity to vote and decline it, it's OK. The reason for these procedures is to *offer* control and ownership, not for students to accept them.

Class Rules

Making rules for students' behavior prior to their arrival is a mistake. There is no action more alienating for students than walking into a room on the first day of school and seeing a list of rules already posted. Human history shows us that people rebel against rules imposed on them without their input or consent. It also shows that the most harmonious and happy societies are those in which the governed create and agree to their own rules by a democratic process. Students, like all citizens, require control and freedom, as well as a right to due process when the fairness of the rule or its application is in question.

To instill a sense of ownership and build a positive relationship with students, teachers must allow them to create their own rules. Otherwise, students and teacher will be locked in ongoing power struggles. Again, you should *never* post rules before students arrive on the first day. Instead, wait for students to get there, then invite them to make the rules.

Here's how.

The Procedure

1.   **Get started right away.** On the first day of school, in the first two hours of instruction, get students started on creating their own Class Rules. This should take 15 to 25 minutes. While you can provide developmentally appropriate breaks, it's best to do this all in one sitting.

2. **Cede ownership of the rules.** Remind your students that as the teacher, you are only in the room to teach, not to own the room. Emphasize that they are in *their* classroom. Ask them to find where in the room the rules are posted. When students realize that rules are not posted anywhere in the room, ask, "Why do you think that is?" Explain that because the classroom is theirs, they must make the rules for themselves.

3. **Invite students to suggest rules for the class and write them on the board.** Point out that these rules are just suggestions for now, and they won't automatically become class rules just because they're on the board. Accept all appropriate suggestions. For this procedure, *appropriate* means that the rule doesn't involve inappropriate language or suggestions that are purposely mean, unsafe, or hurtful. Students can, however, nominate bad rules that would lead to chaos. In other words, "Scream as loudly as you want at all times" can go on the board; "Don't sit next to Tayla because she *@%*ing stinks" cannot.

See Figure 5.1 for an illustration of what the process might look like as you engage your students in refining their list.

Figure 5.1
Suggested, Combined, and Acceptable Class Rules

Suggestions	Combined Rules	Acceptable Rules
Be nonviolent with hands.		Be respectful.
Be nonviolent with feet.		Work hard.
Be kind.		
Be safe.		
Keep balls in lockers.		
Use nice words.	Be respectful.	
Walk.		
Treat people how you want to be treated.		
Listen to the teacher.		
Listen to one another.		
Be helpful.		
You can throw balls.	You can throw balls.	
Yell as loud as you want.	Yell as loud as you want.	
Work hard.	Work hard.	

4. **Reword suggested rules to use affirmative language.** Be sure to explain to students what you are doing ("Let's just state that in the affirmative"). For example:

   - Revise "Don't hit people" to "Be nonviolent with your hands."
   - Revise "Don't talk while others are talking" to "Stay quiet while others are talking."

5. **Allow enough time that each student can each make two to three suggestions.** In addition, refrain from limiting the number of suggestions that one student may propose. The students who keep adding rules are likely the ones who need the most control. By letting them suggest numerous rules, you are giving them that control.

6. **When students run out of suggestions, review your list.**

7. **Express sincere appreciation for having so many wonderful rules.** Then express dismay that there are *too many* rules. Ask students if any of the rules can be combined. There are no human students in existence who need to be convinced that there are too many rules and that they should get rid of most of them. If they have trouble suggesting a combination, model an example:

   - "Listen to the teacher" and "Listen to each other" can be combined as "Listen when people are talking." Any rule beginning with "Listen" can eventually be combined simply to "Listen."
   - "Be nonviolent with your hands" and "Be nonviolent with your body" can be combined as "Be kind" and "Be safe." These can further be combined as "Be respectful." (See Figure 5.1.)

8. **As you combine rules, be sure to explain your reasoning.** If a student suggests a combination, ask the student to share the reason. You want to make sure that the students who suggested a rule understand why it is being combined with another rule so that they don't feel alienated by the process. Erasing specific rules and replacing them with general rules lets students see the process by which they are creating a fair way to govern their classroom. It's democracy in action!

9. **Address rules that will not serve the class well.** You are likely to get some of these, especially with older students. Do not reject a rule unless it is inappropriate or malicious. Suggesting rules like "You can throw balls" or "Yell as loudly as you want" is a way for students to test the procedure's authenticity—and yours. It is important to pass these tests, so let the suggested rules stand until this point. Then, pick a positive rule that contradicts as many

unacceptable rules as possible. In nearly every case, one positive rule (e.g., "Be respectful" in Figure 5.1) contradicts all the unacceptable rules. Next, point to the positive rule and ask, "Who thinks this is a good rule?" (Do not ask if it is the *best* rule, just if it is *good.*) Count the votes.

- In most rooms, a majority of students will like the positive rule, especially if the teacher has been building relationships from Open House until this moment on the first day. Announce that since everyone—or most students— agree that the positive rule (e.g., "Be respectful") is a good rule, then the class must reject the unacceptable rules because they violate that rule. For example, you might say, "Students can't throw things or be as loud as they want and be respectful at the same time."

- If you get lucky and too many students vote *against* the positive rule, then it is your turn to exercise some control. This is OK, because you have been and will be giving enormous amounts of control away as a matter of routine procedure. You can simply say that for any social group or society to work, people must be respectful. At that point, erase the unacceptable rules.

10. **Review your revised—and much shorter—list of rules.** Once you have rejected inappropriate rules, combined redundant rules, and worked out acceptable rules, the list should look something like the third column in Figure 5.2. Marvel that the class was able to combine and delete so many rules. Point out that there are only two rules left!

    Note: "Work hard" might not be on your list. It doesn't matter if it is or not; see the sidebar for more on that. However, "Be respectful," "Be nice," or "Be kind" should be the other (or only) rule. Why? Because these three rules basically mean the same thing, and each is an authentic, pure distillation of any set of rules for human interaction. It is the essence of the Golden Rule as well as the U.S. Bill of Rights, the Declaration of the Rights of Man in the Citizen in France, English common law, and every democratic legal code on Earth. In other words, when people get together to make rules for human behavior, the purest essence of what they come up with is to be nice, kind, and respectful.

11. **Flesh out the final list.** After marveling a moment, express that you still see a problem with the Class Rules. Explain that if the class keeps the list as it is, then you might be tempted to do something that you don't like to do: lecture. "'Be respectful' is really annoying to hear and to say!" you might exclaim ruefully. "Do your parents ever nag you about being respectful? Mine did, and I *really* didn't enjoy it." Request that students change the rule to read something like

"You have the freedom to do anything you want that does not cause a problem" or "You can do you whatever you feel like doing unless it causes a problem." Tell students that with a rule like that, you won't be tempted to lecture them. Students, especially difficult ones, should like this rule more than most rules imposed on them in the past. The same can probably not be said for "Be nice," "Be kind," and "Be respectful." They've probably heard—and been lectured— about these simple phrases *many* times. In addition, the fact that they co-created the rule makes it inherently more palatable.

12. **Congratulate the class on coming up with a fine set of rules!**

Work Hard?

As noted, "work hard" does not need to be a rule. If the class doesn't come up with it, that's fine. If they want to get rid of it, that's OK, too. The teacher can also remove it, claiming that it might be used to lecture students. That can be a good idea with especially tough students.

Teachers should never *tell* students to work, because they can't *make* them work. Instead, the Real-World Workshop procedure (see Chapter 8) teaches students to realize that their life improves when they work hard. Students learn the benefit of working hard, so there's *no need to try to make them work hard*. Note: the procedure does the teaching—not the teacher. If a class does keep "Work hard" as a rule and a student isn't working hard, the teacher can ask, "What is our rule about working?" Other than that, an effective teacher never tries to make a student work.

- If you are like most teachers, you just had a thought akin to "That's ridiculous. That won't work. If I don't lecture kids about hard work and its benefits, they'll all become lazy!" You will just have to trust me on this point until you begin to implement the Real-World Workshop procedure. To hold you over until then, know this: *every single one of the hundreds of students who have used the Real-World Workshop in my classroom became extremely hard workers without me spending any time trying to lecture them into working.*

Does This/That Cause a Problem?

"You are free to do whatever you want as long as it doesn't cause a problem."

This rule is nice because it's *one* rule. It's easy to remember and easy to apply. Still, students will test it, and you want them to. Most won't realize right away just how much it covers. This rule closes loopholes that more specific rules leave open, and you can apply it to any situation. Rather than coming up with new rules for unique situations (assemblies, field trips, field day), you can use this rule. Plus, you're training students for life.

Think about it: the rule encourages students to learn to consider the consequences before they act. Before doing something, they may ask themselves, "Does this cause a problem?" If they did not ask themselves this, or if they answer incorrectly and do something that causes a problem, just smile and ask, "Does that cause a problem?" Most likely, the student will realize that it does and stop. (We'll get to what to do when the student continues the behavior shortly.)

When a student exhibits a dubious behavior, and it's unclear whether it causes a problem, you should still ask, "Does that cause a problem?" The student might offer opinions, in which case you can respond, "I'm not sure. Let's all figure it out later." Let's look at an example of this situation.

The bus riders in a class walk in line to the buses at the end of the day. One student decides to stop and get a drink at the water fountain. The teacher asks, "Does that cause a problem?" The student says that it doesn't. The teacher says, "OK, I'm not sure. Let's all figure it out later." The next day, during the Morning or Afternoon Meeting, the teacher describes the situation and asks, "Does a student stopping to get a drink in this instance cause a problem?" The teacher then manages the discussion, inviting all students to share their opinions, listening to them, and asking targeted questions. Through the discussion, the teacher guides students to realize that, in this situation, stopping to get a drink does cause a problem. Why? Because students are walking in a line. When one student stops, the rest of the line stops or gets jumbled. The student stopping causes a problem because it inconveniences, confuses, or delays others. Therefore, stopping for a drink before going to the buses is no longer allowed under the Class Rules.

Due Process

The Fifth Amendment to the U.S. Constitution reads, in part, "No person shall . . . be deprived of life, liberty, or property, without due process of law." The phrase "due process" means that people have a right to not be punished arbitrarily. They have a right to make their case and be heard. This principle dates back long before the Constitution; it has its roots in the Magna Carta of 1215, and even in ancient Athens, the birthplace of much democratic thought.

Due process is a fundamental principle of democratic governance, and students, the citizens of your classroom, have a right to expect it, too. Therefore, immediately after your class has established your Class Rules, tell students something like the following:

> If you do cause a problem, and can't or won't solve it, then I must do something about it. I might accidently do something that is not fair or say that I am going to do something that is not fair. If you think that I am doing something unfair, then I want you to whisper this to me: "I don't know about that. Could we talk about this later?" We will then talk about it later when it is convenient for me.

This does not let students off the hook. It just means that you and the student will have a private conversation about the matter later. At that time, you should listen without talking. When the student is done talking, consider the student's point of view. If you realize that you were wrong in your assessment of the situation, you can change you mind and pursue a new, fairer course of action. If you are not sure what is the best course of action in light of new facts or this new perspective, you can thank the student and let them know that you need to think about it and will get back to them. Then you can do more thinking or investigating, whatever the situation requires. If you don't need this time, you can skip this step. After this delay—or right away, if you don't need it—ask to offer your perspective on the matter. The original decision can be upheld or changed. Either way, the student received a fair hearing. As a result, you and the student both feel better about the situation, and your relationship is improved.

Class Pledge

The Class Pledge procedure should follow the Class Rules procedure. That's because you will not be posting the Class Rules agreed on by the students and the teacher. Rather, you will guide your students to write a class constitution. First, teach or review the concept of a constitution in an age-appropriate manner (use trade books on the topic if appropriate). After discussing the concept of a constitution as a guiding rule or law, lead students in another Real-World Workshop to turn their rules into a class constitution, which will, in turn, become the Class Pledge.

The Procedure

1. **Reformat the agreed-upon rules.** Rewrite the Class Rule(s) in a format similar to that of the U.S. Constitution ("We, [class name] may do . . ."). This will serve as a rough draft of the class constitution.

2. **Display the draft in a prominent location.** This will now be referred to as the Class Constitution.

3. **Consider how to share control over the Class Pledge.** Before moving on with the rest of the procedure, determine how much control you are willing to share with students regarding how they say the Class Pledge. *What* they say or recite is the class constitution; *how* they say it is what defines the pledge. You should decide ahead of time what elements of performing the pledge your students can decide. Options include whether they sit or stand while saying the pledge, what pose they take, and how they finish it. Keep in mind the age of your students, and keep it easy and safe—finishing the pledge with a round-house kick is probably a bad idea.

4. **Designate constitution work as Later activities.** Prepare for the next Real-World Workshop by listing "Write class constitution" and "Sign class constitution" as Laters. Have poster paper and multiple colors of markers set out. When students have finished with their Nows, they can write the class constitution on poster paper and sign the document. Encourage them to use their best handwriting.

5. **Display the constitution.** Prominently display the class constitution at the front of the classroom, where it will be the focal point of the Class Pledge.

6. **Determine the format for the Class Pledge.** Explain to students that they have written out their class constitution, and now they must decide *how* to say the constitution as their Class Pledge. Tell students what aspects of performing the pledge they will be deciding.

   - Begin by conducting a vote on whether students should sit or stand while saying the pledge. (If developmentally appropriate, allow a student who is being attentive at the time of this ritual to conduct and tally the vote.) The majority rules.

   - Tell students that they will next suggest and vote on a pose or other physical act that students can do as they say the Class Pledge. (Remind students that people stand and hold their right hand over their heart when reciting the Pledge of Allegiance.) Explain the guidelines for any suggested pose: it must not cause a problem, and it cannot be putting your hand over your heart. (Notice that we no longer have to remind kids about the pose being safe and appropriate for school; now we only have to say that the pose must not cause a problem.) Remind students that they can punctuate the end of the pledge with a sound, movement, or both simultaneously.

- Call on each student to nominate a pose or movement. Again, allow students to donate their nominations if they choose. Hold a second vote in which students vote for their favorites. Students may vote either once or twice. Whichever pose/movement gets the most votes wins. In the case of a tie, erase all nominations besides the top vote-getters, and vote again. As before, you might want to let an attentive student lead and tally the vote. By this point, middle and high school teachers should have next to nothing to do with this process.

7. **Celebrate your students' work by practicing the Class Pledge together!** Let students know that you will now be reciting your Class Pledge immediately after the Pledge of Allegiance each morning for the rest of the year.

Sample Class Pledges

Most class constitutions should read like the examples above. How students say the words of a class constitution is what makes it the Class Pledge. Here are some past Class Pledge pose and movement winners from my students:

- Holding hands
- Saluting, hand to forehead
- Covering one eye as if reading an eye chart
- Putting a hand on the shoulder of a neighboring student
- Holding up both hands in a "cat attack" pose (this one came from the Bobcats class; at the end of the pledge, each student swiped down with their "claws" and exclaimed, "Rawr!")

ESPN Goodbye

Just as every student should get an ESPN Greeting when they enter their school and classroom, they should get the same treatment when they leave their classroom and/or school. Recall that ESPN stands for meaningful *eye contact*, genuine *smile*, safe *physical contact*, and the student's *name*.

The Procedure

How you deliver the ESPN Goodbye depends on the departure processes and logistics specific to your class and school. Before the start of the school year, spend some time thinking about the best way to ensure that you can deliver an ESPN

Goodbye to each student when they leave the classroom or the school. You can modify the suggested procedures below to fit your circumstances.

1. **Call for them to line up as you walk toward the door.**

2. **Stand at the door.** Situate yourself with one shoulder blade in and one shoulder blade out of the room. Make sure you can see all students from this position.

3. **When all car riders and walkers are waiting at the door to leave, give each student in line an ESPN Goodbye as they depart.** Make eye contact, smile, offer safe physical contact, and use their name (or nickname).

4. **While giving the ESPN Goodbye, take the time to offer words of encouragement, wish them luck at a game that night, and so on.** Take as much time as you can before they must leave. Not only does taking time with each student help build relationships, but it also creates space between each student. This reduces the likelihood that students will exhibit negative behaviors while leaving the building.

For bus riders who walk out to a parking lot where the buses are waiting:

1. **If possible, walk students to the buses, even if it is not required of you.** This has several positive effects for your students and your school:

   - It shows your students that you want to spend more time with them.
   - It shows that you care about their safety.
   - It creates a much safer school, hallway, and bus lot.
   - It encourages other teachers to do the same with their students.

2. **Put your students in bus order.** This means line them up in the order in which the buses either come or are stationed in the lot. As buses pull up or as you walk by each bus, give each student an ESPN Goodbye. You may not be able to chat much, but try to send each student off with an encouraging word.

If walkers and car riders are dismissed after bus riders, you can reverse the order in which you do things. Line up bussers to receive the ESPN Goodbye as they leave your room, and then walk out the walkers and car riders.

The ESPN Goodbye procedure should be used for all students, preK–12. For many teachers, it may feel awkward using the procedure with older students. Middle and high school students will invariably balk at being walked to buses or a car lot by a teacher. Their opinions on the matter are irrelevant; students at this age will act like their teachers are crazy and/or stupid and/or uncool no matter what their teachers do. How they act is therefore not an indication of whether they like what their teachers are doing or whether what their teachers are doing is effective. The use of the ESPN Goodbye procedure helps you build relationships with students and keep students safe, and it is an essential part of creating a functional, positive classroom.

✢ ✢ ✢ ✢ ✢ ✢ ✢ ✢ ✢ ✢ ✢ ✢

Relationship-Building Procedures allow teachers the opportunity to establish and manage the machinery necessary to build optimal relationships with students, no matter how difficult those students are. Establishing these procedures allows the relationships to be built as a matter of routine, instead of having to find new and novel ways of building relationships on the fly while you are trying to teach. The next chapter will outline exactly how to establish and manage procedures for sharing control of the classroom in a healthy way and on your terms, so that students are less likely to take control on their terms.

Figure 5.2

First Three Weeks of School Schedule

1	2	3	4	5
ESPN Greeting/Goodbye Class Nickname Team Nickname Morning Meeting Lock-It-In Real-World Workshop Silent Sustained Reading	Class Constitution Hire Prompter	Hire Alarm Clock	Hire Prompter	1st Nickname Ceremony Hire Someone
6	7	8	9	10
ESPN Greeting/Goodbye Class Handshake Procedure	Hire Prompter	Hire Alarm Clock	Hire Prompter	2nd Nickname Ceremony Hire Someone
11	12	13	14	15
ESPN Greeting/Goodbye Class Applause Procedure				3rd Nickname Ceremony Hire Someone

Part III

Control-Sharing Procedures

*Give students control on your terms so
they don't take it on theirs.*

I had been warned about Juriah.

I had received his student card with its requisite behavioral and academic information. He disrupted constantly. He would refuse to do anything he didn't feel like doing at any given time. The card indicated that the fact that both of Juriah's parents were in prison was "no excuse" for his behavior. The teacher included a complaint that she had sent him to the Intervention Assistance Team, feeling that his inability to do work or follow directions was due to a severe learning disability. Subsequent assessments of Juriah revealed no such disability.

I was in my 13th year working with extremely difficult kids, and I had requested that Juriah, identified as one of the toughest students in the school, be put in my room.

While teachers were busy working in their rooms two weeks before the first day of school, I asked Juriah's former teacher about him. It was amazing how quickly her pale face turned bright red. It reminded me of my frustrations that I had with students during my pre-strategy, pre-procedure days. She angrily ranted about her frustrations with him, saying how wrong and ridiculous the results of Juriah's assessment were. She suggested that Juriah did not actually belong in school at all: his behaviors were just too extreme and his IQ, regardless of the psychologist's assessment, was too low for him to attend a regular public school. She called Juriah "retarded."

Two weeks later, I met Juriah. Kids who terrorize classrooms have a certain look in their eyes on the first day of class: like a lion overlooking the savannah full of gazelles. These kids often use the first day to assess their new classroom situation and decide how they can best do the worst damage. Juriah had that look in his eyes: he had devoured his kindergarten, 1st grade, and 2nd grade teachers. He was sizing me up to see if I was going to be another gazelle that would soon bite the dust.

Immediately upon his arrival in my classroom, I met him with an enthusiastic ESPN Greeting. Juriah began to understand immediately that I was not a gazelle: I was the alpha lion. I intensely focused on the Relationship-Building Strategies and Procedures detailed in Chapters 4 and 5, giving him a feeling of ownership over his classroom and affection for me. Very quickly, Juriah began to actually like me. He later told me that I was the first adult besides his grandmother that he ever liked.

And yet, the Relationship-Building Procedures and Strategies would not have been enough to get Juriah to be a cooperative, prosocial member of our small society. As I suspected from the beginning, and as I confirmed later, Juriah had been abused and neglected throughout his life. He had been threatened and hit. He had been left alone in his home for days. These are just the horrors that I was able to find out about through a home visit and a cursory investigation. Surely, there were worse stories.

Because of these experiences, Juriah had become a high–control need child (HCNC). Because Juriah felt almost constantly out of control due to the beatings and neglect, he saw threats even when there weren't any, and he continually attempted to get control of any situation and of every person he came across. His brain was always telling him, "Grab all of the control you can right now! We don't know when we'll get any more!"

During Juriah's life at school, his intense need for control manifested itself in predictable acting out: refusing to be cooperative, being disruptive. At school, he was able to get the control that he didn't have in any other area of his life. The Relationship-Building Procedures and Strategies would allow Juriah to feel less threatened and give him some ownership, and thereby some control, of his environment. But they would not give Juriah enough control that he wouldn't seek more control in unhealthy ways (the only ways he knew how).

The only way Juriah was going to use prosocial behaviors was if he was systematically given plenty of healthy control through the use of Control-Sharing Strategies and the establishment of Control-Sharing Procedures.

Starting on that very first day, I gave Juriah control on my terms so that he wouldn't try to take it on his terms. He and his classmates taught the first 30 minutes of every school day. The students were given control of transitions from one activity to another. Students led the hallway line. He and other students followed a procedure for deciding upon voice level for worktime, and the students themselves would tell the class when it was time to clean up or be quiet.

In addition, I almost never told students, especially HCNCs like Juriah, to stop using negative behaviors. Instead, I would use small interventions to gently guide them toward positive behaviors. When I would fail at successfully guiding Juriah, I would calmly use consequences at some point later, when he and I were neither stressed nor busy.

I also gave Juriah a job on the second day of school. It was one of the many jobs I gave to my students. I told Juriah that he was in charge of telling students it was time to throw away their breakfast (we ate breakfast in our rooms). At 8:04, and no later, he was to say, "Three big bites, three big sips, you know what to do." Later, the class came up with another verbal prompt for him to say: "Blip, blop" (see Chapter 6). I told him that he could have that job as long as he always did it right and never forgot. I told him that if I ever looked up at the clock and it read 8:05 before he had given the class our prompt, he would be fired, just like in real life, where if you do your job poorly, you lose it.

How do you think Juriah's newfound employment as a breakfast prompter went? After all, his 2nd grade teacher thought that he was so stupid and terrible at following directions that he didn't belong in our school.

Juriah did that job to perfection every single day for 176 days in a row: a record for any student for any job before or since. He forgot to do it on the second-to-last day of school, and he was fired, with sadness and empathy. He was allowed to make a new hire (per the procedure described in Chapter 6).

Why was such a student able to be so successful? The reason was that Juriah was actually smart, but more important, he was an HCNC. High–control need children will do anything to get, have, and keep control. This is why traditional means of dealing with HCNCs backfire. When we tell HCNCs what to do ("Listen," "Be quiet," "Line up," "Stop touching him"), we make it less likely that they will do any of these things, because just giving these instructions puts the HCNC into fight-or-flight mode. They immediately feel a loss of control and become determined to get it back.

However, if we give an HCNC the *opportunity* to gain control, the student will do whatever works to get that control. In this case, Juriah had such a need for control that he did what no one in his life thought was possible: he acted responsibly. In fact, he acted more responsibly with his job than anyone else!

The reality was that Juriah did not have a learning disability, and our school was exactly where he belonged. He just needed—not wanted, but *needed*—a huge amount of control. No other teacher had given him what he needed. He spent nearly every moment of his school career, up to the moment I shook his hand on the first day of 3rd grade, trying to get his control needs met in unhealthy ways.

This is not to say that I gave Juriah any of the control that I wanted. I did no such thing. In fact, I was incredibly strict with Juriah, as I was with the other students in the class, and I only gave them the control that I didn't need anyway, using procedures and strategies that allowed me to have more time and energy to do my job.

Juriah, the student who was supposed to be incorrigible and stupid, thrived in my room. He had a lot of learning to do, and he tested limits, as HCNCs do. By the time he was fired on that 177th day of class, he had been given enough control and limits that he was able to take the disappointment, hire his best friend for the last two days of breakfast prompting, and move on.

Juriah's former teacher had told me how glad she was to see Juriah go on the last day of school the previous year. My last day with him was quite different. On my last day with Juriah, I could not bear to let him go. He was leaving for another school, and I feared I would never see him again. I walked him to his bus, as I did every day. We gave each other a hug, which, being big, tough men, we had never done before. I told him that I loved him, and then he said the last words that he would ever say to me: "I love you, Mr. Ervin."

✣ ✣ ✣ ✣ ✣ ✣ ✣ ✣ ✣ ✣ ✣ ✣

Control-Sharing Procedures allow you to keep the control that you do need by giving away the control that you don't need. The control you need is determined by one factor: what you feel like you need. If any of the following procedures makes you cringe because you don't want to give that specific kind of control away, don't use it. All of the procedures and strategies in this book are designed to train students to use positive, prosocial behaviors with a minimal use of your energy and time. They are meant to lower your stress level, not to increase it. Just remember that the more control we give away, the more we can keep for ourselves.

The parts of the procedures that give away control are preventive: they allow the teacher to systematically give away control in a healthy way. In addition, there is a reactive element: they also include Procedural Learning Opportunities (PLOs). These are consequences woven into the procedures themselves. A teacher, especially a teacher of difficult students, cannot simply ask children to follow a procedure and then hope and pray that they are cooperative. To this end, behavioral leadership procedures always give students two choices:

1. The student can be cooperative

    or

2. The student can learn a lesson about how to use positive behaviors or be responsible.

    Teachers can be calm when students are always faced with these two choices. Of course, when students are cooperative, it is easier to be calm, and it is easier to be calm when students are learning to be prosocial people by becoming better at using positive behaviors or becoming more responsible when they experiment with using antisocial behaviors. It is the third choice that we do not allow:

3. The student can get what they want by using antisocial behaviors.

    It is very difficult, if not impossible, to watch students use antisocial behaviors to get what they want, since we know that this will destroy our classrooms and lead to tremendous suffering for the student in both the short and long terms.

    This section details procedures for guiding students to choose between the first two choices while giving away the control that you don't need, keeping the control that you do, and systematically applying consequences when students are not cooperative.

6

Student Job Procedures

Giving students jobs in the classroom has substantial benefits. When done correctly, charging students with specific classroom tasks can teach them important life lessons and responsibility. Many teachers create a job chart whereby the names of students are rotated every month, week, or day, and the students do whichever job their name is next to on the job chart. Unfortunately, this takes far too much time and energy, and teaches students unhealthy, unrealistic lessons about responsibility and employment. I suggest that any teacher using a job chart throw it out and recommend to preservice teachers that they never start using one.

Instead, I recommend applying the Student Job Procedures detailed in this chapter. The pros and cons can be summed up simply.

Reasons not to use job charts:

· Making job charts takes time and energy.

· Job charts take time and energy to maintain.

· Taking time and energy to make and maintain job charts tells the teacher and the students that maintenance of the classroom is the teacher's job, not the students'.

· Job charts feel insulting and childish to older students (because they are).

· Arbitrarily forcing students to do jobs that they do not want could create a needless power struggle.

- Arbitrarily forcing students to do jobs that they do not want does not teach any real-world lessons, since forced labor does not occur in a free society.

- Job charts teach students that everyone is entitled to a job, no matter how well they do that job.

- Job charts teach students that it is someone else's place to seek them out and give them a job.

Benefits to implementing Student Job Procedures:

- There is no chart to make or maintain.

- Using Student Job Procedures takes little or no time or energy.

- The lack of a teacher-imposed chart or system sends the implicit message that the maintenance of the classroom is the job of the students.

- Students learn that it is easier to get jobs if people like you.

- Students learn that people are not entitled to a job.

- Students learn that people get to keep their jobs if they do them well.

- Students learn that if people do their jobs poorly, they will be fired.

Student Jobs: Hiring, Training, and Firing Guidelines

Hiring Procedure

Student Job Procedures require you only to hire the first job holder for each job, minimizing teacher effort and maximizing student responsibility and ownership. Hire that first student at random. Do not hire difficult students first. Do not hire easy students first. Do not use the threat of *not* hiring a student to try to change behaviors. All students have the right to an opportunity to have a job, though they do not have the right to keep that job. They also do not have a right to do every job.

When you hire a child for a job, simply hire them. Don't lecture them about the job's importance or the importance of employment in general. Simply say something to the effect of the following:

> *I have a special job for you. It is yours if you want it, and it will help*
> *our classroom. You can have it as long as you do the job perfectly. If*
> *you forget to do it or do it poorly, I will fire you. Your job will be to*
> *_____. Are you interested?*

Training Procedure

After you model how to do an individual job for all of your students, teach the first student who is hired to do that job how to do it *once*. After that, you are off the hook for teaching how to do the job. Previous job holders can train new employees, so you only teach one student one time for each job. Training children more than once is inefficient, and it tricks students into thinking doing a job well is someone else's problem. Also, students learn faster and more effectively through failure (in this case, being fired).

Once you hire a student for any job, do not help, remind, or prompt them in any way. If they do their job perfectly, they get to keep their job for the rest of the year. If they fail to do their job perfectly, they are fired, and they get to hire the next person to take the job. Getting fired is effective failure, especially when done in tandem with a Calm Signal (see Chapter 4 for details).

Firing Procedures

When a student fails at remembering to do their job, or they don't do their job properly, fire them. No warnings, no reteaching, no threats. They are simply fired, but in a specific way. First, you need to use your Calm Signal. Here is a simple script:

> Oh, man. You're fired. You can hire someone to do the job, or I can. Your choice.

Students can choose any student who has never held that job. They can pick their best friend, and they can opt to not pick their enemies. This allows students to learn the lesson that if you are nice, it's easier to get a job. Students can also decline having a job. Again, we don't live in a world where forced labor is legal, so there is no need to prepare our students for this type of world by making kids do jobs.

It is possible that a student could do a job perfectly and have that job all year. This would be incredibly rare, but it should be allowed to happen. That child is doing a service to the rest of the class by modeling an incredible amount of responsibility. Other students will be able to see that this level of responsibility is possible and that it gets people good things in the form of employment and status.

Having looked at the guidelines around initiating and terminating student jobs, let's examine jobs in which students can contribute to the management of their own classroom.

Student Prompter

How often do you have to prompt students to do things in school? Students in K–12 schools are told what to do hundreds of times per day. Every time a person is told what to do, they feel at least some loss of control. The cumulative effect of being bossed around every day, over and over again, is that students will do whatever it takes to get their feeling of control back.

This is especially true for HCNCs. Students who have experienced trauma can be triggered simply by being told what to do, especially in the form of repeated imperatives. HCNCs become determined to get the control back on their terms, possibly through overtly aggressive, passively aggressive, or passive-resistant behaviors. Much of this can be avoided by using interventions instead of making demands (see Chapter 9).

Another way to avoid taking away control from students (and, in fact, give them *more control*) is to have the students themselves prompt each other to do things. This includes students prompting each other to clean up after morning activities, before lunch, and at the end of the day. Students can also be in charge of prompting the class to be quiet. Finally, they can prompt the teacher when it is time for students to leave the room for special education services, occupational therapy, physical therapy, scheduled trips to the nurse, or Title I Reading services.

As with all procedures, the job of Student Prompter is designed to make your life as a teacher significantly easier. You no longer need to keep your eyes on the clock: students are now responsible for this. It isn't reasonable for teachers to have to think about the individual schedules of 25–35 students every day. Using these procedures will leave you with more time and mental energy to do your job.

These are simply prompts to *begin the process* of preparing to transition. This is not having students transition from one thing to the next.

For each category of Student Prompter, begin the year by using the prompt yourself, all the while only taking the control that you need. Then pass the responsibility to your student(s) following the directions below. Modify the directions or script slightly, depending on which prompting routine you are introducing.

Directions

Model the use of whichever prompt you choose for as many days as you feel is developmentally appropriate. During Morning Meeting (this would take place at the beginning of homeroom period for middle and high school) on the fourth day of school (for example), let your students know that you don't like to boss kids around, and for four days you have had to by prompting them (to transition from morning work/cleanup, for lunch/cleanup, for the end of the day/get quiet). Let them know that you will be hiring a student to prompt the rest of the class to (insert prompting procedure here) every day. At some point during that day or period, hire a student according to the Hiring Procedure detailed above. Make sure that the student knows what time to use the prompt. Let them know that they will be fired if you notice that it is even one second past the time when they were supposed to prompt the class. Then manage them according to Training Procedures and fire them according to Firing Procedures.

Only tell students how to do the job *one time per year*, even for prekindergartners. Reminders and lectures about hurrying and transitioning better and faster make it *less* likely that students will hurry and transition better and faster. Instead, prompt students with interventions and use consequences when students are not cooperative and interventions have failed to effectively guide individual students to desired behaviors (see Chapter 9). Students will know what to do with the help of the interventions. More importantly, they will figure things out by seeing what their peers are doing. You can differentiate for younger students or for students with cognitive issues simply by using more interventions. This is preferable to repeating directions and warning students, which takes more time and encourages negative behaviors. When and if an entire class struggles with effectively transitioning to a prompt, implement a wholesale Class Procedural Learning Opportunity (see Chapter 7).

Morning Cleanup Prompter procedures. A teacher has so much to do every morning. Not having to tell students to clean up is one less thing to think about, gives control to your class at the beginning of school every day, and reminds every student every day that their classroom is truly theirs. Whether your class is a high school homeroom, a half-day kindergarten classroom, a 3rd grade classroom where everyone eats free breakfast in the room, or a 5th grade class who stays together throughout the morning for language arts, every classroom has a beginning of the day, so all teachers can use this prompt.

On the first day of school, prompt students when it is time to transition from whatever activity they are doing as they arrive (eating breakfast or doing a quickstart activity, for example) to whatever activity is next. Students should always have an activity to do during arrival. The following teacher prompts take the minimal amount of control from students while still prompting them to stop an activity. There are different prompts depending on the age of the students and the activity being stopped, as well as the activity being started. Notice that these prompts include two assumptions necessary for optimal student cooperation: the assumption of intelligence, and the assumption of cooperation.

- For elementary breakfast (with morning work) to Morning Meeting (see Chapter 8): "Three big bites, three big sips. You know what to do."
- For elementary morning work (without breakfast) to Morning Meeting: "It's 8:30. You know what to do."
- For middle and high school homeroom: "It's 8:30. What's next?"

After modeling the Morning Cleanup Prompter job for an appropriate number of days, hire a student to take on the responsibility.

Lunchtime Prompter procedures. It is very important for students to understand that it is not the job of the teacher to get students ready to go to lunch; that is the job of the students themselves. Never tell a student to clean up or get ready, because you can't control this, and it makes it less likely that HCNCs will get ready. Instead, use one of the following prompts.

- Elementary: "I will dismiss teams that are seated silently at quiet, clean tables."
- Middle school/high school: "I dismiss teams to lunch who are silent, clean, and seated."

If you have a different expectation (you don't care if students are quiet or at clean desks, for example), you can change the prompt—for example, "I dismiss teams who are seated." You can create your own prompt, as long as you are not telling students what to do.

Make sure that your own lunch is available in your classroom. Immediately after giving the prompt, start eating your lunch while comfortably seated at your desk. During these first days of school, make sure your lunch is especially appealing: sub sandwiches, delicious fast food, and so on. Large fountain drinks are helpful. Looking at your computer or phone as you eat makes it even more effective. Simply say your prompt once and start enjoying your meal. Your actions communicate to students, "Your lunch starts when you use the expected behaviors, but whatever you choose, my lunch starts right now."

After modeling the Lunchtime Prompter job for an appropriate number of days, hire a student to take on the responsibility. Do this either during Morning Meeting (elementary) or at the beginning of the period before lunch (middle/high school). So that it makes sense, and so that the student gets ownership of the process, have them change the "I" in the prompt to "we" (e.g., "We will dismiss teams who are seated"), or name them directly in the prompt (e.g., "Devin will dismiss teams who are seated").

End of Day Prompter. Whether you are a prekindergarten teacher or an Advanced Placement English teacher, the end of the school day can be hectic. Not having to remember to tell students that the academic day is over and not having to worry about antisocial behaviors during this time can be the difference between feeling like you had a successful day or an unsuccessful one.

All students, preK–12, should take part in Afternoon Meeting (see Chapter 8) at the end of the day. For students who retrieve their backpacks and get mail, homework, and so on before Afternoon Meeting, use the following prompt:

- "I will dismiss teams whose tables are clean and whose things are ready to go."

Students who will get their things on their way out the door after Afternoon Meeting merely need to be quiet and have everything put away. In this case, use the following prompt:

- "I will begin Afternoon Meeting when everyone is seated quietly," or, "Devin will begin Afternoon Meeting when everyone is seated quietly."

After modeling the End of Day Prompter job for an appropriate number of days, hire a student to take on the responsibility. Do this either during Morning Meeting (elementary) or at the beginning of the last period of the day (middle/high school). So that it makes sense, and so that the student gets ownership of the process, have them change the "I" in the prompt to "we" (e.g., "We will begin Afternoon Meeting when everyone is seated quietly").

If you find yourself running behind and need a few extra minutes to finish assessing a small group, for example, simply tell your student prompter to wait until slightly later just for that day. For example: "Big Sal, could you wait until 3:02 instead of 3:00 to prompt us to clean up, please?"

Prompt for Quiet procedure. This procedure is designed to be used when students will be transitioning to another activity but will remain in place. (If students are going to transition to another location after the prompt, use the Lock-It-In procedure in Chapter 7.)

Trying to get students to be quiet is one of the most common problems in schools. Teachers often have nightmares about their futile efforts to "make" their students be quiet so they can teach. Using this procedure means you will no longer need to struggle to have silent students and will enjoy more pleasant dreams.

Telling students to be quiet is a common mistake. You cannot make students be quiet, and when told to be quiet, difficult students will often endeavor to prove that point. Instead of telling students to be quiet, you can tell them when you will go on to the next activity or lesson (when they are quiet), and then use consequences for classes or students who are not quiet.

- "I will begin when everyone is seated quietly."

If certain materials are required for the upcoming activity or assignment, the prompt can be altered accordingly:

- "I will begin when everyone is seated quietly with their math books turned to page 32."

To calmly encourage cooperation, you can do as many interventions as you wish, with an emphasis on moving closer to students who are standing or talking (see Chapter 9). Keep in mind that the number of interventions that you wish to use could be zero. If students continue to engage in antisocial behaviors, enact the appropriate consequence procedure, depending on the number of students still using antisocial behaviors after you use the Prompt for Quiet (see the description of Procedural Learning Opportunities below).

After modeling the Prompt for Quiet job for an appropriate number of days, hire a student to take on the responsibility. So that it makes sense, and so that the student gets ownership of the process, have them change the "I" in the prompt to "we" (e.g., "We will begin when everyone is seated quietly").

Remember, the prompt for cleanup is prompted by the clock, and the prompt for silence is prompted by the teacher. The prompt for silence can be given by the teacher, especially when in a hurry, or it can be given by a student. That student can be a hired prompter, or any students can be prompted at any time by the teacher. If there is no prompter hired, only students who are using prosocial behaviors should be prompted.

Fun, easy ways to prompt both hired and temporary prompters include throwing a safe, soft, non-bouncy object at students whom you want to give the silence prompt. Have the student always put the object back in a predetermined place. If a hired prompter forgets, they are fired. If a temporary prompter forgets, don't use them again.

Student-Created Prompts

Whenever it is convenient for you, you can allow students to create, nominate, and vote for the format of their prompts. You can have the same prompt for all of your cleanup/transition prep prompts (Morning Cleanup, Lunchtime, End of Day, etc.), or you can have a different one for each. Your students can also create a prompt for silence. Make sure to make the silence prompt different than any of the cleanup/transition prep prompts, or confusion will ensue. Use the same procedure for nomination and voting as you did for Class Handshake or Class Applause. Students may choose any number of silly sounds or phrases: "Sha-na-na!" "Bleep-blorp!" and "Shebang!" would all be acceptable.

What If They Never Get Quiet? Procedural Learning Opportunities

Since many students have been trained by parents and teachers that when adults say things that they don't really mean them, they have learned to ignore prompts for quiet. Through Class Procedural Learning Opportunities (PLOs), Small-Group PLOs, and Individual PLOs, those students will learn one of the most valuable lessons you can teach them: that when authority figures say things and set limits, there will be consequences for testing those limits. Whether children learn this can be a matter of life or death, and successfully teaching this concept to students may be the most important thing that you do in your lifetime.

When five or more students continue to be disruptive after a Prompt for Quiet and a period of waiting and, if you wish, after a few interventions have been used, it is time to implement a Class PLO. If the number of students still engaging in the antisocial behavior of talking after the prompt is less than five but more than one, skip to a Small-Group PLO. If only one student continues to talk post-prompt, be disappointed that more students won't learn this valuable lesson, and continue to an Individual PLO.

Procedural Learning Opportunities are not punishments. They are opportunities for students to learn how to master being an effective part of the school community. In this way, they are similar to Delayed Learning Opportunities (see Chapter 9), which offer the same benefit. PLOs are consequences that are woven into the fabric of procedures that allow students to learn how to be effective within the parameters of the specific procedure.

If you have already hired a student for a prompting job, give the student the choice to participate in PLO practice sessions, but do not require it. Many students, especially HCNCs, will enjoy being a part of student consequences, and it is a fantastic means of giving those students a tremendous amount of control on your terms. Make sure, however, that they are merely giving the prompt, not trying to manage the behaviors of their fellow students. To the extent that it is appropriate, student prompters can express frustration with classmates' inability to be silent to a prompt. If the student prompter deals with this frustration inappropriately, they should be fired.

A Word on Group Consequences

When a classroom is in a state of general disarray because of widespread use of antisocial behaviors, many teachers make the mistake of trying to use "retail discipline": providing each individual with specific, tailor-made consequences. Sometimes, though, "wholesale discipline" is necessary when "retail discipline" becomes too difficult to administer and causes more chaos than it alleviates.

The logical group consequences described here teach a valuable lesson to the entire class. They show everyone that people's actions affect other people, especially people on the same team. If a basketball player doesn't play defense, does it affect the entire team? If a person in an office doesn't pull their weight on a project, does the entire business suffer? If a parent is arrested for driving under the influence, does the entire family's life become more difficult? Of course, the answer to these questions is "Yes." School, then, should prepare students by teaching these lessons today instead of waiting for our students to learn them as adults, when the amount of suffering involved for them, their coworkers, their teams, and their families will be significantly higher, and possibly more dangerous.

You may have noticed that there were no consequences for students who did not clean up and prepare to transition at a reasonable pace (the definition of a reasonable pace is entirely up to you). This is because the Behavioral Leadership Classroom is set up so that the natural and/or logical consequences for doing things lackadaisically will befall students either during the prompt's PLO (if students are not changing locations) or during the Lock-It-In procedure and PLO for students who are changing locations.

PLO for Prompt to Quiet Failure

When you have used the Prompt to Quiet procedure and performed as many interventions as you feel like, and five or more students are still engaging in an undesired behavior (usually, talking), you can say the following:

> *Oh, man, [class nickname]. I will be doing something about this later.*
> *Don't let it ruin your day.*

You can then either begin the PLO right then and there, or move on with the lesson with the students still using antisocial behaviors. They will learn not to—later.

PLOs during instructional time. If you choose to, you can go through the PLO steps immediately. Very often, teachers will begin PLOs during instructional time because of how many students are exhibiting antisocial behaviors (talking, standing, or not cleaning up, for example). Implementing the Class PLO can usually get the number of students still using antisocial behaviors down below five so you can administer a Small-Group PLO later. If you wish to get back to teaching before your class can successfully practice responding to the prompt as a whole, delay the consequence and resume practice at a noninstructional time.

PLOs during noninstructional time. The other option is to administer this PLO during a noninstructional time. Possible noninstructional times for PLOs include before school, recess, lunch (never withhold food), after school, weekends, during a noninstructional school event, or during a behavioral Now (see page 158). Class PLOs can also be done during the Real-World Workshop procedure (see Chapter 8) if and when all students have completed their Nows. If using one of these times for consequences creates a burden that you don't want to endure (you feel that Saturdays need to be a time for rest), or the use of this time does not fit into your or your administration's value structure (you feel that kids should always be allowed to run around at recess), don't use that time to give consequences. For students older than 5 without cognitive disabilities, you can wait days before giving a PLO; for students over 8, you can wait weeks. For kindergartners, you can wait until the next day. For students with cognitive disabilities, use your best professional judgment. Remember, delaying a PLO for even 15 minutes still gives you the benefits of delaying a consequence. Be in no rush to find a time that is convenient for you.

PLOs as Practice Sessions

Procedural Learning Opportunities are essentially practice sessions for procedures that students haven't yet mastered. When collecting and herding students to participate in this practice session, whether it's your whole class or a small group, keep a smile on your face. You can use a prop, like a cup of coffee or a snack. These nonwork activities and your smile will give students the implicit message that you are not worried about the PLO, that this situation is not a problem for you, and that it might be a problem for them. You will be able to be calm because this and all other Delayed and Procedural Learning Opportunities always give students two choices, and two choices only:

1. The student(s) will be cooperative (in this case, practice being quiet to a prompt)

   or

2. The student(s) will learn a valuable lesson about being cooperative next time.

Say the following one time:

> *We will begin practicing when everyone is seated, and everyone is silent.*

While smiling, use interventions (see Chapter 9) or wait silently for as many seconds as feels comfortable for you if any students are not seated quietly. If the group or entire class is cooperative, move on to the Class and Small-Group PLO script below. If there is even one student not being cooperative once you decide that you would like to move on, say the following:

> *Oh, man. Looks like you all need to practice an extra time.*

You will then add to the amount of practice sessions the class chooses. Move on immediately to the Class and Small-Group PLO script.

Class and Small-Group PLO Script

> *Oh, man, [class nickname]. It looks like you all are struggling with being quiet when it is time to listen. No worries. I'm not mad at you. When you struggle with something, you need to practice doing it until you are an expert. So now I'm going to give you the chance to practice and become an expert. If you can become an expert today, that's fine. Otherwise, you will be coming in to practice this every _____ for the rest of the year until you become an expert. That's fine too.*
>
> *I am going to give you all a chance to talk to each other. You don't have to, though. Then I will give the Prompt to Quiet [or the student hired for the Prompt to Quiet job will give the prompt]. If you all are completely quiet once you hear the prompt, that will count as a successful practice. This is team practice. In order for a practice attempt to be successful, everyone must be perfectly silent the second I am done giving the prompt. Tell me, how many times do you need to practice, five times or six times?*

Have students vote. If they are cooperative and choose a number, accept it as the number of times they will have to practice. If they refuse, or chaos ensues when the question is asked, pick the greater number for them. If the class was not able to be quiet when prompted for the practice session, let them know that you will be adding an extra practice session.

The preceding example includes an appropriate choice of times for 3rd grade or above. For preK and kindergarten, one or two practices is appropriate. For 1st and 2nd grade, three or four practices is best.

Now begin the practice session. Say the following:

I may try to trick you by saying my prompt very quickly or very quietly.

OK, you all can talk now if you want.

You can wait however long you want—usually between 5 and 30 seconds—before you say the prompt. Start with a louder, slower prompt, and make the prompt quieter and faster as you go on. If you are using a hired student prompter, you can coach them on this as well.

Mentally prepare yourself. If you are used to hoping and praying that students are cooperative, shift your paradigm. Remember that uncooperative students, by definition, need to learn that being cooperative can get them what they want: in their respective pasts, being uncooperative has been more effective in this endeavor. Be happy that you are about to successfully teach uncooperative students that being uncooperative will not get them what they want. They will not be able to create chaos, they will not be able to feel the freedom of doing whatever they want without consequences, they will not be able to control the emotions of an adult, and they will not get approval from their peers. In short, start hoping that students are uncooperative so that they can learn to be cooperative.

It can be helpful to be involved with another activity when monitoring practicing the Prompt for Quiet procedure. Checking your phone, grading papers, or working on your computer shows students that this session may be a challenge for them, but it is not a challenge for you.

When Classes and Small Groups Are Successful

Do not spend a lot of time and energy praising successful practice attempts. Simply say the following:

That's one successful practice. ___ more to go. Feel free to talk.

Repeat this after every successful practice. The number of successful practice sessions needed to reach the goal needs to be cumulative. It should not be that number of successful practices in a row. Once the class has completed their practices, say the following:

Are you all experts at being quiet when it's time to listen?

If anyone says "No," have them stay in their seat. Have them go through an Individual PLO for the Prompt for Quiet procedure once the other students have gone.

If multiple students say "No," have them do a Small-Group PLO once the other students are gone. Allow all other students to go to whatever noninstructional activity they were missing. Feel free to use an ESPN Goodbye on their way out.

When Classes and Small Groups Are Unsuccessful

When a class is not unanimously silent to the prompt during the PLO, use your Calm Signal. Then say the following:

> *That's an unsuccessful practice attempt. No worries. You can try again.*
> *Feel free to talk.*

Repeat each time students are unsuccessful. When students have a successful practice, follow the instructions for when they are successful, above. If the same students continually fail to practice successfully, allow them to fail until they have been successful at frustrating a significant number of the cooperative students. This allows the uncooperative students to learn that being uncooperative will no longer get them positive regard from a majority of their peers. It is highly likely that the number of students who are not cooperative will be lower than the number of students who were uncooperative when the practice session began.

Once the cooperative students are significantly frustrated with the uncooperative students, say the following:

> *Oh, man. It looks like almost all of you are experts at being quiet when*
> *you are supposed to listen. Chris, Jaquata, Ashley, and Brandy, are you*
> *all experts?*

If they answer "Yes," give them an ESPN Goodbye as they adjourn to whatever noninstructional activity they have been missing. Dismiss groups of students in the same way. Use student nicknames if they have them. If students say that they are not experts, tell them to have a seat.

The students who remain have shown, through their actions or by their own admission, that they are not yet experts at being quiet to a prompt. If more than one student remains, use this procedure again. If only one student remains, have the student practice using an Individual PLO.

Individual PLO

When you have given your prompt and only one student is still using an undesired behavior (e.g., talking), you can say the following:

> *Oh, man. I will help you do some learning later. Don't let it ruin your day.*

Just as in the procedure explained above, you will give this consequence during a noninstructional time. Bring the student into the room in the same manner: calmly, while smiling and doing some other leisurely activity.

Individual PLO Script

The Individual PLO script varies only slightly from the one for the whole class or small group. Say the following with sadness and empathy:

> Oh, man. It looks like you are struggling with being quiet when it is time to listen. No worries. I'm not mad at you. When you struggle with something, you need to practice doing it until you are an expert. So now I'm going to give you the chance to practice and become an expert. If you can become an expert today, that's fine. Otherwise, you will be coming in to practice this every _____ for the rest of the year until you become an expert. That's fine, too.
>
> I am going to give you the chance to talk. Just pretend that there are other people here. You don't have to, though. Then I will give the prompt. If you are completely quiet once I am done saying the prompt, that will count as a successful practice. How many times do you need to practice, seven times or nine times?

If the student chooses a number, accept it as the number of times he or she will have to practice. If the student refuses, pick the greater number for the student.

> OK, nine times it is.

The preceding example includes an appropriate choice of times for 3rd grade or above. For preK and kindergarten, one or two practices is appropriate. For 1st and 2nd grade, three or four practices is best.

Now you can begin the practice session. Say the following:

> Now, I may try to trick you by saying my prompt very quickly or very quietly. OK, you can talk now if you want.

You can wait however long you want to—usually between 5 and 30 seconds—before you say the prompt. Vary the amount of time before you give the prompt. Start with a louder, slower prompt, and make the prompt quieter and faster as you go on. Mentally prepare yourself for the possibility that the student will be uncooperative, as those practices have gotten them what they wanted in the past. Embrace the opportunity for them to learn the opposite.

When Individuals Are Successful

Do not spend a lot of time and energy praising successful practice attempts. Simply say the following:

That's one successful practice. ___ more to go. Feel free to talk.

Repeat this after every successful practice. The number of successful practice sessions needed to reach the goal needs to be cumulative. It should not be that number of successful practices in a row. Once the student has completed the number of practices chosen (or assigned), say the following:

Are you an expert at being quiet when it's time to listen?

If the student says "No," have him or her take a seat and start the entire procedure over, this time giving two choices for the number of practices sessions that are higher than the original choices.

When Individuals Are Unsuccessful

When a student is unsuccessful at being silent to the prompt, use your Calm Signal. Then say the following:

That's an unsuccessful practice attempt. No worries. You can try again.
Feel free to talk.

Repeat each time the student is unsuccessful. When a student has a successful practice, follow the instructions for when they are successful, above.

Human Alarm Clocks

In most preK–12th grade classrooms, students may be required to leave at scheduled times for a multitude of reasons: Title I Reading, speech, gifted, special intervention, occupational therapy, physical therapy, and going to the nurse for daily medication or treatment. Remembering when to send students to the many corners of the school universe at various times per day is difficult, if not impossible. Besides the extra, significant, and unnecessary mental strain of remembering multiple schedules every day, there are three other significant problems with keeping tabs on these schedules and dismissing students every day:

- It gives students the false impression that the maintenance of their lives, health, and education is the job of the adults around them. (It isn't.)
- It forces the teacher into telling students to do things, which takes away a feeling of control from students.

- It isn't any fun.

Using Human Alarm Clocks solves all of these problems. It teaches kids that their schedules, health, and well-being are their responsibility; it keeps you from bossing around your students; and it is a fun and funny way to share control of the classroom with students. The "fun" quality encourages students to remember their appointments. It helps even more due to the general rule of thumb that students who have scheduled appointments throughout the day have higher control needs than those who don't.

The Conversation

The initial conversation for the Human Alarm Clocks procedure can happen with all students with scheduled appointments, with different groups, or with individual students. Talk to students who leave the room at any scheduled interval about the fact that everyone in the class needs to keep track of their own schedules: teachers are responsible for their schedules, and students are responsible for theirs.

Let students know that you will not be reminding them to leave to go to an appointment. Instead, after being told one time per year what time they are to leave and where they are to go, they will be remembering that it is time for an appointment by looking at the clock. It will then be their job to notify you in any way they would like with a sound and some kind of movement. Alternatively, you can give them a notification method, but it should be something fun and at least slightly silly. In any case, make sure they know that they are allowed to interrupt you, no matter what you are doing, when it is time. Tell them that whether you are teaching the entire class, helping one student, or talking to your principal, they are responsible for walking directly in front of you and performing their notification sound and motion. Besides all of the aforementioned benefits of using Human Alarm Clocks, students brazenly walking directly in front of you and doing something distinctive with sound and motion makes it nearly impossible for you to think they are out of their seats for no reason or in line to get work checked.

You should have a method that you use to "shut off" the Human Alarm Clocks. This interaction ensures you always know when a student is leaving the room so they don't quietly use their notification strategy and slip out without you noticing. For example, I would always tap the tops of my students' heads when they came to me with a notification, as if I was turning off my morning alarm clock. Some teachers do a fist bump, high five, or forearm tap.

While you can allow students to come up with their own individual notification strategies, and this may be best practice in terms of giving away an optimal amount of healthy control, I never did. It was calming for me to have everyone going to a certain destination doing the same notification strategy. This way, I would have constant reminders about where the students were going. Also, if a student went to more than one place throughout the week (e.g., occupational therapy at 10:15 on Tuesdays and Title I every day at 2:00), it was just one extra reminder of where that student was going and sometimes, frankly, what day it was.

In my classroom, students going to Title I Reading would approach me and put their hands on top of their heads with the tips of their five fingers touching their scalps and make the following noise, mimicking the obnoxious sounds of an old alarm clock—"MAH-MAH-MAH-MAH!"—until I "turned them off" and they made a beeline out the door. Kids going to special ed pullout would cross their arms in front of themselves, lean back, and give a high-pitched "MEEP-MEEP-MEEP-MEEP!" before I tapped their crossed arms. Any students who had a scheduled appointment to see the nurse would grab their forearm as if it were broken and say "OUCH-OUCH-OUCH-OUCH!" until I tapped their "injured" arm (this completely horrified new students and guests to my room). I would have students going to occupational therapy or physical therapy hop on one foot and say "WHIP-POOR-WILL–WHIP-POOR-WILL–WHIP-POOR-WILL!" I would dismiss them by tapping them on the back. (Don't try to make sense of that one.) Students going to get speech services would stand directly in front of me, make a mini-megaphone with their hands, put the megaphone to their mouths, and then, mimicking a foghorn, say, "SPEEE-EEECH!"

Imagine how much control this gave these students! Imagine how much fun it was, especially when there were visitors to the room. In these circumstances, it was wonderful to watch students approach me, looking at our visitors with a "Wait'll they get a load of this!" look on their faces. I still remember the giggles after they got "turned off." This is yet another way that our classroom felt less like a classroom and more like a clubhouse where we learned things.

For middle and high school students, it's usually a good idea for them to come up with their own signals. Often these students, the Most Mature People in the World, would rather not do anything as attention-grabbing as the aforementioned ideas, so allow them to propose anything as long as it is appropriate and involves a verbal notification from the student and a physical confirmation from the teacher. It may be as innocuous as the student walking up to the teacher and saying, "Going to OT," with a fist bump then given to the student by the teacher.

For preK, kindergarten, and 1st grade students and for students with special needs, telling time and remembering to keep track of time may be an unrealistic expectation. While you can err on the side of having too high expectations, you should also use technology to scaffold learning these skills. While it is important that the students take responsibility for their own schedules, remember that your requirements should be developmentally appropriate. Some tips for scaffolding can include making sure preK/kindergarten/1st grade classrooms have both analog and digital clocks visible for all students (which is probably a good idea whether or not you use this procedure). Make digital clocks available for students who need them at their desks. Provide desktop personal alarms, set by the students, perhaps with the help of a teacher, turned on every day by the students themselves.

What If They Forget?

As previously stated, students using these notification strategies are more likely to remember their appointments. Also, keep in mind that many students going to appointments go with other students. This is often true of students going to gifted, special ed, or Title I Reading sessions. One student or more can remind others that it is time for an appointment, and they will all congregate and do a group alarm clock.

Even when using the Human Alarm Clocks procedure, students will sometimes forget to be aware of the clock. Just as with other jobs, we fire the student using the same, simple script we always use when firing students:

> Oh, man. You're fired. You can hire someone to do the job, or I can. Your choice.

Then, the new hire will become the fired student's alarm. The new hire will adopt the fired student's notification strategy and, instead of going to the teacher, she will use the alarm on the fired student. At that point, the fired student will know to go to the teacher, get the dismissal signal (tap on the head, arm, etc.). The student can then leave.

For instance, at 10:15 every day, a 6th grade student may walk over to a fired student, grab his forearm with his hand and say, "OUCH-OUCH-OUCH-OUCH!" The person going to the nurse would then walk to the teacher, the teacher would tap his outstretched arm, and he would go to the nurse. Or, at 2:00 every Tuesday, a high school senior might go up to another student and say, "Dude. Go to OT." That OT-bound student would just walk up to his teacher, stick out a fist, get a fist bump, and leave the room for his therapy session.

Do not underestimate how powerful the Human Alarm Clocks procedure can be. Students love being in charge of themselves, and after being hired, students love being in charge of other students. Once a student forgets and loses control over their own alarm clock, and either the student or you hire a new one, at some point you can let the first student know that you will be watching them throughout each school day. If you notice that they have become more responsible during other parts of the day (by fulfilling their duties as a student and as a classmate by turning in work, being kind to others, etc.), you may ask them if they would like to become their own alarm clock once again. This will supercharge the Strategic Noticing of "I notice that you are being responsible." In my classroom, students were able to earn back their own alarm clock job after several weeks, a month, several months, or not at all.

Getting the Alarm Clock Job Back

If Human Alarm Clocks can get their job back, why can't other students get their classroom jobs back after being fired?

We allow students to get these jobs back because, unlike other classroom jobs, Human Alarm Clocks jobs require students to only be responsible for themselves. Each time a student is fired and rehired, it teaches that student an important lesson about being responsible for yourself.

Comfort Keeper

One student in your classroom should oversee all the duties that involve keeping the classroom a comfortable place to live and learn. Adjustments need to be made throughout a typical day to maintain an optimal classroom environment, and these adjustments cannot be made by the teacher. The class Comfort Keeper will be prompted by either the teacher or by various situations to close the classroom door when another class or the hallway gets too loud, to open or close a window to regulate the classroom temperature, or to keep the classroom dry when a storm moves in. The Comfort Keeper is in charge of turning lights on and off. You may even choose for the Comfort Keeper to be in charge of running any and all technology, air conditioning, fans, and heat. All of this is, of course, at your discretion.

Attendance Keeper

As every school administrative assistant I ever worked with before I developed this procedure will tell you, I always had a serious problem with remembering to take attendance. A *serious* problem. To this day, I still feel badly about the levels of complete and total exasperation I created in the hearts of those hard-working secretaries.

When and if it is appropriate, and if it is acceptable to your administration, you should have an Attendance Keeper on staff in your classroom. Doing the job correctly, and thus keeping the job, involves remembering to take attendance, taking it with 100 percent accuracy, and, if necessary, walking the attendance report to the office.

Class Greeter/Executive Assistant

One of the best ways to delegate important authority to your students is by hiring a Class Greeter/Executive Assistant. This student will be in charge of greeting visitors to the classroom and often answering questions for the guests. Younger students tend to merely greet visitors using the script below. The older and more mature students are, the more they should assume the role of an Executive Assistant: taking messages, grading, collecting work, and managing any number of tasks. Most high school students can do the job of a student teacher and should be allowed to do all appropriate tasks that can be done by a student.

Especially with older students, use your best professional judgment in hiring and managing this job. Only hire students who can realistically do what you ask of them and proficiently complete their own schoolwork. Do not stop these students from doing enriching activities just so they can assist you. If you do give this job to a student who is not as academically inclined, you should pull back on the job expectations so that the student is being enriched academically while also being able to gain the sense of efficacy that this job can afford.

It is important to note that, even in preK, this is not a cutesy, figurehead job that is merely designed for visitors to think, "Oh, how adorable!" when a 4-year-old greets them. On the contrary, this job is designed to give you more time to teach while affording you the status that you deserve. Teachers are the most important people in any school or school district, and they should be treated as such. No one, including principals, superintendents, mayors, governors, or presidents of the United States should be allowed to walk into your classroom and interrupt your instruction. You and what you are doing are too important for that. Your Class Greeter/Executive Assistant will be trained not only to greet visitors to the classroom with a script, but also to answer questions and help the visitor in any ways possible, according to their developmental level. You are the executive of the classroom; the students are the managers.

Hiring and Training

One major difference between this job and all others is that it requires students who wish to have the job to rehearse and then audition for it. For kindergartners and 1st graders, I suggest sending a letter home to parents that looks something like this:

Dear Parents,

As you know, part of being a Behavioral Leadership Classroom is that we allow students to help manage their own classroom as a way to create a more functional and efficient learning environment and so that students feel more ownership of their classroom. One way they do that is to be hired by me to do certain jobs, including Class Greeter/Executive Assistant. For this job, the student will be required to greet visitors to the classroom with the script below. I will be auditioning interested students next week on _____. The student who can best deliver the script while shaking hands and looking me in the eye will get the job.

If your child is interested in having this job, feel free to work with him or her on rehearsing this greeting. Below is the Class Greeter script:

"Hello, I'm _____. [Shake hands.] Welcome to the _____ Classroom. Right now, we are _____. How can I help you?"

Thanks!

To further "screen" students for this position, offer free coaching at some point on shaking hands and looking people in the eye. Put up "Rehearse Student Greeter Script" as a Later during Real-World Workshop. Then take some time to audition students for the job, making sure you keep in mind how well they shake hands and look you in the eye. Hire the most proficient student, taking special care to make sure that they genuinely want the job.

Inform your new Class Greeter/Executive Assistant of any people who should be exempt from having to be greeted. The list should be short but may perhaps include a teacher with whom you plan from across the hall or a special ed teacher who works hand-in-hand with you. Anyone who enters your room more than once per day may be ignored by your Class Greeter/Executive Assistant, but they should greet everyone else. You should train them to answer any question and solve any problem that they can, depending upon their intellectual and developmental abilities.

7

Transitions: The Lock-It-In Procedure

It goes without question that our goal is for all of our students to use prosocial behaviors while transitioning efficiently from one activity to the next. But that will never happen with students whose negative behaviors during transitions get them attention, allow them to feel free of consequences, give them the feeling of control over their teacher's emotions, and get them positive regard from their peers. Only when students are unable to get these things as a result of their negative behaviors will they turn to using positive behaviors to get what they—and we—want.

Unfortunately, traditional means of attempting to elicit positive behaviors from students during transitions often produce the opposite results—and the worse the behavior, the more students reap the negative benefits, and the worse it will *continue* to get. From repeatedly stating the rules, to bossing students around, to punishing them, to lecturing them, to sending them to the principal's office, traditional methods for trying to get students to comply fail them, and most profoundly fail the most difficult students.

The reason for this failure is twofold. First, difficult students, by definition, are the "behavioral pioneers" who will challenge the rules first and most often, so they will have their antisocial behaviors most often reinforced. No wonder teachers often say that they have "tried everything" with a student, and nothing seems to be working. The reason is that the methods being tried are inherently ineffective, so the more you use them, the worse the behavior will get.

Second, when ineffective procedures for transitions fail, teachers have an understandable instinct to take increasingly more control away from students. This serves to make a less pleasant environment for all students, but it is absolutely devastating to the HCNCs, who usually then engage in some form of rebellion.

The Lock-It-In procedure prevents students from getting any of the benefits for negative behaviors that traditional transition techniques give students. This is why the Lock-It-In procedure is effective and traditional techniques are not—and why the procedure deserves its own chapter.

How to Begin Modeling the Lock-It-In Procedure

On the first day of school, immediately before your class makes their first transition from one location to another, say the following. Say it clearly and well, because this will be the only time that you discuss transitions for the rest of the year.

> *The way you all will be transitioning from desks to the carpet, from the carpet to desks, and from the desks and carpet to the line is going to be different than what you are used to. I am going to do something called "locking it in." The way that I will do this is to notice which team is the first team to have a silent and clean table and lock it into my brain. Then I will notice which team is second to be silent and clean, and third, and so on. I won't say anything when I notice these tables. I will wait until everyone is ready. Then I will dismiss the teams in the order in which they were ready. I will do this today, and sometime soon, I will ask one of you to do it. I am going to start locking it in now.*

At this point, simply look around at your class using any of the four Eye Interventions (see Chapter 9 for details), probably starting with the Curious Eye and then going to Confused Eye, occasionally to the Crazy Eye, and once in a long while to the Evil Eye. Be very obvious and intentional with these interventions. Keep in mind that you are modeling the proper way to Lock-It-In for students who will start leading this transition shortly.

Feel free to move around the room, maintain proximity, or, rarely, use a question from the Question Matrix (Chapter 9). Keep these interventions very low-level, and don't use more than a couple outside of Eye Interventions. The reason for this is that the procedure itself has a powerful immediate consequence at the center of it, and there are also delayed consequences in store for students who are continuously uncooperative. You don't want to work too hard to save students from these consequences, since consequences are the best and most effective teachers of positive behavior.

While you are doing interventions, silently and with no external reaction, mentally note and "lock in" which team is silent and clean first. Then note which team is silent and clean second, then third, and so on. As soon as all teams are silent and clean, dismiss each team one at a time in the order in which they were ready. During this procedure, if a team is ready and they were locked in first, but a student on that team talked, they are no longer locked in, and the second team, in this case, moves up. (Don't worry about the mental strain of this; no one will know if you confused the order since you are making these notes silently and mentally.)

Dismiss teams at a speed that does not create a traffic jam. The speed necessary to accomplish this will differ depending upon where the students begin and where they are going. Elementary students who are lining up at the door can be dismissed from their desks fairly quickly. High school students who can be released directly to the hall can be dismissed even faster.

The Lock-It-In procedure can be used for any transition, regardless of grade level. Remember that these transitions may be happening after a prompt for cleanup from the student or teacher. Once it is time for the actual transition, supplies, books, and trash should be taken care of already. The transition will not have to include putting anything away or cleaning up: those things will already have been done, and they will have been done in more of a relaxed environment, where students are able to talk and socialize while taking care of their classroom.

Remember that there have been no consequences for slow transitioners. Those consequences will happen naturally, either by not being prepared to transition during Lock-It-In or as Failure to Get Locked In PLO.

How to Pass the Responsibility to Your Students

When you are ready, tell your students that you don't want to boss them around, that this is their classroom, and that they are going to get to be in charge of their own transitions. Let them know that from now on, you will simply pick a student who is already doing what they are supposed to be doing (sitting quietly at a clean workspace) to Lock-It-In. To be clear, the person whose job it is to Lock-It-In is not hired and fired. Instead, you will pick a different person each time. Simply say, "_____, you are ready. Could you lock it in?" Say it so that other students can hear, but don't make it an announcement.

The benefits of this procedure are tremendous:

- It gives a significant amount of control to your class.
- Instead of taking control away from your HCNCs every time the class needs to transition, it gives them a chance to *get* control by being quiet and ready.
- It systematically trains HCNCs that being cooperative *gives them more control.*
- It gives you back hours, if not days, per year. While a student is locking it in, you can be preparing for the next lesson, grading papers, or eating a snack.
- It shows that the maintenance of your classroom is your students' responsibility, not yours.
- If you feel like it, allowing a student to lock it in gives you the time and energy to do low-level interventions to guide students toward compliance.
- It is one less thing you need to worry about.

Allow your "Lock-It-Iner" to take plenty of time—up to four minutes is fine if it is OK with you and you are not inconveniencing anyone. Keep in mind that this is time that you can spend relaxing or getting things done, all while showing students that the management of the class is their responsibility.

As soon as all students are silent, your Lock-It-Iner will begin to dismiss one team at a time. When students first begin to lead this procedure, they may require some coaching, even in high school. Stand or sit near them so that you can coach them to slow down or speed up. Students may occasionally dismiss a team first when they should have dismissed them last. You will be able to correct this when necessary, though it will happen rarely. You may be surprised how well the Lock-It-Iner naturally uses the Eye Interventions from Chapter 9 if you have modeled them properly and for enough time. As the Lock-It-Iner dismisses teams, you will have the time and energy to stand between where the students are coming from (carpet, desks, etc.) and where they are going (carpet, desks, the door) and use interventions or a Failure to Transition Correctly PLO.

The number of days that you will model the Lock-It-In procedure will depend on your comfort level and what you see as developmentally appropriate for your students (in that order). Here is a suggested number of days depending on grade level:

- 6th and up: after 6 days of modeling
- 5th: after 7 days of modeling
- 4th: after 8 days of modeling

- 3rd: after 9 days of modeling
- 2nd: after 10 days of modeling
- 1st: after 11 days of modeling
- K: after 12 days of modeling

If an unreasonable amount of time elapses without *every student in your class-room* being silent and ready, or if you see your Lock-It-Iner getting frustrated that a team is not complying, go to the Failure to Get Locked In PLO.

Natural Consequences of the Lock-It-In Procedure

The natural consequences of being locked in later than others and therefore transitioning later is woven into the procedure. This is highly effective with students in preK–5th grade, who typically want to be the first to do things. After 5th grade, this natural consequence begins to be less effective with every passing year. It is still a great organizational tool, although students new to this procedure will have to learn about proper behavior by relying more on the logical consequences that befall students in the Failure to Get Locked In PLO.

In addition, taking a long time to line up for lunch or specials classes is its own natural consequence. Use this as much as is functional for you and your school. A rule of thumb: as soon as this causes a real problem for someone outside your classroom, it is time to stop allowing this natural consequence to befall your students. This is OK, since the natural consequences are not necessary in training your students. Consider them to be a bonus: when you can use them, great; if you can't, no problem. In other words, if you are worried that the lunch server is going to slash your tires because your class has been late to lunch every day for a week, it's time to go beyond the natural consequences of being late to lunch and bring on the PLOs.

Failure to Transition Correctly PLOs

If students fail to transition correctly, there are simple, immediate consequences that can be used to prompt the expected behaviors. If a student exhibits a negative behavior while transitioning, use your Calm Signal, but then ask the student to go back to their seat:

Oh, man. Could you please take a seat?

If at any point multiple students from the same team exhibit negative behaviors while transitioning, so much so that picking out which students did what becomes difficult in any way, simply have the entire team go back and sit down. If you let team consequences be your default position for the first three weeks, you should rarely, if ever, have multiple students on a team consistently exhibit negative behaviors afterward.

Failure to Get Locked In PLOs

Nearly all classrooms will have at least a few students who have gotten what they wanted by being uncooperative over a sustained time period. These students will continue to use those behaviors during the Lock-It-In procedure before being effectively trained not to. For them, Failure to Get Locked In PLOs provide another excellent opportunity to learn the lesson that being uncooperative doesn't get them what they want.

Failure to Get Locked In PLOs differ from Prompt for Quiet PLOs in that students are held accountable by their team, at least initially. This means that if even one student is uncooperative on a team, that entire team is held accountable. In 99 percent of cases, students will be held accountable with either a Class Transition PLO or a Single Team Transition PLO. It is easy to determine which practice procedure to use. If you have one team that fails with the procedure (read: is not perfectly cooperative), use a Single Team Transition PLO. If two or more teams fail, use a Class Transition PLO. In either case, say the following:

Oh, man. I will help you do some learning later. Don't let it ruin your day.

Then dismiss one team at a time, starting with the teams that were perfectly cooperative, in order of how quickly they became cooperative.

Once cooperative teams have transitioned, stop transitioning. For transitions to lining up at the door, allow cooperative teams to begin leaving the room *before* uncooperative teams get called to the door. Do not say anything to uncooperative teams or students about their behavior. For students who are not lining up but just walking out the classroom door, make sure all cooperative team members are gone before uncooperative team members are able to leave. For transitions within the room—carpet to desks, desks to carpet—make sure there is some kind of natural break between the cooperative and uncooperative teams. This is usually best done by beginning some small part of instruction before the uncooperative teams are asked to transition. Even transitioning cooperative students and then sitting down with them for a read-aloud before inviting the others to join you is enough to make cooperative behaviors functional and uncooperative behaviors nonfunctional.

Class Transition PLO

Notice that we did not give the opportunity for students to practice the procedure repeatedly during instructional time, since we have already done that by waiting patiently and perhaps even using some interventions. The students have already shown that they can't be successful with this behavior right now.

When students *on more than one team* are unwilling to create a quiet and clean team environment in what you find to be a reasonable amount of time, it is time to let the entire class know that you will be utilizing a Class Transition PLO. Say the following with sadness and empathy:

> *Oh, man, [class nickname]. It looks like you all are struggling with cre-*
> *ating a quiet, clean environment when it is time to transition to another*
> *activity. No worries. I'm not mad at you. When you struggle with some-*
> *thing, you need to practice doing it until you are an expert. So now I'm*
> *going to give you the chance to practice and become an expert. If you can*
> *become an expert today, that's fine. Otherwise, you will be coming in to*
> *practice this every _____ for the rest of the year until you become an*
> *expert. That's fine, too.*
>
> *I am going to give you all a chance to talk to each other. You don't*
> *have to, though. Then I will say the prompt [or have the Lock-It-Iner*
> *give the prompt]. I will then give you 30 seconds to create a quiet and*
> *clean learning environment while I lock it in. I will count in my head. If*
> *the entire class has created a quiet, clean learning environment before 30*
> *seconds, I will dismiss you all in the order that you were ready, and that*
> *will count for a successful practice. Tell me, how many times do you need*
> *to practice successfully: two times or three times?*

Do this until everyone has successfully practiced for the amount that they chose, or until all but one team has practiced successfully and that one team has annoyed the rest of the class. At that point, dismiss successful teams one at a time and continue with a Single Team Transition PLO.

Single Team Transition PLO

Use the same script and procedures as you did with the Class Transition PLO. If you have transitioned from the Class Transition PLO to a Single Team Transition PLO, start with the same number of practices you had left when the cooperative teams left.

Single Individual Transition PLO

You should only use a Single Individual Transition PLO in the most extreme cases. If a student has been the only one to be unsuccessful for more than 30 minutes, have the student practice individually. Allowing the student to annoy teammates with their behavior is productive: it is an opportunity for the student to learn that being uncooperative is not going to get positive regard from peers.

How to Utilize Lock-It-Iners for PLOs

Lock-It-Iners may walk up to teams and use such delicate interventions as "Hey! Be quiet!" Let this go as long the student is not being abusive or threatening and as long as this fits into your value structure. If the student does become abusive, fire that student and hire another Lock-It-Iner. If you feel that other logical consequences are necessary, have the student do Lock-It-Iner practice later. Otherwise, let the Lock-It-Iner proceed with their own interventions, though it's a good idea to monitor them. After all, this is a student doing what used to be your job. If necessary, you can intervene by saying the following:

> Oh, man. Looks like this team needs to practice being quiet when prompted. [Turn to Lock-It-Iner.] Would you like to help them to practice later, or do you want me to do it by myself?

Prompt the Lock-It-Iner to only dismiss teams who are being unanimously cooperative. Once the cooperative teams have lined up, or sat on the carpet, or sat in their seats (including the Lock-It-Iner), you can begin the next activity in some small way. If beginning a read-aloud, for example, you could sit down with the book in hand. Upon beginning this instruction, dismiss uncooperative teams. When lining up, make sure you line up uncooperative teams immediately *after* you have prompted the cooperative teams to leave. If possible, walk out of the room before the uncooperative students cross the threshold while still being able to observe all of the students. These interventions say to uncooperative students, "We love you, we're not mad at you, your antisocial behaviors don't work here, and we are moving on without you."

8

Academic Control-Sharing Procedures

Teachers are tasked with delivering a tremendous amount of material to students. It may even be unrealistic for a teacher to impart this amount of content to students during the time allotted, especially considering how much teachers are asked to differentiate for abilities and learning styles. This causes stress for the teacher, which may often be transferred to the students. For many classrooms, academic learning time is a time of high anxiety, when teachers hoard control as a natural human defense mechanism: when we feel out of control, we hold on to the control we do have for dear life.

Teachers are often at their worst while trying to deliver instruction and monitor work. While instructing, some teachers hoard control by badgering, lecturing, warning, and threatening students. In addition, it's not uncommon for teachers to yell and try to intimidate students into doing their work.

The problems with this dynamic are many. First, students are skilled at identifying and trying to avoid stressful situations. They avoid stressful academic situations by using negative behaviors to get out of class, retreating into their own minds (daydreaming), being off task, or doing work half-heartedly. Second, when academic time is the most stressful time of the day, students come to dislike learning and hard work, even if they have an inherent interest in the subject matter.

Ultimately, when students learn to see learning and work as bad things that make them sad and stressed, it has a devastating effect on their effectiveness as people, their chances to become lifelong learners, and their prospects for happiness in school and beyond. The stress created by these dynamics is even more damaging for HCNCs who have experienced significant trauma in their lives.

It is for these reasons that filling the entire academic portion of the day with choices given by a calm teacher is essential to the short- and long-term happiness of both students and teachers. It is also essential that these procedures be facilitated by the students themselves before the end of the third week of school, if not sooner. The only way for this to occur at an optimal level is by providing teachers with the procedures necessary to avoid all instances of anger, lectures, threats, and warnings. Simultaneously, teachers need to be able to give away any unnecessary control while confidently keeping the control that they do need.

The following procedures are described in the order in which they may take place throughout the day. Not every class will have an opportunity to use all of these procedures every day, due to grade level or type of class, but every teacher can use all or parts of these procedures to create procedures of their own. See pages 155–157 for guidelines for making your own procedures that best fit your grade level and specific circumstances.

Morning Meeting

Successfully getting started every morning for every student every day depends on an effective Relationship-Building Procedure (ESPN Greeting) and a Control-Sharing Procedure (a Morning Meeting), both working their magic immediately upon the students' arrival. Remember, you have no idea what has happened in the lives of your students over the weekend or since you saw them the day before. They may have experienced difficult or even traumatic events since they last left your classroom. All students, but especially your most difficult ones, need these relationships and this feeling of control immediately when they walk into your room, and you need to fulfill those needs.

Something else that they need is consistency. Keep in mind that your students' lives may be a haphazard, random series of events from the moment they leave your classroom in the afternoon to the moment they arrive in your room every morning. You standing in exactly the same place giving an ESPN Greeting every morning will be the first building block in creating a consistent, calm, predictable, caring environment for your students. The second building block is a consistent Morning Meeting, starting with a Quick Start Activity. The content of this meeting will change daily, but it has the same components every single day—by design.

The Control-Sharing and Relationship-Building elements of the Morning Meeting procedure will successfully encourage most students to cooperate in the successful participation in and maintenance of this procedure. The thoughtfully created structure of this procedure includes logical consequences for those remaining students who are uncooperative. Limits should be set once *per year*. After that, Gentle Guidance Interventions (see Chapter 9) should be used to gently guide students toward cooperation. In rare cases, consequences not already woven into the procedure can be used; most of these will be delayed.

Quick Start Activity Guidelines

As soon as your students have participated in the ESPN Greeting, have them put their belongings away and get to work on a Quick Start Activity. This activity must be aligned with standards; it is not playtime. If you do not require students to begin working as soon as they arrive, your class will lose weeks of instruction per year. A Quick Start Activity also gives the implicit message that, first and foremost, school is a place for learning.

Furthermore, the conditions under which students start working on their Quick Start Activity immediately create a relaxed, calm environment to start out each and every school day. Students should be allowed to socialize during this time. If students eat breakfast in the room, they can eat while doing the activity. Again, logical consequences await students who do not finish this activity in time, so students will learn how to concentrate within the context of these freedoms.

If the activity is something that needs be to put out by the teacher, distribute all of the materials (perhaps just papers) to team mailboxes, rather than putting each paper on each student's desk. If the activity is to be done in journals, write the activities on the board. The activities themselves can vary in content as widely as the preK–12th grade standards vary, so obviously the content will be at your discretion. A Quick Start Activity should meet the following criteria:

- *Able to be finished by the end of Morning Meeting.*
- *Includes a question that must be answered or a task that must be completed.*
- *Able to be checked by a teacher or student who will make sure it is completed.*
- *Easily completed (at first).* Make sure everyone is able to do the activity, and err on the side of it being too easy. The idea is to get students addicted to the feeling of success first thing in the morning every day. Very gradually, increase the difficulty. Differentiate insofar as it is possible. Allow students to be helped by

teammates, but as time goes by, encourage students to try to find answers on their own.

- *Aligns with the standards you teach.*
- *At least a little fun.* Funny word problems for 4th graders with students' names in them are usually better than 20 multiplication problems. A question asking for an opinion for a high school social studies class about a current event that happened the day before is preferable to a question asking students to describe the three branches of government. At least at first, fun and funny is better than challenging and frustrating.
- *Something that can be created quickly.* You are a teacher. You have no extra time, and you have to make this Quick Start Activity every day. Some savvy teachers create a template to simplify the process. As a 3rd grade teacher, I always did one daily edit and one daily math problem. I created a template, and each day I would change its contents and project the "new" activity onto my board. Feel free to use templates created by others in your school or online.
- *Draws upon old information.* You should be the one teaching new concepts, and that should be done during regular lessons throughout the class day.

Team Captains

Each team should have a new team captain each day. On the first day of school, select one student as team captain from each team. The function of that student during Morning Meeting is to get Quick Start Activity materials for the team, located in the class mailbox or materials bin. It is also the job of the team captain to pass out papers to the team throughout the day.

Each day, the position of the student who is the team captain rotates counter-clockwise. It is up to the students to manage this order. If there is a disagreement, allow the team to attempt to work it out. If it becomes a problem for you, or if you are asked by the students to resolve the issue, simply give the choice, "Would you like to solve this yourself, or would you like me to solve it?" If the students ask you to solve it, or if they are unable to solve the problem immediately, select a student from *another* team to be the team captain for that team for the day, creating a very high likelihood that next time, the team will be able to solve the problem on their own.

Team of the Day (TOD)

Every day, one of the class's teams will be the "team of the day" (TOD). That team will have special responsibilities during Morning Meeting, detailed here, and during Afternoon Meeting, described later in the chapter. The team of the day will rotate from day to day based on an order decided by you. The only responsibility that you have in maintaining the TOD is to make a colored dot on a spot on the board before students arrive every day. The team whose color matches the color of the dot is the TOD.

Every day, place a note in the TOD's mailbox or on their team table or desks that involves a friendly greeting, any announcements that need to be made, and the day's schedule. The TOD can immediately get to work on writing the day's schedule on the board. The title of my schedule that I handed the TOD to post every day was "Fun Things to Do Today." This implied that the school day is meant to be enjoyable.

For classes that are self-contained, or for classes that switch once throughout the day, each lesson should be referred to, in order, as a lesson that is to be learned, not an activity that must be done. Therefore, you should not write "math" as one of the "Fun Things." The word "math" holds little or no value by itself, and perhaps no word in the English language produces less excitement in the average human brain than the word "math." "Learn about rays and angles" is significantly more compelling: "What is an angle?" students might ask themselves. "What's a ray? Is that like a stingray? I like stingrays. I don't really like math, but maybe I'll find out if a ray is like a stingray. Hmm. I am sort of looking forward to that."

One extra step you can take is by communicating with teachers about what will be learned in their classes, so that instead of listing "PE" as just something that every-one has to do, you could have students write "Learn to accurately throw a ball at a target," for example. Listing the things to be learned instead of just showing your stu-dents what they will be doing makes a profound difference in buy-in and excitement about learning every single day.

For classes and grade levels that teach patterns and multiplication, consider sharing a "rule" (adding by 7, subtracting by 2) or a pattern (ABBC). Have the TOD incorporate the pattern and rule into the schedule list, and see if the other students can figure out what they are (see Figure 8.1).

Tip for TOD Schedule Writing

For a more relaxed, comfortable way for the TOD to design and post the daily schedule, you may want to create a removable dry-erase board so the students can work together on the schedule at their desks or on the floor. Simply take a portable dry-erase board, at least three feet by two feet, and apply magnetic tape to the back so students can place it on the magnetized board at the front (as long as it can be placed securely) when they've finished. Alternatively, you could hang the board on designated hooks—whatever works best in your classroom.

Figure 8.1

Sample Schedule Incorporating Pattern and Rule

Fun Things to Do Today
4 Morning Meeting
^ 6 Learn about adding doubles
^ 8 Learn about writing a personal narrative
^ 10 Lunch
# 12 Recess
^ 14 Read The Sisters Grimm
^ 16 Learn about map grids
^ 18 Readers' Workshop
# 20 Afternoon Meeting
Pattern:
Rule:

The TOD has their work cut out for them every morning because they must get the schedule up on the board *and* get their Quick Start Activity completed. Do not require students to do one before the other, and do not require students to participate in putting up the schedule. The schedule does not need to be completed, though when you remove all potential power struggles from this process, students will tend to want to do it. If the schedule is not completed, add this task as a Later and have the TOD representative verbally announce the schedule to the class.

For intermediate students who change classes once during the day, a bit of communication between morning and afternoon teachers may be necessary to find out what is happening in the afternoon so that it can be added to the schedule, or two different schedules can be made for morning and afternoon. For middle and high school students, you may choose to not do a schedule at all, but simply have students write what is for lunch, a news headline, or important announcements. Some teachers don't ask students to write anything. Having students verbally making announcements and running the room in general during a nonacademic homeroom is essential in middle and high schools. It communicates to students not only that it is their class but also that it is their school. You might even encourage middle and high school students to add to these announcements in any appropriate ways that they would like:

creating news desks, comedy sketches, and so on. Homeroom, perhaps more than any other period, should be like a clubhouse where students like to be. A fantastically welcoming, loving middle or high school homeroom can improve student attendance *and* promptness!

When appropriate for the grade level, the TOD can also be in charge of arranging the calendar, weather report, and so on. Any and all activities that you do routinely that are not being done by a hired student in the morning should be done by the TOD.

Get Started

At a time of your choosing, you or your student prompter will prompt the class to prepare for the student-led Morning Meeting. If students are moving from one place to another to begin the meeting (usually desks to carpet for younger students), after a reasonable amount of time, ask a student who is silent with a clean workspace to start the Lock-It-In procedure (see Chapter 7). As students transition, the TOD team captain will go in front of the group and begin Morning Meeting as soon as all students are silent and seated. For students who are not transitioning locations, skip the Lock-It-In step and simply have the TOD team captain begin Morning Meeting. After each activity, members of the TOD will select another TOD member. Once all TOD members have run part of the meeting, the TOD starts over, going through the students in the same order.

Of course, these components are merely suggestions. As a teacher, you are the expert in what elements of the Morning Meeting are most appropriate for your class. How you run Morning Meeting is more important than its elements. Make this procedure your own, but ensure that the time is owned and operated by your students and that you are barely working, or not working at all, during this period of time.

All this being said, on the first day, you should run most or all of Morning Meeting yourself for modeling purposes. It will be exhausting, but don't worry: you won't do this again until the first day of school next year. Make sure you communicate to your students that, starting tomorrow, they will be taking over some, most, or all of these responsibilities (depending on their developmental levels). Daring teachers of older students may want students to do parts of Morning Meeting without any modeling. For all students, hand over these responsibilities as soon as possible.

The following directions for elements of a Morning Meeting are presented from the perspective of a classroom whose students are fully in control of Morning Meeting. You decide when that should be. Generally, all aspects of the Morning Meeting should be handed over in the first three weeks of school for grades 3 through

12. Kindergarten–2nd grade classes may take around six weeks before full student ownership.

Pledges. The TOD team captain has the honor of running the pledge or pledges. When prompted by the teacher, the team captain uses the Prompt for Quiet procedure (see Chapter 6). Remember, your students will be managing behaviors along with you, according to the procedures described in earlier chapters. They will take the lead, with your guidance; you will facilitate students setting limits on each other.

If your school does not do the Pledge of Allegiance all at once, do it at this time, led by the TOD team captain, and follow it with the Class Pledge.

Schedule. The TOD team captain then chooses another TOD member who is seated and ready. That TOD member can read the entire schedule, perhaps chorally with other students, as well as any lesson that is tied in with the revealing of the schedule (e.g., detecting patterns or rules). Keep in mind that students can learn practically anything if it is taught every day. For years, every one of my students was proficient in naming patterns and finding rules for operations because we did it every single day.

Date. The date should always be posted by the TOD somewhere in the room, and the next TOD member selected should announce the date. This can also be the time to share a daily fun fact, weird news, and so on.

Weather. The next selected TOD member can go over current, low, and high temperatures; atmospheric conditions; or even detailed weather forecasts. Draw data from thermometers and other meteorological instruments or from an online weather information source.

Character education. Many schools already have prescribed character education programs. These programs can be woven into the Morning Meeting and put here. One member of the team of the day can lead a discussion in any way that makes sense. The key is for the discussion leader to truly lead the discussion. For example, in my classroom, we used a "Word of the Week" format, where we would have a character education word ("respect," "responsibility," "self-discipline," etc.) every week, and a student from the team of the day would lead a quick discussion about that word by asking questions like "What is the Word of the Week?" or "What does 'responsibility' mean to you?" or "Who can think of an example of someone being respectful?" You can help facilitate these discussions, but make sure the student takes the lead, insofar as they are able.

The next TOD member is the lead teacher in charge of reviewing the Quick Start Activity of the day. If and when necessary, you can assist, but giving the responsibility for the review to a student frees you up to use Gentle Guidance Interventions to create and nurture a positive learning environment. Of course, you will need to scaffold appropriately for the student teaching. Never send students into a situation that they cannot handle, but challenge them by giving them just enough support to be successful.

Once the answer is written on the board and all teaching is done, allow an appropriate amount of time for students to complete their work, if necessary. Students should be done or nearly done by the time teaching is done. Allow them to copy the work off the board at this point. Remember that most students should have had significant time to work on this already: it has been available since the moment they arrived at school.

The following means of holding students accountable will supercharge hard work without anyone but the students working hard.

Tagging

From the first day of the school year, once it is possible that a student may be done with the Quick Start Activity, say the following:

> I will tag students who are done with the Quick Start Activity and have
> their hands down. Once you have been tagged, you may _____ and
> talk with your friends, or you may sit and wait silently.

Fill in the blank with the actions necessary for students to be ready for the next activity. Depending on grade level and circumstances, the blank could be filled in with the following:

- Take out your math book and open it to page 33.
- Sit on your square on the carpet.
- Get out your writing journal.
- Stare off into space.

At that point, you may walk around and tag those who are done, while helping those students who ask for help. Ignore students who are not working hard. The procedure itself will teach them to work hard. At the appropriate time, say the following:

> Feel free to finish any time in the next 120 seconds, or after your other
> Nows are done during Real-World Workshop, or at recess [or lunch if
> there is no recess].

Do not lecture or warn or threaten. Just make the statement. With 10 seconds remaining, walk around with a clipboard and write down the names of students who have not completed the Quick Start Activity. When done correctly, you will never have more students not getting done in any given week than you had the week before. If you do, you are not following these procedures correctly, not giving enough time, or giving work that is too challenging for some students.

This procedure requires too much work for you to do for very long. Second through 12th grade teachers should move on to the Tagging Taggers subprocedure below within the first three weeks of school; preK–1st grade teachers may take up to six weeks.

Tagging Taggers

This subprocedure is identical to Tagging in all ways but one. When you tag taggers, you will have help holding students accountable for finishing their work. Say the following once the TOD member is done reviewing the Quick Start Activity:

> We will be starting something fun today that we will do for the rest of the year. Instead of me tagging everyone when they are done, I will simply tag the first person who is done on each team. That person will become the tagger for their team and will be in charge of helping their teammates and tagging them when they are done. Finally, they will be in charge of telling me if anyone didn't get done in time so I know who has to finish their Quick Start Activity after their other Nows during Real-World Workshop or at recess/lunch.

Then go around and find one student on each team who is done first. This will have the side effect of students not allowing other students to copy off their work before a tagger is chosen from each team. Also, the first person done on each team is almost always quite proficient at the skills necessary to complete the work and will be similarly proficient at teaching and helping other students. Once you have chosen a tagger from a team, ignore that team—they have a new teacher.

Many teachers, myself included, don't give the option for students to complete the Quick Start Activity during Real-World Workshop, but allow them to do so if they ask. In a decade of using this procedure, I've never had a class who didn't quickly figure out that they could get their work checked by their teacher during workshop instead of during recess. This, of course, increases ownership of the work.

Real-World Workshop Procedure

The way teachers traditionally organize independent work time for students prepares students for a world that no longer exists; systematically disincentivizes hard work;

forces teachers into time-consuming, unwinnable power struggles; takes time away from instruction; and systematically encourages belligerent and resistant behavior.

Traditional work time usually proceeds as follows:

1. The teacher introduces and teaches a standard.

2. The students practice the standard by completing an assignment.

3. Once the assignment is completed, the student is made to complete more assignments to practice the use of that standard or other standards that have already been taught until it is time to learn something else or until the school day or class period ends.

4. Students who do not do the work or do not work hard enough, are told—often repeatedly and with increasing emotion—to do their work or to work harder.

This process repeats itself thousands and thousands and thousands of times over the course of a student's educational life . . . and it's all wrong.

How Traditional Work Time Prepares Students for a Way of Life They Will Never Actually Encounter

Traditional "work time" creates an environment in which students who work hard to get work done get one thing immediately after the completion of said work: more work. This model, not coincidentally, coincides perfectly with training students to be part of the workforce that existed during the time when compulsory public schooling was coming into existence. In the early and mid-20th century, more than half of working Americans worked on farms or in factories. Traditional work time in schools follows the "9 to 5" (factories) and the "sunup to sundown" (farms) models for work.

American public schools were designed to train students to be part of an economy in which participants were expected to work hard from the beginning of their workday to the end. But this type of economy hasn't existed for 50 years, and it will never exist again. It's time to stop preparing students for a world that no longer exists.

In today's economy, hard work is as important as ever, and people still have essential work that they must do, *and* they face far more choices about what work they enjoy and how to pursue that work with enthusiasm. In today's economy, the efficacy of a worker is more often based on the product or output of work, not the consistency and steadiness of input.

How Traditional Work Time Destroys the Work Ethic

This contrived way of organizing work prevents students from learning an existential truth about hard work: the harder people work, the better their lives become. When students understand this truism, they will work harder without teacher input. They will equate hard work with pleasure instead of pain.

This should not be construed as any kind of "pull yourself up by your own bootstraps" political statement about hard work. Nor should it be taken to mean that hard work leads to a generally happy life in the distant future. What it actually means is that, in a real-world setting, working hard enough to get specific tasks done makes your life better and more pleasant *instantly* because you *no longer have to do those tasks!* In real life, when you are done with your work, you get to do things that you would rather do.

How Traditional Work Time Creates Power Struggles and Encourages Belligerent and "Lazy" Behaviors

Many students don't enjoy learning for the sake of learning. And many are wired to be difficult, control-seeking, attention-seeking, and stubborn. For those students, traditional work time is very frustrating. I should know, because I was one of those students.

If a student can't feel the control and satisfaction of being done with work, they often try to replace those feelings by controlling something that they can *always* control: whether or not they do the work. Over the years, tens of millions of teachers have spent billions of hours trying to get students to complete work. This creates anger, resentment, and power struggles that teachers are bound to lose, because they cannot *make* students work—and the students know this. The more stubborn the student, the more their stubbornness is reinforced and heightened. This stubbornness can become belligerence or overt aggression. Most often, though, these behaviors are misunderstood as laziness. In actuality, "laziness" is usually just a passive-aggressive or passive-resistant reaction to being told to do work. Many students (like me) would rather win an unlosable power struggle than actually do the work, especially when the reward for doing work is . . . more work.

The Alternative to Traditional Work Time

The Real-World Workshop procedure creates an environment whereby students' lives get better *instantly* when they work hard enough to complete quality work. On the other hand, just like in real life, not getting done with their work is its own consequence because they still have work to do so they are not able to do the things they would rather do. Real-World Workshop trains students to work hard and teaches them, through experience, the essential life truth that life improves when you work hard.

How to Use the Real-World Workshop Procedure

In order to teach every detail of this procedure, we will examine the most complicated version first. Simpler differentiated versions of the procedure will follow, though none of the versions is truly complicated. Approximately 95 percent of the necessary information can be found in the first descriptions, as all versions are nearly identical. Once the basics of the procedure are detailed, and differentiations are given for preK, kindergarten, and intermediate, middle, and high school, we will look at Procedural Learning Opportunities for setting and enforcing limits regarding voice level with individuals, small groups, and whole groups.

The first version is designed for a 3rd grade self-contained classroom—that is, a classroom that teaches all non-enrichment subjects (typically everything but physical education, art, music, and technology). Kindergarten through 2nd grade Real-World Workshop is exactly the same in procedure and process, though the preK and kindergarten procedures involve some very simple differentiations, mostly to accommodate for nonreaders. And 4th–12th grade Real-World Workshop is significantly simpler than preK–3rd.

Relax and Trust the Procedure

The procedure itself will teach students all the necessary lessons about hard work. Simply follow these directions to put the procedures in place. Fight the urge to nag students about working hard. Such actions will have the opposite of the intended effect. Instead, let the natural consequences built into the procedure work their magic. The Real-World Workshop's incorporation of "Nows," "Laters," and "Mystery Laters" is the basis for the procedure that teaches these lessons about hard work.

Nows

Nows are activities that correspond to direct instruction. Just as with traditional work time, the teacher teaches to a standard, and then students practice that standard using a Now activity. Nows are generally put on the Nows and Laters Board one at a time, immediately after the corresponding standard has been introduced. Once students are done with the Nows, they can move on to the Laters. When more standards from different subjects are introduced, more Nows are written on the Nows and Laters Board. If students fail to complete a Now before the class moves on to the next lesson, they need to complete the Now that goes with the next lesson, and then double back to the first Now. Just like in life, work that goes unfinished piles up.

While Nows are usually academic, they can also be Behavioral Leadership Classroom ownership or management tasks. For example, your first Now, done on the first day, could be "Choose team name"—hardly academic, but very important. Of course, lessons, Nows included, should be as interesting, stimulating, and compelling as possible.

Laters

Laters are the activities that students can do once they complete their Nows. These activities should also align with Common Core standards; they are not play-time. With only occasional exceptions, Laters should be academic in nature (or Behavioral Leadership activities) and something that the students already know how to do on their own. At least one should be something that is impossible to completely finish, for example, "Read" or "Play math board games." This prevents the ever-pop-ular cry of "I'm *done!* What do I do now?"

Though mostly academic, the Laters should also be *fun!* As a rule of thumb, every student needs to have at least one academic Later that is extremely appealing. Students need the incentive of seeing that their life will get better when they apply the effort necessary to get done with work (exemplified by the Nows).

Laters can also be tasks that students choose to serve their classroom. This builds ownership of the classroom while making your life easier. If you know you need to have something done and a student can do it, make it a Later. Do your students need to have mail delivered to their mailboxes? Have "Deliver mail" be a Later. If it has to be delivered every day, keep it up as a Later every day! This is an alternative to having Mail Carrier as an assigned and fireable job. Neither way is right or wrong—the only wrong way for mail to be delivered in a classroom is for the teacher to do it!

Worried that students are missing too much class time? No problem. Simply stop putting nonacademic Laters on the board for a while. Concerned that a student keeps picking the same academic Later? Remove it. Varying which Laters are available to students makes each individual Later more reinforcing anyway. Add more and more Laters as the year goes on. There is nothing wrong with having 15 Laters in a 3rd grade Real-World Workshop in November.

While you can't control whether students do their Nows, you have *total* control over how appealing, fun, exciting, educational, and wonderful your Laters are. Students who are left alone to decide whether to do their Nows without teacher prod-ding, lecturing, or warning will eventually start work if the Laters and the Mystery

Later (see below) are appealing enough. However, if you turn doing the Nows into a power struggle, many students will refuse to do them just to win, no matter how appealing the Laters are.

Laters could include the following:

- Vocabulary-related word games
- Any number of computer-based academic games or activities
- Writing and sending a letter to a celebrity
- Math whiteboard challenges
- Delivering mail
- Any number of the hundreds of possible activities provided by your curriculum

Celebrations: A Character Education "Later"

One Later that I always had available was Celebrations. Once they had completed their Nows, students could take a sticky note and write an example that they have seen of a schoolmate or teacher exemplifying a characteristic of good character: "I would like to celebrate DeMarcus for being respectful when he said "please" and "thank you" to the lunch server yesterday." We always had a Celebrations Board available where students would post their Celebrations. Then during Afternoon Meeting, students who had posted Celebrations, if called on, would have an opportunity to read their Celebrations with the class.

Mystery Later

The Mystery Later is a Later that is not shown to the students immediately. It is signified by a question mark below all other Laters. It is generally not academic, it is especially appealing, and it does not have to be provided every day, though the question mark should always be on the board. It is meant to do an especially effective job of encouraging students to complete their Nows to your satisfaction every day. It teaches the real-world lesson that when you work hard and get your work done, if a fantastic opportunity for fun presents itself, you can take advantage of it! Mystery Laters should usually be revealed on the board once most students who have been working hard are on their Laters. For self-contained classrooms, this will usually be during the last 45 minutes of your academic day. Mystery Laters could include activities like the following:

- Recess
- Play basketball with Principal Jones

- Play on Chromebooks
- Play dodgeball with Coach Johnson
- Relax under a tree
- Do relay races on the track

The possibilities are endless.

Of course, some of these involve some logistical organization, but perhaps not as many as you might think. If Principal Jones shows up unannounced in your doorway with a basketball under his arm, you know you can reveal the corresponding Mystery Later, and students who are on their Laters can leave with him to play basketball. The same is true when Coach Johnson shows up with a dodgeball. If you team-teach or do inclusion with another teacher, and you erase your question mark and put up "Recess," one teacher can take those who are working on their Laters and wish to have recess outside, and the other teacher can work with those still on their Nows. If you teach alone, you can put recess up as a Mystery Later, line up your entire class, and have students who are not done with Nows bring those Nows outside to work on in a designated area while those on their Laters play. The same can be done with relay races or any other outdoor activity.

Now that you understand how to use Nows, Laters, and Mystery Laters, the text below will show you how to enact the Real-World Workshop procedure starting on the second day of school. Recall that you already used the procedure on your first day, without even having all the details under your belt.

On Day 2, you may begin some academic work; for example, you might start your first math lesson. (Please note that this book offers no suggestions about any academic content; this is purely an example.) Let's say you are doing a review of 2nd grade addition. You have taught the lesson, and students will practice their skills by doing a workbook page. Your board may look like this:

Nows

Math book, page 1, #6–12

Laters

Create team tags

Read

?

Note that your board will look like this at the beginning of Day 2 only if all teams successfully and unanimously chose team names on Day 1 (the only Now for that day). If there is even one team who has not yet chosen a team name, that Now remains, although it applies only to teams who have not yet completed it. Under those circumstances, your board will look like this:

Nows

Math book, page 1, #6–12

Unanimously decide on a team nickname

Laters

Create team tags

Read

?

In circumstances like this one, teams will tend to discuss the name while they do their academic Now. Accept their choice at any time.

As students complete their Now, they will, one at a time, be able to move on to their Laters. It is essential that you don't allow students to do Laters until they have completed their Nows. Also, make sure that the Nows are done to whatever level of quality that you require. Keep in mind that this procedure has already given you significantly more time and mental bandwidth with which to hold students accountable, since you are no longer trying to convince, cajole, bribe, or lecture students into working.

Have students demonstrate accountability in any way that works for you; whatever you have done in the past will be easier to do now due to this procedure. Here are some strategies that have worked for me during my career, starting with the most time-consuming and ending with the least time-consuming.

1. *Grade for 100 percent mastery.* In short, students need to get everything right to show that they completely grasp the standard being practiced. This works quite well for certain elementary school math lessons or for PE lessons of all levels, for example. Keep sending the student back until the work is perfect. Write down scores in a gradebook.

2. *Grade for a certain level of proficiency.* Using an established rubric, have a certain level of proficiency necessary for you to accept a Now. Send the student back if they do not meet that minimal standard. Write down scores in a gradebook.

3. *Just make sure it's not garbage.* This is a lower level of scrutiny. It is helpful for when you can grade the work later and, frankly, when you are especially busy. Using this method, you have students submit work to you, you look at it to make sure that the writing/math/art is not a travesty against humanity, and, if not, you accept it. You can simply put a dot in the correct spot in your

gradebook and "overwrite" the dot with a grade later. The dot helps you easily see that the student completed the Now.

4. *Trust, pray, and spot check.* When you are in a *huge* hurry, you may want to resort to this once in a long while. This tactic involves allowing students to simply turn in work to a designated place when they are done with it. When and if you have time, you can look through it and hand back work not done to your satisfaction, at least to make sure it isn't garbage. (Numbers 3 and 4 require the same very low-level demonstration of proficiency.)

In order to facilitate strategies #1–3, call on students who indicate they have completed their Nows by raising their hands and remaining seated. You can either sit at a desk or reading table with your gradebook or walk around with it; a reading table is optimal for interacting with multiple students while checking their work. If you are seated in one spot and are sensitive to noise level, you can set the following limit: "Feel free to stay in line as long as you are silently checking your work."

If a student who is in line to have their work checked speaks or stops checking their work, use the following script:

Oh, man, [student name], could you please have a seat? Thanks.

The student can then sit down, raise their hand, and wait to be called upon again. This limit should be the same no matter what voice level your students choose with their vote and their behavior choices (which will be discussed further below). I use this silence expectation simply because it is difficult for me to concentrate when several students talk right next to me, even at the appropriate "soft talking" voice level. If this doesn't bother you, ignore this advice.

Realistic Differentiation Using the Nows and Laters Board

In most real-life classrooms, traditional work time practices make it extremely difficult to implement quality differentiated instruction, especially in classrooms with wide-ranging ability levels. Real-World Workshop makes it possible and, in some cases easy, to differentiate instruction.

Notice that as each student completes the Now on Day 2 and moves on to the Laters, which are self-directed, you will have fewer and fewer students who are still on their Nows. These students may need help refocusing (see Gentle Guidance Interventions, Chapter 9), or they may need more help academically. Either way, Real-World Workshop creates a more advantageous student-to-teacher ratio for them with every student who completes their Nows. In this way, the students scaffold for themselves simply by not having the proficiency to complete their Nows.

Eventually on Day 2, only those truly struggling academically or having problems with focus or refusing to work (which is fine) will still be on their Nows—perhaps three students or so. When it is time to teach another lesson, do so. Once you finish teaching that lesson, add the corresponding Now to the Nows and Laters Board.

Nows

Math book, page 1, #6–12

Write introductory narrative paragraph

Laters

Create team tags

Read

?

Now everyone has a new Now ("Write introductory narrative paragraph"), and that is what they all should work on until they are finished. Once that task is completed, the three students who did not finish their math task should double back to complete it. Everyone else, once done with the narrative paragraph, can do their Laters. Trust that your students will come to recognize this reality *on their own*. Pointing it out or, worse, lecturing kids about it, will have the opposite of the intended effect. Trust the procedure to do the teaching.

Students will complete their second Now with the benefit of your expert instruction while you are also holding them accountable by not allowing them to get to their Laters before finishing all of their Nows. Again, you will notice that you are more and more able to help those who need help as more and more students move on to their Laters.

The same pattern will happen in the afternoon when a reading lesson is added:

Nows

Math book, page 1, #6–12

Write introductory narrative paragraph

Answer reading questions #1–4

Laters

Create team tags

Read

?

With perhaps 45 minutes left in the academic day, you can reveal your Mystery Later. On Day 1, you added "Recess." For simplicity, we'll add the same Mystery Later here:

Nows

Math book, page 1, #6–12

Write introductory narrative paragraph

Answer reading questions #1–4

Laters

Create team tags

Read

Recess

Again, let the procedure do the teaching. Instead of lecturing students about the consequence, allow them to learn from the consequences.

Further Differentiation

Aside from the inherent differentiation detailed above, Real-World Workshop can create a fantastic platform for more fully differentiating for all students, regardless of their academic levels. Special education students, gifted students, and students with cognitive issues and other special needs can all be served optimally using Real-World Workshop. Below are various ways to differentiate. For some students, these differentiations may be planned and facilitated, at least in part, by gifted and special education intervention specialists. Feel free to use any methods that are appropriate for the students that you serve.

The first, simplest, and most conventional way to differentiate is to simply create different Nows for different groups of students. Having different groups for math and reading, for example, could involve two different assignments for each of these subjects, designated by two different colors:

Nows

Math book, page 1, #6–12/ page 1, #6–9

Write introductory narrative paragraph

Answer reading questions #1–4/#1–2

Laters

Create team tags

Read

?

This grouping may be enough to sufficiently differentiate for most students. Those who need more can have their own Workshop Folders that they keep with them. For some students, their folders may include additional and enriching Laters that other students might not be ready for, such as the following:

Laters

Create Team Tags

Read

Advanced sudoku

Write a letter to Bill Gates

Number puzzles

Other advanced students might have either extra Nows or completely different and more challenging Nows that still correspond to the same lesson (or both); or they can go without the lesson if they don't need it and go straight to their Now; or they could leave during the Now and get a lesson from the gifted intervention specialist that corresponds to a special Now in their Workshop Folders. Their folder may contain a list that looks like this:

Nows

Complete addition art puzzle

Write narrative survey possibilities

Answer all reading questions on page 46

Laters

Create team tags

Read

Advanced sudoku

Write a letter to Bill Gates

Number puzzles

Conversely, students who require simplified or specialized work due to cognitive disabilities might have a list that looks like this:

Nows

Practice making 10 with blocks with Ms. Frank

Write a sentence about myself

Read leveled reader book 3 with Mr. Levy

Laters

Create Team Tags

Make more 10s with blocks

Read

?

Real-World Workshop is a platform that allows students who need accommodations to remain in the least restrictive environment and feel that they are part of the Behavioral Leadership Classroom so that they can reap all of its benefits!

Old Homework

When you list "old homework" as a permanent Now, you will never, ever have to talk to students about whether they did their homework again. All they have to do is make sure that it is completed before they do their Laters. If a student says that they didn't do their homework, you can just say, "Don't worry about it. You can do it today before you do your Laters. I'll like you whether you do your homework at home or at school!"

Today's Homework

Allowing students to do the homework assigned that day as a Later has a profound effect. Students who love learning and working hard often love to get homework done in class to feel good about themselves and perhaps to benefit from your expert instruction before going home where there is no teacher to enrich their intellectual exploits. Other students want to get done with their homework at school so they can go out and play basketball immediately after arriving at home. Either way, having "Today's homework" as a Later can be a game-changer.

Recess Work

If a particular assignment or assignments have remained undone for a length of time that you find to be unreasonable, and if it is acceptable to your administration and consistent with your value structure, you can move that assignment from the Nows column to a new column: Recess Work. When this happens, students must stay in from recess until their Recess Work is completed. If you deem it to be appropriate, "Old homework" can become Recess Work.

Nows

Write introductory narrative paragraph

Answer reading questions #1–4

Recess Work

Math book, page 1, #6–12

Old homework

Laters

Create Team Tags

Read

?

Behavioral Nows

Once all academic Nows have been completed, those students who need to do so can practice a positive behavior, solve a problem that they caused, or destress an adult or student as a behavioral Now. (There will be more discussion of these Delayed Learning Opportunity techniques in Chapter 11.) In this case, your Nows and Laters

Board may look like this, with perhaps just a few students needing to do the behavioral Now:

Nows

Math book, page 1, #6–12/ page 1, #6–9

Write introductory narrative paragraph

Answer reading questions #1–4/#1–2

Practice not touching people in line

Laters

Create Team Tags

Read

?

Real-World Workshop During Indoor Recess

When using Real-World Workshop, you may see some amazing things happen during indoor recess. Let students know that they are allowed to do their Laters at that time even if they haven't finished their Nows (it is recess, after all). Of course, they are also allowed to play any indoor recess games, as they always have.

This is a test of the quality of your Laters. If no one ever chooses Laters during indoor recess, your Laters are not good enough. Improve them. Allowing students to do Laters during indoor recess will help to get students who have not been consistently getting to them during Real-World Workshop addicted to these educational activities. They will realize that when recess is over, they will have to go back to doing Nows more or less all day long *unless they work harder*. They then realize that if they work hard, they can "play" much or most of the day!

Additionally, you will find that many students, even students who have never worked hard in their lives, will start doing Nows *during recess!* I have had students look around during indoor recess, turn to me and ask, "Wait . . . is this recess, or is this Workshop?"

Start Off Easy and Get Them Addicted to Success

Keep in mind that you may have students who have had success in the past with acting "lazy" and becoming belligerent. These students will reveal themselves in the first few days of school. It is your job to create the optimal environment for all of your students to become successful in working hard and using positive behaviors. No procedure better accomplishes this than Real-World Workshop.

Think about the outlook that most of your difficult students have on their first day of school: they generally don't like school because it's too hard, it isn't fun, and their teachers are mean. They see themselves as being not smart enough to succeed in the ways their teachers want them to be successful—being human and wanting to be competent at *something*—so many try to be competent at being disruptive and at controlling their teachers' emotions.

One important way to make this procedure more immediately effective is to simply set the academic expectations of the Nows significantly lower than you otherwise would. Of course, you should differentiate for students, and you shouldn't make assignments *insultingly* easy, but err on the side of assignments being a little too easy, at first. The first three weeks of the school year are not the time to be challenging kids. The first three weeks are most important for building your routines, sharing control, building relationships, showing students that negative behaviors don't work in your room, having fun, and getting students *addicted to success*. By the end of the first three weeks, you want your students to think, "This grade is easy, and I am good at it!"

Once you have hooked your kids, as the year goes on, slowly increase the difficulty of the Nows, eventually challenging students on a level that they never dreamed they could attain. By the end of the year, *all* of your students will be able to experience success—not just when things are easy but also when things are extremely difficult. This will greatly improve their self-confidence and self-concept. This progress over the course of just one year will be profoundly life-changing for these students.

While some students love learning for the sake of learning, many don't. The use of Real-World Workshop gets students' motors running and gets them addicted to working hard. Once the motor is running and they are energized to do work, they are likely to find work that they like or even love. Whether they find that they love math in 2nd grade or that they love industrial drawing at a career-based high school as a junior, Real-World Workshop can keep students motivated so they can find out what they love to learn!

Close Down School

On the very first day of school, I always said the following to my students. Consider trying something similar with your own students.

> Look, folks, I'm a different sort of teacher. I don't believe in making kids learn for no reason, and I don't believe in hard work for the sake of hard work. There will be a bunch of things that you are supposed to do every day. I will only ask you to do work that will help you to learn important things. I'll never ask you to do extra work. When you are done doing everything you have to do, which are your Nows, you can do stuff you'd

rather do, which are your Laters. Here's the thing: when everyone in the room is done with all of their Nows, we're done. School is closed. There's a law that says that we have to be here until [dismissal time], but as far as I'm concerned, our school day will be over. We can sort of do anything you want to do. I don't really care what we do. Now I'm not saying everyone must get done with their work every day. I'm just saying that I'm here to help you learn a certain amount of things every day. Once everyone learns them, we're done. We can go outside; you can hang out. You can fall asleep under a tree for all I care. Some of my students like to goof around. Last year, we all silently snuck around the school and pretended to be ninjas. It freaked everyone out. Anyway, the point is that once we're done, we're done.

Allow your students to come up with what they want to do if and when everyone in the room is done with their Nows. Accept any ideas that do not cause problems and that allow you to monitor all of your students at all times. Keep in mind that "closing down school" may never happen all year long, and that is OK. Even the possibility of this outcome can have tremendous benefits. Students being able to shut down their classrooms with their hard work reinforces positive behaviors in a profound way.

Prekindergarten–First Grade Differentiation

Although all of the aforementioned elements of Real-World Workshop also apply to grades preK–1, a few modifications are necessary. The most obvious is that you may have to accommodate for nonreaders. One way to make this accommodation is to draw pictures of Nows and Laters instead of writing them, when possible. Another difference is to have fewer Nows and Laters, especially at first, and especially in preK and kindergarten. All grades preK–1st should start out with no more than one Now and one Later, with 1st grade possibly being an exception if the extra Later is "Read." Therefore, on Day 1, your preK or kindergarten Nows and Laters Board might show just two symbols. Under Nows, there could be an icon of a paint palette indicating fingerpainting. Under Laters, there would be a picture of a book, indicating independent reading.

For 1st grade, the Nows and Laters Board might look like this:

Nows

Math book, page 8, #1–6

Laters

Play apple counting game

Read

Differentiation for Grades 4–12

As stated previously, 4th–12th grade differentiation is actually a simplification because, in most U.S. schools, grades 4–12 involve specialized classes. (If you have a self-contained classroom in any grade, follow the above procedure without these modifications.)

For Secondary Grades

As a teacher of only one subject, your simplifications may be obvious to you:

- Your academic Nows will only correspond to the subject that you teach.
- Your academic Laters will only correspond to the subject that you teach.
- You will have significantly fewer Nows. If you have a 48-minute class period, for example, you will typically only have one or two Nows.
- In the first three weeks, you should plan so that the hardest-working students are able to complete all Nows in the first 25 to 30 minutes of class. Remember not to challenge students too much during this time, and make sure to have a great Mystery Later at least four out of five days.
- "Work in office" can be a fantastic Later in schools where school administrative assistants need help answering phones or filing non-HIPAA-related papers. For secondary students in schools that have adjoining elementary schools, helping with younger students can be a Later. Anything that is OK with your administration can be a Later.
- If your administration stresses "teaching bell-to-bell," you will tend to lean on excellent academic Laters instead of nonacademic or classroom job Laters to encourage hard work. Remember, an academic Later still involves academic work to academic standards. In addition, you should ask your administrator to read this Real-World Workshop section of the manual so that they might then allow you to get your students more quickly addicted to hard work using nonacademic Laters, Mystery Laters, and Closing Down School.
- If and when your students can work hard enough to Close Down School, let that time be as fun as your students can make it without causing problems for you or for them. Your students should be eligible for this possibility near the end of every class period. Truly let students do whatever they want unless it causes a problem. If it does not contradict your values, you can even allow students to check their phones, watch ridiculous (but appropriate) internet videos on the class SMART Board, have an impromptu dance contest, and generally goof off. Slowly increase academic rigor over time so that this outcome eventually

happens only very rarely, but the first three weeks of school are not the time for significant academic rigor. Hopefully, each one of your classrooms' hard work will be able to close the room down a couple of times in the first three weeks.

For Intermediate Grades

This section refers to grades that split the day in two, generally in situations where math is taught during one half of the day, language arts is during the other half, and science and social studies are taught one on each side of the midday break. This way of doing things is most typical in grades 4, 5, and sometimes 6. The differentiations here are a hybrid between the self-contained procedure and the secondary grades procedure:

- If you teach two subjects during your half-day, only allow academic Nows and Laters from those subjects.
- Your students should have half as many Nows compared with students in a self-contained, full-day classroom.
- Close down your half of school when appropriate.

Voice Level PLO

The instructions for creating Real-World Workshop given thus far are nearly all-inclusive in terms of using a procedure to create a real-world situation whereby working hard becomes a functional behavior and not working hard becomes dysfunctional. Not getting into power struggles over work makes cooperation functional and belligerent behavior dysfunctional. But getting hard work and cooperation from students in Real-World Workshop is only two-thirds of the equation. The final piece of the puzzle is the procedure for establishing and enforcing a proper voice level during Real-World Workshop.

A vast majority of teachers fail miserably at this. There are two essential reasons for this failure:

1. *Students feel bossed around regarding voice level.* Teachers tend to feel out of control when it comes to trying to maintain a proper voice level since, up until the publishing of this book, they have not had a surefire procedure for setting and enforcing limits about voice level. When their need for control is not met, some students rebel with louder and louder voices. The problem is compounded when all students try to talk over each other in order to be heard, resulting in a noise level that makes it difficult or impossible to learn.

2. *The use of warnings.* Students "need" as many warnings as they are given. Astute students take note that when a teacher constantly warns about, in this case, the voice level of the room being too loud, that teacher has proven themselves to be someone who takes no action, even after repeatedly warning that action will be taken. Difficult students quickly realize that they can be as loud as they want, and it will only cause the teacher to become angrier and perhaps more entertaining.

The Voice Level PLO solves both problems simultaneously: the teacher bombards the entire class with choices about voice level and music to be played (or not) while never, ever warning students about their voice level.

Setting limits. At the beginning of *every single Real-World Workshop*, overwhelm your class with choices in a simple, scripted way. Feel free to read the script verbatim or paraphrase, using developmentally appropriate language while introducing Real-World Workshop. The first part will be said only once—right before the first Workshop of the year:

> [Class name], we are about to begin Real-World Workshop. We will do this hundreds of times this year. Each time, I will give you three choices on which voice level you prefer. You will vote, and we will keep using that voice level for as many seconds as you can stay on that voice level as a group. I will describe each voice level one time, right now, and I will never bother you all about it again.
>
> One voice level you can choose is silence. Silence, as you know, means absolutely no noises made verbally or with your body.
>
> [Put your index and middle finger on your throat and speak in a whisper.] Whispering is talking like this. I am going to show you a cool trick for determining whether or not you are whispering. If you would like to do this with me, feel free to put your fingers on your throat like I am doing. [Pause.] On the count of three, say your name with your normal speaking voice, and notice if you feel vibrations on your fingers. One, two, three: [say your name]. Did you feel the vibrations? Me too.
>
> [In a whisper.] Now, on the count of three, whisper your name. One, two, three: [say your name in a whisper.] Did you notice that you couldn't feel a vibration? When we are in Whispering Workshop, if it helps you to remember, you can put your fingers on your throat before talking.
>
> Soft talking is the third option. Soft talking means that someone at another table cannot hear you, but the people at your table can hear you.

I will also ask you all if you want to listen to music or not, and then I will give you two choices of music.

For elementary students, continue with the following:

Some of you may struggle with tuning your ears to being able to hear the proper voice level and talking at or below that voice level. That is totally normal. Everyone is different. If you accidentally talk above the proper voice level, I will give you a chance to put your head down and listen carefully to the voice level so you can tune your ears to what it sounds like. Sometime later, I will come to you and ask if you can hear our silence. If you think that you have properly tuned your ears, you can tell me using the proper voice level, or give me a thumbs-up if we are on silent. If you need more time, you can tell me, or give me a thumbs-down if we are on silent, and I will give you more time so you can go back to ear tuning.

For secondary students, say the following:

Here's the deal, folks. You have probably dealt with teachers nagging you about your voice level in class for a long time. You are in ___ grade, which means you've probably been nagged about voice level for ___ years. That has to have been annoying, and I'm sorry about that. We all know what happens: one person speaks 1 percent louder than everyone else, and then everyone speaks 1 percent louder than everyone else, and then everyone gets louder, and so on. It's just kind of natural, and in some ways it isn't really anyone's fault. Then the teacher gets frustrated, and then you get annoyed by the nagging teacher, and so on and so forth.

The good news for you all is that I will never nag you and none of us will have to be in a room where it's too loud—ever. The reality is that when anyone is in a room that starts to get loud, your ears and voices just "go out of tune": you lose the ability to hear the right voice level, and your voice just naturally gets louder. What we are going to do is have a system for not letting our ears and voices get "out of tune." Once you all choose your preferred voice level and we get started, I, or one of you, will be in charge of retuning people. If you talk above the chosen voice level—and it isn't a big deal if you do—the Retuner will go and give a sign that you need to retune. We'll vote on a signal later if you want, but for now the sign is just quietly saying, "Retune," and tapping the person gently on the shoulder. Don't embarrass the person by saying this loudly. Then, if you were the one who went out of tune, just put your head down so no one can see your eyes, with your entire head above the desk or table. Just retune your ears by listening to the correct voice level. The Retuner will then wait between 1 minute and about 10 minutes before they come back to you, tag you, and quietly say the word "tuned." If you are retuning someone for the first time, it should be closer to 1 minute. If it is their third or fourth time, it should be more like 10 minutes. Sometimes three or four students sitting next to each other may all need to be retuned at the same time. In that case just tag each one and say, "Retune," to each.

Now, if more than four students need to be retuned at the same time, we're just going to give up on that voice level for a bit and we will go to the next quietest voice level. The reason for this is that the lower voice levels like silence and whispering are easier to retune to. We may go from soft talking to whispering, or whispering to silence. If more than four people need to be retuned at silence level, we'll just have the whole class retune until it's time to go on to the next thing. The Retuner will say, so everyone can hear, "You have chosen [whispering or silent] workshop" when more than four students need to be retuned.

For the first few times we have Workshop, I'll be the Retuner so that you all can see how I do it. Very soon, though, I'll just pick someone at the beginning of Workshop who has the tuned-in voice level right away. If you are the Retuner, that means I'm not, so if I speak too loudly during Workshop, you can retune me if I need it. The only difference is that I will sit with my head up, since I have to be observing the classroom. The Retuner will still come and tag me and say, "Tuned," anywhere between 1 minute and 10 minutes later. Just like for you all, have me retune for something like 1 minute if it's my first retune and more like 10 minutes if it's my third or fourth. By doing this, no one gets nagged, no one gets angry, and we'll never have to be in a room that is too loud.

Take questions from the group at this point.

Giving Choices

The following script should be the same every time you do Real-World Workshop. Keeping it the same every time makes it easier for you to remember it, allows you to do it faster, and creates consistency in the lives of students who may not be getting consistency anywhere else. Feel free to read it yourself at first, but turn the task over to students as soon as it is developmentally appropriate. The minimal amount of time this takes is well worth the control you are giving away each time this procedure is executed. The script can be shortened and made to be more casual, especially when being led by secondary students. Of course, manage and monitor that all musical artists and songs are school-appropriate. The script for giving students choices about voice level and music during Real-World Workshop is as follows:

> OK, here we go. Show of hands: who would like silent workshop? [Count hands.] Who would like whispering workshop? [Count hands.] Who would like soft talking workshop? [Count hands.] Who does not want music? [Count hands.] Who does want music? [Count hands.] We will listen to either Beyoncé or Taylor Swift. Who wants Beyoncé? [Count hands.] Who wants Taylor Swift? [Count hands.] [Musical artist] it is. I will begin playing the music when I hear [chosen voice level here].

Find the artist on a device, put your finger on the "play" button or mouse, look up at your class with a smile, and begin playing music when the proper voice level is achieved. If the proper voice level is not achieved within 10 seconds, say the following:

> Oh, man. No music today.

Then immediately enforce the limits that you just set.

Note that students will choose soft talking workshop 95 percent of the time, but which level they choose is 100 percent irrelevant. What is relevant is that they are systematically, repeatedly, and on an overwhelming basis given a feeling of control. Secondary students are guaranteed to roll their eyes and act annoyed by this procedure. Again, their acceptance of doing this as "cool" (or whatever teenagers say) is irrelevant. The point is for the students to be bombarded by choice, even to the point that it becomes "uncool." Actual counting of hands is not necessary, unless it looks like either silent or whisper Workshop might get the majority vote, which will be rare.

Enforcing the Limits

Individual and Small-Group PLOs. Remember, there will be absolutely no warnings. When one, two, or three students choose to speak above whichever voice level has been voted upon, the consequence is always the same, and it is expressed by walking near the student(s) and saying the following:

> [Elementary] Oh, man. Could you put your head down and listen for the [current voice level]?
> [Secondary] Oh, man. Retune.

The students will then put their heads down on their tables or desks for anywhere between 25 seconds and 10 minutes, depending on the age and developmental level of the students and how often they have had to listen to the voice level in the past. The idea of the listening consequence is that they are fine-tuning their ears to be able to notice and use the proper voice level in class. This is often difficult at first for students for whom loud voice levels are common in their homes.

After a period of time, whisper the following to the students with their heads down:

> [Elementary] Do you hear our [voice level]? [Pull on your earlobe.]
> [Secondary] Retuned. [Tap student on the shoulder.]

After any affirmative response from your elementary students, return an affirmative response indicating that they can get back to work. After this procedure has been in place for a few weeks, you can merely say the student's name and pull on your earlobe with a quizzical expression, get an affirmative, and give one back, and the student can get back to working with only the student's name being uttered. For secondary students, just assume intelligence and walk away.

Proper head-down position involves the student's eyes not being able to be seen by anyone and their head being fully above the desk or table. If a student fails at this, simply say the following:

> Oh, man. Looks like you need to practice putting your head down the right way. You can either practice now by doing it perfectly, or you can practice later. Either way is fine.

If the student puts their head down properly while tuning their ear to the voice level, no further action needs to be taken besides spending more time, right then, with their head down. Students who continue to not put their head down correctly will practice doing so later, during noninstructional time. For more details on how to do this, see Delayed Learning Opportunities in Chapter 11.

If one to three students do this repeatedly, simply repeat the procedure, giving them more head-down time each time to tune their ears to the proper voice level.

Whole-Class Voice Demotion PLO. Remember that, when developmentally appropriate and properly monitored, older students will be administering this PLO. For the purposes of this manual, the directions below indicate that you will be doing this as the teacher. Just keep in mind that, when appropriate, a student could be administering the PLO. Utilizing students for these PLOs is optional. If you don't think your students are up for it, or you think this might cause more problems than it solves, don't do it.

To review, the possible voice levels are, in order, the following:

1. Soft talking
2. Whispering
3. Silent

Each level is more enjoyable for the students than the one that comes after it. The trouble is that the most enjoyable voice levels are the most difficult to maintain: soft talking involves lots of thoughtful awareness. Silent involves almost no awareness.

When four or more students speak above the voted-upon voice level, that is the class's way of telling you, "We cannot yet handle this voice level; we need an easier one." When this happens, you should oblige. If they voted for soft talking Workshop, and four or more students talk above that level, say the following:

> Oh, man. Looks like you guys have chosen [start whispering and put two fingers on your throat] whispering Workshop.

Again, this script can be more casual with secondary students, and if you have a volunteer Retuner, this is even more the case. If you are the Retuner, however, do not omit your Calm Signal, no matter how casual your language becomes.

The expectation is that everyone is now in whispering Workshop. Whispering Workshop is quieter and easier to monitor anyway! Hooray for you! Once in whispering Workshop, when four or more students talk above whispering, say, while still whispering:

> Oh, man. Looks like you all have chosen silent Workshop.

The expectation is that everyone is now in silent Workshop. Silence! Yes! You thought you would have to wait until the end of the day, and now you get it early. Plus, silence is incredibly easy to manage!

Do you see how you have flipped the script? Do you see how, without this procedure, you have to hope and pray that students don't get too loud, but with this procedure, you will hope that they do get too loud?

Once in silent Workshop, when four or more students talk or whisper say, while still whispering:

> Oh, man. Looks like you are not ready to do Workshop at all. Could everyone please put their heads down and listen to our silence while I get some work done? Thanks.

Students should then have their heads down for as long as Real-World Workshop was supposed to last. Use this Class Head Down PLO when necessary. If you have three minutes left, their heads will be down for that amount of time. The same is true if you have 45 minutes left.

In all my years of teaching, I only had to "shut it down" three times. Two of those times, there were less than 10 minutes left. That makes sense—it should take a long time for four or more students to fail over and over. Because of this, you will usually only have a few minutes for "shut down time." One time, I did have to shut it down with 45 minutes to go. After a couple of whispered uses of the Class Head Down PLO, everyone sat with their heads down silently, and I got 44½ minutes of grading done.

I also never had to shut them down again.

Preventive Movement

As detailed in Chapter 4, Preventive Movement is an essential part of the Real-World Workshop procedure. Make sure that you are moving around as much as is feasible for you. Instructing, grading, and holding students accountable for their Nows while walking around with a gradebook is one great way to prevent negative behaviors with your movement.

Instructing, grading, and teaching from a seated position at your desk and, optimally, from a reading table also has its advantages, especially if you can have several students immediately around you. When you lead the class from this position, it is important to occasionally do a Preventive Sweep by getting up and moving around the room before sitting back at your table or desk. The goal of both of these Preventive Movement strategies is to create intermittent reinforcement so your students will have to think twice about negative behaviors, since you could be just around the corner.

Strategic Noticing

This strategy, also detailed in Chapter 4, is likewise essential to Real-World Workshop. One simple statement can be used to supercharge the effectiveness of this procedure:

I noticed you using the right voice level.

Refer to Chapter 4 for more about the "why" of Strategic Noticing and with which students this should be private/individual, public/individual, or whole group, but this statement should be made every four minutes, at least, at the beginning of the year during Workshop.

Your students want to be noticed. Even older students will often get visibly happier when they are on the receiving end of Strategic Noticing. Your difficult students have been noticed in the past for being loud in class; that is *why* they have been loud in class in the past. By noticing them having the appropriate voice levels over and over again, you are giving them and everyone around them instructions about how they can use their voice level to get attention in your classroom.

Gentle Guidance Interventions During Real-World Workshop

Only use all of the fantastic and helpful Gentle Guidance Interventions (GGIs) that you will learn in Chapter 9 when guiding non-voice-level behaviors. In other words, any other behavior can be dealt with using these interventions, but do not use them for voice level infractions. For instance, you can use GGIs for two students grabbing at each other, a student being out of their seat, or a student eating in class, but you would use the in-built PLOs for two students talking above an agreed-to voice level.

The only "sort of" exception to this guideline is when you are not quite able to tell if students are above the class-prescribed voice level. In that circumstance, you can consider using an intervention—usually an Eye Intervention (#1–4), and nearly always one of the nonverbal interventions (#1–24). Feel free to skip over to Chapter 9 for a sneak peek at those interventions.

Put It All Together

Real-World Workshop is, by far, the most involved procedure described in this book. Relative to other procedures, it takes the longest to learn. But it is also a highly effective tool. Remember, all independent work that can be done while students are allowed to talk or work cooperatively should be done through Real-World Workshop!

Silent Work Procedure

Times that students are not allowed to talk or work independently (e.g., state testing or Silent Sustained Reading time) call for the Silent Work procedure. Fortunately, you have already learned it! The Silent Work Procedure is just the Real-World Workshop procedure without any choices about voice level. You can even do music choices (if appropriate) and turn the music off as an immediate consequence for less than perfect silent work behavior. All PLOs for voice level infractions are the same, including shutting it down. You are just starting off on "silent."

You can use the Silent Work procedure for mandated testing, though in this case you cannot use the ear-tuning PLO. You will only be able to use interventions and Delayed Learning Opportunities for voice level infractions, since you cannot take time away from the tests. For all other learning activities for which you have an expectation of silence, you can use the PLOs for students who talk just like in Real-World Workshop. The only caveat to this is that if you are giving a *non*mandated test and you use the head-down PLO, you must give that student the time back later (preferably during noninstructional time) so they have the same amount of time to finish testing as their classmates.

Silent Sustained Reading

Use the Silent Work procedure for any Silent Sustained Reading (SSR) time. Without the procedure and PLOs, it is nearly impossible to have students read and work silently, as called for in many reading curricula, while the teacher works with small, usually leveled, groups. This is true for Silent Sustained Reading from preK through high school. Following are additional techniques that will enhance the Silent Work Procedure during SSR.

Three weeks of modeling. Kids have a hard time emulating what they have never seen, and some kids have never seen an adult read a book. If they have never seen an adult read a book, at worst, they might feel like they are having to read as some sort of punishment. At best, they may feel alienated from the process of reading. If they have never seen an adult read a book, they will never see reading as "just a thing that people do," and they will be very likely to be resistant to reading. That is why, for the first three weeks of school, the only job assigned to you during Silent Work is to read a good book that you enjoy while following the procedure. Taking time to model reading during the first three weeks of school will result in getting that time back many times over throughout the year. In addition, you actually get to take care of yourself by relaxing with a good book in the middle of the school day!

Lock it in. If your curriculum calls for you to teach a reading lesson, do so at the beginning of your reading period or block. Once finished, dismiss your students to get books and begin Silent Work using the Lock-It-In procedure (see Chapter 7), taking special care to do it slowly enough that each team is mostly out of the way and reading before the next team is called.

If you have made it to the point where students are locking it in, start reading immediately after picking your Lock-It-Iner (the first student you see who is sitting quietly at a clean desk or whatever your expectation is).

An advanced move that will help you simultaneously build relationships, share ownership, and share control is to pick the Lock-It-Iner and direct them to dismiss *you* when you are ready: "Damien, you are ready. Could you lock it in? Remember to treat me like a team and dismiss me to Silent Work when you notice that I am ready." Then sit at your desk or table if students are at their desks, or sit on the carpet if students are at the carpet. Alternatively, you could sit with a team and be Locked-In with them. This can be particularly useful in order to create proximity with a team who is having trouble being ready.

Position yourself by putting a chair in a Power Position (see Chapter 3), and assume an assertive, seated stance while reading. This tells students that you are in charge; nothing they can do will change that. Knowing who the alpha is (and not having to figure it out for themselves) is calming for students.

Combine reading with Preventive Movement. Read your book for a minute or two. Make sure you have a drink, snack, or both. Again, this alpha move *shows* that you are in charge without telling your students so. Then, without taking your eyes off your book, do a Behavioral Sweep. Slowly walk around the room while reading. Just like in Real-World Workshop, use Gentle Guidance Interventions *only for behaviors that do not have to do with voice level.* Again, only use your PLOs for talking.

Afternoon Meeting

All students, preK–12, have an end to their day, and all students, preK–12, are human. In order for humans to feel an optimal sense of satisfaction with an experience, they require closure. Both students and teachers can obtain this sense of closure through the Afternoon Meeting procedure. Part of this closure literally involves checking off the class's to-do list. The Morning Meeting allows students to say to each other, "This is what we will achieve. This is the reason why we are here today." The Afternoon Meeting allows them to say, "This is what we achieved today."

In addition to creating a sense of purpose and closure daily, the Afternoon Meeting procedure gives students a feeling of control by allowing them to run this part of the day. As a teacher, you will do very little and exert minimal energy during a time when most teachers have very little energy left. Finally, after achieving closure to the academic day, students will have the opportunity to end each day with a fun, nonacademic game or activity to end on a good note.

The procedure for Afternoon Meeting detailed below is generally for elementary students who are in a self-contained room all day or intermediate students who switch classes midday. Secondary teachers should read this procedure with an eye toward picking and choosing small parts of the procedure for the end of each class period, or only for their last class period of the day. Of special importance is that all secondary class periods have some kind of closure to the lesson and connection to what will be learned the next school day, and that the last period of the day has that element plus at least some token closure statement for the day and some kind of announcement about the following school day. This trains everyone, including you, to think, "I accomplished something today, and I will accomplish something tomorrow," instead of "There went another time period of random activity; I suppose another one will happen tomorrow." Secondary school closure statements may sound like the following:

- (Single class period closure) Student: "Today we learned about elements of quadratic equations. Tomorrow we will learn about using those equations to solve real-world problems."
- (Last period closure) Student: "Today we learned about elements of quadratic equations. Tomorrow we will learn about using those equations to solve real-world problems. Remember to wear school colors for Spirit Day tomorrow. Goodnight, everybody! Be safe driving home!"

As always, give away as much control to students as is effective and appropriate on how this is done and what is said. Secondary teachers should also see below for specific secondary Activity Choices.

At every level, the Afternoon Meeting procedure allows students to proclaim every day, "This is our classroom, we are awesome, and this is what we accomplished together!"

Afternoon Prompt

The student hired as End of Day Prompter (see Chapter 6) prompts the class to prepare for Afternoon Meeting at a predetermined time. When selecting the correct time for the End of Day Prompt, do not make the mistake of giving the students considerably more time than they will need to get ready for the meeting in the future. Teachers who do this accidentally train their students to be slower at this transition than they need to be. Instead, assign a time that you think will be appropriate for your students all year long. If you pick the right time, students will feel challenged to be ready in a timely manner. Give extra support at the beginning of the year in the form of Gentle Guidance Interventions, with an emphasis on the questions from the Question Matrix (see Chapter 9). Allow students to rise to the challenge with your calm guidance. Most important, remember to use Strategic Noticing with students and teams who are transitioning quickly:

- "I notice Red is being efficient and quick."
- "I notice the Dinos taking care of business."

The possible exceptions to this rule of thumb are for preK and kindergarten. These students develop physiologically and neurologically so rapidly and their ability to complete tasks increases so quickly that the teacher should usually shorten the amount of time given to prepare for Afternoon Meeting once or twice as the year goes on.

Team of the Day Responsibilities

When prompted, the TOD goes into high gear. Besides the responsibilities placed on all students at this time (see below), TOD tasks can include the following:

- Custodial duties: sweeping, vacuuming, taking out the trash, wiping down doorknobs, wiping down boards, etc.
- Closing windows and blinds
- Cleaning and organizing common and teacher areas: reading tables, reading chair, teacher desk

Who does what on any given day is not your concern; TODs should be left to decide who does what. Any attempt on your part to try to manage the process will have extensive negative effects on student ownership, student cooperation, and student enthusiasm. When left alone, students work out an infinite number of ways to divide up and complete labor. Some students just do the thing they like to do all year: kids who find sweeping to be satisfactory sweep every time their team is the TOD. Some kids love organizing the reading area. Some teams come up with complicated rotations of duties. Some teams have had one rotating person do all TOD responsibilities while the other members of the team gather that person's personal items. After many years of using this procedure, I have been amazed by how creative and cooperative students are. It is extremely rare for students to refuse to pitch in, as long as you can keep yourself from interfering. Don't intervene when a student isn't contributing; you will find that the natural consequences of laziness and not being helpful will almost always change their behavior toward being more helpful.

Just as with TOD disagreements during Morning Meeting, you should avoid being tricked into owning the TOD's problems. If there is any kind of disagreement that does not involve activities that may cause lasting harm, respond by saying:

Oh, man. Can you solve this, or would you like me to solve it for you?

If the person who asks this responds that the TOD will solve the problem, wish them good luck and walk away. If they say that you should solve it, hire another team to be TOD for the rest of the day—which includes running Afternoon Meeting.

Team Captain Responsibilities

Each team captain's Afternoon Meeting responsibilities may include the following:

- Wiping down all team desks or tables and all team areas with a bleach wipe
- Delivering mail from mailboxes to student desks
- Anything else that is specifically for the benefit of each team that can be done by a student

Again, if teachers stay away from the inner workings of the teams, it is rare that team captains will refuse to do their duties. If they do start refusing during Afternoon Meeting, instruct the next student in line for team captain duties to take over for the rest of the day and continue as team captain the next day.

Student Responsibilities

Students should be responsible for organizing their own materials and having them ready to go on their desks. All mail should be put away in folders. Students should be seated silently. At this point, classes that gather their belongings on their way to be dismissed and do not go to a carpet for Afternoon Meeting are ready for Afternoon Meeting. Students who gather their belongings before Afternoon Meeting should be dismissed using the Lock-It-In procedure (see Chapter 7). If they are to go to a carpet, that is where they go. If they are to go to their desks, they go to their desks.

Celebrations

When students have completed their responsibilities, the TOD team captain stands up, goes to the front of the room next to the Celebrations Board, and says the following:

I will start Celebrations when everyone is seated silently.

This is a good time for the teacher to sit among the students and use Gentle Guidance Interventions (Chapter 9). If students are not quiet after a reasonable amount of time, consider a Delayed Learning Opportunity.

The TOD team captain then chooses students who wish to celebrate their classmates, teachers, administrators, or anyone in their lives for living up to words that are used as part of their class's character education program. Once the Celebrations have all been read or the teacher notices that the class is running out of time, the TOD team captain reviews the day's schedule.

Daily Schedule Review

A review of the day's accomplishments is an essential part of Afternoon Meeting. For older students, this review will almost always be less specific and more casual in nature, since middle and high school students sharing their last period class will almost never have done all of the same lessons. Nevertheless, some sort of final review or checklist should be performed by a student for the benefit of all at the end of the day.

The TOD team captain can also use this time for announcements or reminders about upcoming events. Middle and high school students will likely be better at this than their younger counterparts, and they should be allowed to take as much ownership of these duties as they'd like. For younger students, it is necessary to review the lessons and events of the day in terms of what was done and what was learned. In this case, the TOD team captain points to each item on the list and asks for a choral response from the class.

TOD team captain: "Did we do Morning Meeting?"

Class: "Yes!"

TOD team captain puts a check mark next to "Morning Meeting."

TOD team captain: "Did we learn about rays and angles?"

Class: "Yes!"

TOD team captain puts a check mark next to "Learn about rays and angles."

TOD team captain: "Did we write a thank-you card to Officer James?"

Class: "No!"

TOD team captain circles "Write a thank-you card to Officer James."

TOD team captain: "Did we learn to throw a ball at a target in PE?"

Class: "Yes!"

TOD team captain puts a check mark next to "Learn to throw a ball at a target in PE."

. . . and so on.

Besides giving a tremendous amount of healthy control and ownership to students, this schedule review subprocedure gives you the added benefit of being able to look at the daily schedule and see, at a glance, what was and was not accomplished that day. Any circled items can appear on the next day's schedule.

Activity Choices or Ceremony

At this point of Afternoon Meeting, you can either allow the students to choose a game or hold a Nickname Ceremony (see Chapter 5). The daily game choices must be given by you, at least at first. If and when appropriate, and if and when you are ready, students can run this part of the day. Secondary teachers should turn this procedure over to students almost immediately. Activities should be fun, generally not academic, and often team-building exercises. Fun exercises at the end of the day make all of Afternoon Meeting more functional because it becomes a motivating situation (MS). When students are in an MS, the natural consequence of losing out on the MS trains them to be cooperative—as long as you allow the natural consequence to befall students without anger or lectures, and as long as you don't save students from that consequence. Students quickly realize that the faster they get through Afternoon Meeting (and depending on the school and grade level, get their belongings and be ready to leave), the more time they have to take part in the Afternoon Meeting activity. As long as the ceremony and games are fun and developmentally appropriate (so that the students enjoy them at least as much as going home), you can maintain an MS that will, more than any other procedure, create and allow you to maintain a functional end to your school day. You should recognize this same dynamic from Real-World Workshop: the harder students work and the more responsible they are, the better their life becomes, and the better the lives of the people around them become.

Extremely entertaining and compelling activity choices at the end of the day are the engine for a successful Afternoon Meeting: transitions will be more efficient, students will use more positive behaviors, and they will be more likely to hold each other accountable. Just like with Laters and Real-World Workshop, you cannot make students do things, but you can control how compelling, fun, and awesome the Afternoon Meeting activity choices are. These can be games that you know to be favorites of your students, or any other activity that is fun and appropriate. Introduce them one at a time throughout your day as "brain breaks." Do this multiple times per day during the first two weeks as beta testing to find out which activities and games your students enjoy most. Use their favorites as Afternoon Meeting activities.

Potential games are listed below, but here is a word on activities. One of the three choices you give should be more of an activity; "sit around and talk" is one choice that was usually available at the end of the day for my students. "Pull up (appropriate) videos on the internet" can be another. Even if you know what your students' favorite activity or game is, you still need to give them a choice every day. Remember, within every choice is a healthy rejection: when a high school senior chooses "sit around and talk" five times in a row while rolling her eyes, she is rejecting *on your terms* your suggestion of two other games that she might think are stupid and beneath such a cool, mature person such as herself. Make sure you cycle through all games and activities, and don't have any game or activity available every day.

How to Begin Activity Choices

Say the following from a Power Position:

I will give activity choices when everyone is seated silently.

Then wait.

Do nothing but wait and pray that your students keep talking until all time is gone and everyone has to leave. Hope that this happens on multiple days. As previously stated, this is an MS: not being able to participate in the situation is a consequence in and of itself. In very, very rare cases (I have never experienced it during the use of this procedure), you can give whole-group, small-group, or individual Delayed Learning Opportunities for the failure to be silent to a prompt once that student or those students have sufficiently frustrated their classmates over the course of several days.

Once everyone is silent, offer three activity choices, even if you are 100 percent sure you know what the students will pick. (Hopefully you were able to teach and beta-test three activities on your first day.) Have students vote. Play the winning game and have fun!

The Magic of Choices

When I was teaching, after the TOD team captain completed the review of the daily schedule, I would walk to my chair in front of my students before giving the Activity Choices prompt: "I will give activity choices when everyone is seated silently."

Every single year, for 10 years of doing this procedure, something magical occurred in the first three weeks of school. Before I could even sit down in my chair, students would say the same word to each other—the same word for 10 straight years: "Choices! Choices!" they would say, often followed by some shushing. After four or five weeks, the class would consistently go silent before I could make it to my chair.

This can happen for any teacher who picks games and activities that are at least as stimulating as going home.

Games

Red Ball. Students and teachers stand in a circle so that everyone can see each other. The teacher pantomimes catching an invisible ball thrown from an invisible person and says, "Thank you." The teacher looks at the ball and says, "Red ball." The teacher then makes eye contact with a student.

The teacher pantomimes throwing the ball toward that student in a deliberate manner, slowly following through toward the targeted student. The student repeats all of the above actions, choosing another student or throwing the ball back to the teacher.

Once students seem to have achieved a reasonable amount of fluency, the teacher repeats the above actions, this time accepting an invisible "blue ball" from the invisible ball thrower. There are now two invisible balls in play. The teacher adds a new invisible ball (of a different color, of course) every 30 seconds or so.

As long as the students are successful, keep adding balls of different colors. When students are keeping a normal number of balls going for their developmental level, use normal "boring" colors (red, blue, green). Once they start to keep a number of balls going that seems to be particularly impressive, start adding ball colors that ignite the imagination a bit (silver, gold, rainbow, white fire, indigo). If you can remember and repeat the same color order on different days, it can add to the excitement for kids, especially ones who have been raised using leveled video games.

This game teaches kids to listen quietly, to concentrate, and to work cooperatively, but *don't tell students what they should be learning.* Instead, let the game do the teaching.

Czechoslovakia Boom-Sha-Boom. This game involves the students and teacher standing in a circle so everyone can see everyone else. The teacher slowly and methodically demonstrates a basic clapping motion as students join in: *clap, thigh slap, clap, thigh slap.* The teacher tells students that the first time through this weird song, they should just listen, unless they start to figure out the pattern and want to try joining in on the first run-through.

The teacher begins singing the following song to the beat of slow clapping/thigh slapping:

Czechoslovakia boom-sha-boom

Yugoslavia boom-sha-boom

Who's got the rhythm of the hands? (clap-clap-clap)

We got the rhythm of the hands. (clap-clap-clap)

Who's got the rhythm of the feet? (stomp-stomp-stomp)

We got the rhythm of the feet. (stomp-stomp-stomp)

Who's got the rhythm of the hips? (ono-mato-poeia) [while doing a running motion with fists and shaking hips from side to side with each part of the word]

We got the rhythm of the hips. (ono-mato-poeia) [same motions]

Who's got the rhythm of the eyes? (wooooooo!!!!) [while throwing hands in the air]

We got the rhythm of the eyes. (wooooooo!!!!) [same motions]

The teacher then says, "Everybody!" and goes through the song slightly faster. The song gets faster each time until students can no longer keep up.

This game teaches kids to listen, concentrate, and work cooperatively.

Shake It Out. This game involves students and teachers standing in a circle so everyone can see everyone else. The teacher briefly describes how to play the game, and asks for students to join in. The teacher shakes a hand limp-wristedly, as if to flick something sticky off, counting each shake up to 10: "1-2-3-4-5-6-7-8-9-10." The teacher then does the same with the other hand, then with one foot (kicking a limp foot forward off the ground 10 times) and then the other foot.

The group then repeats the sequence of shakes, counting only to 9 each time: "1-2-3-4-5-6-7-8-9." Next, the sequences go to 8, 7, and so on, speeding up slightly as the game proceeds. The game ends when everyone very quickly counts to one with each appendage: "1-1-1-1!"

This game teaches kids to listen, concentrate, and work cooperatively.

Mr. Ervin Dodgeball. This game should be played in a gym or outside with one or two foam dodgeballs. Play this game at your own risk and *do not use anything other than official foam dodgeballs*. Using anything else will likely *cause injuries*, and Ervin Educational Consulting is not responsible for any injuries incurred by playing this game. In any case, make sure your administrator approves the playing of this game.

Create boundaries for play. The field of play should be small enough that students can all be eliminated by being hit with balls in a reasonable amount of time, but big enough that they can run freely without running into each other. If physical boundaries (lines on a gym floor or trees, bushes, or outer walls of the school) are not available, use cones, or ask four students who do not wish to play to be the four corners of the field of play.

Rules

- The objective of the game is to be the last player remaining.
- The teacher is the all-time thrower of balls. If the teacher hits a student anywhere on their body, they are out.
- If the student catches the ball, they are out.
- If the ball bounces off the ground and hits the student, they are out.
- If the ball bounces off another student and hits a student, both are out.
- If a student goes outside the boundaries, they are out.

- If a ball is motionless on the ground, a student may pick it up and throw it back to the teacher. That student cannot be a target for one throw from the teacher. Once that teacher throws the ball at someone else, that student can be a target again.

- If a ball goes outside the boundaries, students may retrieve it and give it to the thrower without being counted as out.
- As each student is hit and is out, they stand along the barrier, forming a physical rectangle around the playing area.
- The last student remaining wins.

Variations

This game can be played with one ball and one teacher, two balls and one teacher, or two balls and two teachers. The winner can become the thrower in the next game, which can be played without the teacher, but the teacher being the thrower helps greatly in building relationships with students, so be a thrower whenever you can. Finally, the teacher can be a thrower at the same time as a student.

Remember, the key word is "fun." Make sure *you* are having fun. Make sure *the students* are having fun. If the last thing you do before you do your ESPN Goodbye is enjoy the company of your students, and your students see you enjoying them, it will go a long way toward building relationships with your students.

ESPN Goodbye Procedure

The final Control-Sharing Procedure is an ESPN Goodbye. Where you give the ESPN Goodbye will depend upon where, according to the logistics of your school, you last see your students. Secondary teachers can even do this at the end of each period. Though this form of the ESPN Goodbye may only be a high five or fist bump or some other "tap" for reasons of timing, it will go a very long way to show your students that you care about them.

Usually, secondary teachers will last see their last period students as they walk out of the classroom. Elementary teachers could be dismissing bus students, car riders, and after-school care students from the room or dropping them off in bus lots, after-school care, or car lots. Wherever you last see a student, that is where you should use the ESPN Goodbye procedure.

You can decide when to use a standard handshake and when to use the Class Handshake. Often, teachers use the former in the morning and the latter at the end of the day. This is most consistently true of secondary teachers, who prefer the quicker (remember it has to last less than a second for secondary school) Class Handshake when they have less time at the end of the day. For all grade levels, doing an ESPN Goodbye from any location offers the added benefit of staggering the relocation of your students to any given space, whether it is the hallway outside your classroom, a bus lot, a car lot, or an after-school care room or area.

The main benefit of the ESPN Goodbye is so very important: to let each and every student know that, even though you are not required to do it, you are taking the time to say "goodbye" to them because you care about them and like them enough to do it. This consistent routine will improve the lives of your students, especially those who may not be experiencing consistent routines and expressions of care at home.

By now you should be noticing that these procedures complement and enhance each other: procedures that build relationships also share control, and procedures that share control help to build relationships. When used together, these procedures turn classrooms into control-sharing and relationship-building machines. If you set the machine into motion in your first three weeks, it will create and perpetuate a classroom environment that is safe, calm, and kind—a place where students can work, struggle, grow, and learn.

Part IV

Control-Sharing Strategies

Hold students accountable without power struggles.

Michael's oldest brother was in prison for murder. He had another brother, still a minor, in juvenile detention for manslaughter.

Michael was 7.

Michael did not start the year in my 1st grade classroom. He was in Ms. Crusher's room. Five weeks into the school year, while in a lunch line, he grabbed another student and threw him face-first into a lunch table. The student's open mouth slammed into the side of the table in such a way that the table edge split both sides of his mouth all the way up to his jaw. The injury required hundreds of stitches extending from the edge of each side of his mouth almost all the way up to each ear.

Michael was suspended for the last three weeks of our year-round school's trimester before a three-week break. During those six weeks, it had not crossed the mind of our principal that the victim should not have to spend the rest of 1st grade in the same classroom with the student who had permanently disfigured him. Instead, she made this decision the morning we returned from break. I was informed that Michael would be in my class for the remainder of the school year just five minutes before the start of the first school day of the second trimester.

This was less than optimal, as my classroom during my second year of teaching was already a mess of a place. Chaos reigned. A vast majority of my students came from homes in crisis, and they ran the room. No amount of yelling and attempts at bossing students around had done anything but cause more chaos. As rough as most of my students were, I knew that Michael was on another level. Of course, I knew all about the attack. I knew that Michael lived a traumatic existence at home. I knew all about how both of his brothers had killed people.

I also knew that Michael, and students like him who had lives filled with trauma, had brains that had been short-circuited by these traumatic experiences. I knew that they were often hardwired to have problems with attention and making good choices, and that they were more prone to being aggressive or belligerent when faced with challenges and problems. They would perceive and react to threats that weren't really there.

I also knew that I had 300 seconds to prepare for Michael's arrival.

As I walked my students (including my new one) from the gym where we congregated every morning for breakfast, I was overwhelmed by just how totally useless all of this knowledge was. I knew that this student's trauma had turned him into a person who used aggression, belligerence, and potentially homicidal actions to get a feeling of control.

Well, so what? What was I supposed to do about it? Having had no instruction on how to interact with a student like this (or any of my other students, for that matter), I attempted to "manage" Michael with the only two possible strategies I could think of: being really nice to him so as not to anger him, and ignoring his negative behaviors.

As he walked through the classroom doorway, I immediately realized that there would be no "honeymoon period." In Michael's first 60 seconds in the classroom, he used belligerent aggression to establish his dominance as the alpha in the environment—and I was powerless to do anything about it. Yelling at me, challenging other students to fight, and grabbing things out of people's hands all happened in that first minute.

"Just ignore him," I said to my students and myself, over and over, as he walked around the room destroying school and student property. Ignoring negative behaviors started to seem like an insufficient strategy as the dollar amount of destroyed property started to tally up, and Michael's yelled questions of "What are you looking at?" intensified to death threats.

As I attempted to ignore negative behaviors and be nice to Michael, his behaviors escalated, as did my blood pressure. After 40 minutes in the classroom, I abandoned the strategies of "ignore" and "be nice" all at once.

"ALL RIGHT, THAT'S IT!"

If you ever hear yourself saying these words, try your best to stop talking. No one has ever followed up "ALL RIGHT, THAT'S IT!" by saying something smart or helpful.

"YOU ARE NEVER GOING TO RECESS EVER AGAIN!"

I was so far gone and so fully controlled by my brain stem that I am surprised now that I was able to form words of any kind. This ridiculous, unenforceable punishment notification sent Michael into the stratosphere. Formerly targeting his belligerence toward specific people and things, his path of destruction now became an arbitrary and violent tantrum. As he began to roar and tear things off the wall, kicking and hitting anyone around him, I reacted.

"NOOOOOOOOOOOOOOOOOOOOOOO!" I bellowed, as I grabbed Michael by the arm and pulled him out of the classroom and down the short hallway to the principal's office. As Michael and I burst through her office door, she was sitting in a meeting with another adult whose job appeared, at that moment, to be significantly easier than mine. Taking Michael by both shoulders now, I extended my arms forward toward my principal.

"HERE!" I said, before storming out of the office.

Translation: "YOU DID THIS TO ME, AND NOW I AM DOING THIS TO YOU!"

✤ ✤ ✤ ✤ ✤ ✤ ✤ ✤ ✤ ✤ ✤

Michael came from a profoundly unsafe, unpredictable, dangerous home environment where he practiced extremely negative behaviors such as stealing, lying, and physical assault. These behaviors elicited anger, yelling, and physical abuse from his mother and grandmother. These reactions from the women in his life began and perpetuated the "Bad Kid Cycle."

You have learned how to break this cycle; you have learned to remain calm and not give students the anger that they are trying to elicit with negative behaviors by using the Calm Signal. You have learned how to systematically give students attention when they are using positive behaviors by using Strategic Noticing. For Michael, the use of the Calm Signal and Strategic Noticing would still not be enough to break the Bad Kid Cycle.

Even if Calm Signals, Strategic Noticing, *and* the procedures were used, it would not have been effective enough for Michael to be successful at being a positive contributor to his class in the short term and to his world in the long term. Because of his level of trauma, Michael would use so many negative behaviors at such a high frequency rate that those negative behaviors would have overwhelmed his class and teacher before the Bad Kid Cycle could be reversed, before the procedures were able to offer enough healthy control, and before they could build enough of the necessary relationships. The final, missing piece that Michael would have needed is the content of this section: Control-Sharing Strategies.

Control-Sharing Strategies help you react to negative behaviors and change them into positive ones in ways that are minimally intrusive and less likely to trigger explosive behaviors from students. They include Delayed Learning Opportunities (DLOs) and Gentle Guidance Interventions (GGIs).

There are *hundreds of thousands* of Michaels all over the country. They deserve to have a chance at success, and without these Control-Sharing Strategies, used over time, their chances of success are minimal.

✢ ✢ ✢ ✢ ✢ ✢ ✢ ✢ ✢ ✢ ✢ ✢

Control-Sharing Strategies are also important for Mykeshas.

Mykesha was a happy, healthy student from a functional family, and she was in the same class as Michael. She exclusively used positive behaviors, and she was pulled out of my class by her parent because my room was physically dangerous and she wasn't learning anything. There are tens of millions of Mykeshas in our country: students who cannot learn anything in their classrooms because their schools are being destroyed by Michaels.

The bottom line is that both Mykeshas and Michaels deserve a positive, loving environment in which they can feel safe, have fun, and learn. It is a civil right. It is a human right. The following chapters will show you Gentle Guidance Interventions that will allow you to mitigate low-level negative behaviors and gently guide students away from those behaviors without creating power struggles that make behaviors worse. One of these chapters is about a special GGI called a Mindfulness Break, which allows students to take as much time as they need to regain the composure necessary to again be a positive, prosocial member of the classroom.

Delayed Learning Opportunities are the terminal destination for repeated or serious negative behaviors not prevented by Relationship-Building Strategies, Relationship-Building Procedures, and Control-Sharing Procedures and not mitigated by Gentle Guidance Interventions. When all of these strategies and procedures have failed, it means that the student is waving a flag at the adults in his or her life as if to say, "I need a real lesson about how to use positive behaviors or a lesson about responsibility." This chapter will show you how to notify the student of this lesson, and then it will show you specifically how to teach the lesson.

Once you have learned these Control-Sharing Strategies, you will possess the full arsenal of behavioral leadership procedures and strategies. You will be ready to be a behavioral leader!

9

Gentle Guidance Interventions

As anyone who remembers their own childhood can attest, students sometimes get slightly off track by dabbling in negative behaviors in such a way that it doesn't cause a major problem, and they just need to get guided back to the right path. Unfortunately, the traditional ways of guiding students back to using positive behaviors (warnings, demands, lectures, and threats) will drive explosive, unhealthy students into worse behaviors while being less than effective with all students.

A vast majority of the time, negative behaviors can be dealt with by using Gentle Guidance Interventions (GGIs). GGIs are ways of calmly guiding students to use positive behaviors that do not frighten or intimidate students, even if those students have a propensity for being easily frightened or intimidated. GGIs are the first intervention to use to help Michaels and Mykeshas learn the most important lessons they will ever learn: that negative behaviors don't work and that positive, prosocial behaviors are the pathway to success and happiness.

Avoiding the "Impossible Choice"

When a student uses a minor negative behavior that causes problems for other people but does not require what are traditionally called "punishments" or "consequences," traditional discipline requires that educators make an impossible choice.

The outcomes of this choice are both bad, and they destroy classroom environments over time. The two choices are as follows:

1. The teacher can ignore the behavior

    or

2. The teacher can make a declarative statement that the behavior should stop.

The Problem with Ignoring

When a student uses a somewhat disruptive behavior—playfully poking a friend under a desk, for example—and the teacher ignores the behavior, the message is communicated that the teacher either is unaware of the behavior or tacitly approves of it. Either way, the behavior is reinforced and will be more likely to be used by that student and by all other students who see the behavior being ignored. Students will react in various ways to this ignoring. Some will be only slightly more likely to mimic this playful but negative behavior. Some will immediately mimic, heighten, and explore this behavior: poking softly becomes poking hard, and poking hard may become grabbing hard and hurting people. Negative behaviors that get ignored tend to spread and get worse.

The Problem with Declarative Statements

The other traditional, "commonsense" option is to make a simple statement declaring that the behavior should stop. It seems innocent enough. After all, if you want someone to stop doing something, it makes sense to tell them to stop doing it. For some students, this can, at first glance, appear to be successful.

The problem, however, is a pesky reality about human beings called "psychological reactance." This phenomenon occurs when an "*unpleasant* motivational arousal emerges when people experience a threat to or loss of their freedom" (Brehm & Brehm, 1981, p. x; emphasis mine). These people will then work to get back freedoms that they perceive were taken away. In other words, people don't like to be told what to do, and when told what to do, they don't react well, often doing the opposite of what was asked of them.

Therefore, telling individuals or entire classrooms full of students what to do in a declarative way is not an effective means of getting cooperation. It ignores the reality presented by psychological reactance. When a demand is made through a declarative statement ("sit down," "work," or "get in line"), even students who are generally cooperative will eventually become resistant in passive, reactive, or even overtly aggressive ways.

The "Impossible Choice" and the Most Vulnerable Students

This binary choice is most acutely apparent when working with students with high ACE scores who have high control needs. Any experienced teacher using traditional discipline practices has dreaded making the "impossible choice" with these students. From experience, teachers know that they will repeat, intensify, and explore low-level negative behaviors when they are ignored. They also know that if they use a declarative statement, even politely worded, to try to stop the behavior, this type of student is likely to explode, stopping all education and perhaps ruining the rest of a class period or even an entire morning or afternoon.

The Solution to the "Impossible Choice"

The good news is that there is a third option for attending to low-level negative behaviors. This third and most effective option is the use of a Gentle Guidance Intervention. These interventions are ways of gently guiding students toward positive behaviors, ways that are far more pleasant than declarative statements, even when those statements are said calmly. GGIs do not embarrass, coerce, threaten, or scare students into using positive behaviors. They merely guide students toward positive behaviors without the use of such tactics. They are highly effective in this effort when used in the context of the rest of the procedures and strategies in this manual. GGIs are not intended to teach students lessons about behavior. When the GGIs fail to guide students to positive behavior, Delayed Learning Opportunities (DLOs; see Chapter 11) will do the teaching about behavior.

How to Use GGIs

The 42 GGIs are listed as a menu, ordered from least time-consuming and least intrusive to most time-consuming and most intrusive, although none of the GGIs are truly time-consuming or intrusive. Use this chapter like a menu at a restaurant. Don't feel the need to order the first thing on the menu, then the second, then the third, and so on. Instead, pick and choose the GGIs that you find to be the most appealing. Ignore the ones that you don't want to use. As you experiment, try to use the GGI with the lowest number that you feel still fits the situation. These are the interventions that are the best for you because they take the least time, and they are the best for the student because they are the least intrusive. If the behavior doesn't change, strongly consider moving to other GGIs down the menu before proceeding to Delayed Learning Opportunities.

Remember to have fun. These GGIs will not only make your life easier but also make your "impossible choices" a thing of the past.

Eye Interventions

The first four interventions involve merely looking at students. They are called "Eye Interventions." The benefits of Eye Interventions are that they take no time or energy: you can continue teaching while you use them. The weakness of these GGIs is that the student must be looking at you. Of course, use these whenever possible. If you can change a student's behavior just by looking at them, why would you do anything else?

1. **Curious Eye.** Simply look at a student with a curious look. This, as with all interventions, stimulates student thinking. ("Why's the teacher looking at me? Oh, maybe I should stop doing this.")

2. **Confused Eye.** Look at a student with the most confused look that you can muster. With just one look, this intervention separates the student from the behavior. It says to the student, "You are so wonderful, and that behavior is not wonderful. What's happening? I'm confused."

3. **Evil Eye.** All parents and teachers seem to have this one in their tool belt.

4. **Crazy Eye.** This one is extra-fun! Make your face look as crazy as possible as you look at the student. How much thinking would this stimulate on the part of the target student—and everyone else, for that matter? There is only room for one crazy person in any situation. When working with students, *be that person first!*

Reactive Movement Interventions

Interventions #5–10 involve stopping behaviors using teacher movement. This is in contrast to the Preventive Movement strategy described in Chapter 4, which prevents negative behaviors before they start. To an observer, they would look the same. The only difference is that Reactive Movement Interventions occur in response to a negative behavior.

5. **Reactive Movement.** Move nonchalantly toward the site of the negative behavior without drawing any attention to it with eye contact or verbal reaction.

6. **Hover.** Simply stop your movement next to the site of the negative behavior. Do not initiate eye contact, but if the student attempts to initiate it, smile.

7. **Stretch the Classroom.** Although this GGI is a bit more involved, it takes no time because you don't need to stop teaching to use it. This is used when a student or another educator is answering a question, or speaking to the class for any reason, and a negative behavior that requires a GGI takes place. Without breaking eye contact with the speaker, move so that the line of vision between you and the speaker intersects with the student(s) using the negative behavior. You can be 5 feet or 50 feet from the speaker; it doesn't matter. Doing this has an almost magical effect in neutralizing the behavior.

8. **Hand on Shoulder.** While hovering and, when appropriate, while continuing to teach, gently place your hand on the shoulder of a student. Again, if the student tries to create eye contact, simply smile or use Eye Interventions #1, #2, or #4. You may want to continue enthusiastically teaching while keeping your hand on a shoulder. (Remember that this is a menu; you don't need to use all the GGIs. If you are uncomfortable with touching any students or your administration doesn't want you to touch students, don't use this one. If you have students who don't want to be touched, don't use this with them. Use your best professional judgment!)

9. **Hand on Chair.** If you don't want to put your hand on a student's shoulder, you can, instead, put it on the back of their chair. When the chair back of many plastic chairs is pushed down, it will gently bend to push on the student's back, making them sit up straighter!

10. **Sit at a Student Desk.** This is a fantastic intervention that has many benefits. First, sitting is great. Your legs deserve a break. Second, it allows you to hover around students while using less energy. Third, you have a chance to assume the assertive seated position, which allows you to calmly assert dominance.

    To assume the assertive seated position, sit in an empty student chair. If one is not available, pull up your own and place it near students. Lean back. Extend your legs forward with heels on the ground. Cross your legs at the ankles if you like. Put your hands behind your head and interlace your fingers. Sitting in this way at a student desk says to your students, "You all are so easy to handle that I can do it while sitting down and relaxing."

11. **Point Down.** This is highly effective with students who are not sitting properly in their seats. If a student is kneeling, sitting on an undercurled leg, or sitting on the back of a chair, casually pointing down can be highly effective and minimally intrusive. This GGI can be combined with Confused Eye. Of course, if none of these ways of sitting bother you, there is no reason to use this GGI!

12. **Point to the Side.** For students who are not quite in the right place, pointing to the side is far less intrusive than bossing students around regarding their exact placement in the room. This can be effective in being strict in what you allow as far as student desks being in the right place, students being in the right place in line, sitting on the right spot on a learning carpet, and so on. Again, feel free to combine with Confused Eye.

The Stop Matrix

These are three ways of stopping instruction that stimulate thinking, take no effort, and take very little time. They can be used to scaffold the management of negative behavior as the behavior continues, or they can be used as stand-alone GGIs.

13. **Stop.** This GGI, like many others, is one that teachers have been using for years that was created simply through trial and error. When a student is using a low-level negative behavior, simply stopping instruction without making any other movement or change in eye focus is highly effective in getting students to stop their negative behaviors and does not bring attention to the student(s) using the negative behavior. Once the behavior stops, teaching continues.

14. **Stop/Look to the Middle Distance.** This intervention is the same as #13, but it also involves you lifting your gaze over the heads of your students toward, usually, a back wall.

15. **Stop/Look at Student.** This can be done in tandem with any of the Eye Interventions.

16. **Stop/Use a Mindfulness Center.** See Chapter 10.

17. **Shoulder Drum.** This can stimulate thinking in students who are not in the right place in the room or can gently bring space cadets back to Earth. It must be done exactly as described here. While passing by a student, take your index and middle fingers on each hand and gently tap on both shoulders of a student, playing a rhythm: *bum-da-bum*. Do not stop walking. Do not look at the student.

18. **Work Tap.** This is a simple GGI that allows teachers to gently refocus students on their work if that focus has waned. In order to make sure this is effective, it needs to be done as described here, with nothing added. Walk by the student and calmly and gently tap the student's work without initiating eye contact and without stopping for more than a second. This is just a gentle refocus. Remember, you should never try to *make* a student work: the Real-World Workshop procedure will do that for you.

19. **Desk Tap.** This is exactly the same GGI as the Work Tap, except you simply tap the desk to refocus the student.

20. **Contraband Tap.** Contraband is something that is, on its face, illegal. Cocaine and plutonium, for example, are illegal to possess. In classrooms, some other things are never allowed, for example, cell phones, trading cards, or food. The possession of contraband in classrooms needlessly causes power struggles for educators who aren't using GGIs. Instead of making demands of students, simply tapping the contraband while walking by can give the student an opportunity to put away the phone, the food, or the Lebron James card while saving face and not being threatened. Only look at the contraband enough to make contact with your fingers—two gentle taps on the object, and never make eye contact with the student. Again, do not stop moving before, during, or after the tap.

21. **Problem Stimuli Tap.** This works exactly the same way as Contraband Tap but does not involve something that is inherently disallowed in the classroom. Instead, it involves something that has become a problem because of the way it is being used. A slap-bracelet that is being used not as wrist décor but for its slapping properties on another student and a pencil that is being used for its poking properties have both become "problem stimuli." Just tap them and walk away.

Notice that GGIs #1–21 have allowed the student the opportunity to correct their own behavior without it being "corrected" in any way! Remember psychological reactance? Being corrected, as anyone can attest, is unpleasant. This is even more true for students with a high ACE score. Using GGIs #1–21 allows teachers to sidestep this unpleasantness and the resistance that it can generate.

Notice that students who are able to change their behavior with the use of GGIs #1–21 were smart enough to do so? We know this because no one had to tell them what to do: they "told" themselves. This is called the "assumption of intelligence." When you assume intelligence, students act smarter, and you build relationships with them. This idea stands in stark contrast to the implicit "assumption of stupidity" aligned with traditional discipline practices, when teachers demand that students do things that they already know they should be doing. It hurts relationships and tends to make students act like their IQs are lower than they actually are.

You should have a very good reason to use a GGI above #21. Don't correct students unless you have to.

22. **Curious Eye/Quick Head Shake.** This is a combination GGI. Use Curious Eye (#1) while also shaking your head "no" very quickly. The idea behind the "quick shake" is that it shows the student that you are trying to allow them to save face—you are trying not to embarrass them, just giving a quick head shake before anyone notices. This can build the relationship, while calling them out would hurt it. It says to the student, "Let's keep this between us, but please stop."

23. **Confused Eye/Quick Head Shake.** Another combination that is exactly the same as #19 with a different look.

24. **Request Thinking (Nonverbal).** This involves a quick tap of your temple. That's it! The silent message is that it would perhaps be a good idea to use some increased brain power to be able to use the correct, positive behavior.

Here is a good place to stop and look back at GGIs #1–24. Do you notice anything important? More specifically, do you notice something missing? Something that is a particularly important part of traditional discipline?

Did you notice that there has been absolutely no talking?

That's right, you have not made a single sound! You haven't spoken a word. Talking takes energy that you don't need to spend. If you can stop a behavior without talking, why would you talk? No teacher in the history of the world has ever walked to their car at the end of the school day thinking, "Today I wish I had talked more to my students about discipline." While using a GGI above #21 demands a good reason to do so, you should have a *great* reason to use an intervention higher than #24! Rest assured, however, that you will have plenty of students who give you some great reasons to use GGIs #25–42, so let's keep going!

25. **Request Thinking (Verbal).** You are finally going to speak! This one is done exactly like #24, but when you point to your temple you calmly say, "Think." This will be helpful scaffolding for students who do not yet know where their brains are. I have traditionally used the verbal request for thinking once per year with my students to make sure everyone is familiar with their own brain location, and then I fall back to the nonverbal intervention.

26. **Noticing Misdirect.** This GGI is sometimes called "the perfect intervention." It is simultaneously a preventive pre-intervention for one student who is using a positive behavior and a GGI for another student who is using a negative behavior. What's more, while most of the other GGIs minimize attention of negative behaviors, Noticing Misdirect gives no attention to these behaviors. Even better, you already know how to do it.

Noticing Misdirect is done exactly the same way as Strategic Noticing, but with an extra effect. You simply notice the positive behavior of a student or of students: "I notice you playing this game cooperatively," for example. The only difference between Noticing Misdirect and Strategic Noticing is *when* you do it. You can make Strategic Noticing also become Noticing Misdirect by using it with students who are playing cooperatively near students who are *not* playing cooperatively. Again, this reinforces the positive behaviors, completely ignores the negative behaviors, and gently guides the students using the negative behaviors toward positive behaviors. Perfect!

27. **Preventive Helping.** This one is highly effective if done correctly, but it can be highly destructive when done wrong. Teachers who attempt something close to this with traditional discipline often destroy their environments.

When a student appears to be getting angry and frustrated, but other students have not yet noticed or only noticed in a very minimal way, ask for some Preventive Helping. Have a teaching tool of some kind at the ready—a stapler, a hole punch, or an empty flash drive. Give it to the student and ask them to take it to another specific teacher relatively nearby. You will have already talked to this teacher and they know to simply accept the teaching tool and say, "Thank you." This minimizes attention given to the emotional buildup, and it gives the student a chance to take a break and briefly change environments.

What many teachers do is wait until the student is angry in a way that everyone sees, then allow the student to "take a lap" whereby they are allowed to wander around the school. *Do not do this.* The effects of regularly responding to student emotion this way will usually be catastrophic. Besides the fact that you are allowing a very angry student to wander around the school unmonitored, you are also letting all of your students know that they can leave the room whenever they want as long as they act very, very angrily and dramatically first. In a matter of days after this action, you may find yourself in a room full of very angry, dramatic students.

28. **Assumption of Intelligence.** Ninety-nine percent of the time when we tell students to do something, they already know what they should do. When we tell students to throw away their food or put away their materials because the bell rang, we are needlessly taking away control, implying that we think kids are unintelligent and making them feel bossed around.

This statement simply tells the student that you know that they are so smart that you don't even need to tell them what to do next: "You know what to do." Say it in passing, without eye contact. Think about how many demands you could replace with this single GGI.

29. **Statement of Fact.** This is a simple statement that assumes intelligence, most often used when students or teams are being less than responsible. It is just a statement of something that is true but should not be. Examples may include the following:

   - "Your desk has stuff under it."
   - "Purple Foxes have some things to do before Afternoon Meeting."
   - "There's a coat on the floor."
   - "The Astronauts still have mail in their mailboxes."

   These simple statements prompt students to do what they are supposed to do without nagging them.

The Question Matrix

While asking questions is a time-honored part of the teaching of academic subjects that goes back to Socrates, questions are woefully absent in the world of discipline. The effects of this absence are often catastrophic.

The words "question" and "demand" are antonyms. Demands stimulate psychological reactance and make students less cooperative: human beings don't like being told what to do. Questions, on the other hand, have an almost magical ability to allow the person being questioned to take ownership of their life and answer the question, at least in their mind. Questions also allow the questioner to assume cooperation, assume intelligence (asking a question makes the assumption that the questionee can answer it), and avoid being anxious about trying to figure out what students should be doing. After all, when you tell someone what to do, you must first determine what they should be doing. Doing this for 25 to 35 students at a time is exhausting. By using the Question Matrix, you can avoid this dynamic. Replacing demands with the following questions can revolutionize your classroom.

30. **"What's next?"** A great prompt for a space cadet lost in space for a moment.

31. **"What now?"**

32. **"Where should you be?"** For when the cadets start to leave the Milky Way.

33. **"What should you be doing?"**

34. **"Is now the right time for that?"** Most behaviors that are negative (problem-causing) in school aren't inherently "bad." Running, yelling, and chewing gum are not the actions of an evil person; they just aren't appropriate for certain locations and times in the school day. Asking this question allows you

to respectfully let the student think about why the otherwise OK behavior is a negative behavior in a school context.

35. **"Does that cause a problem?"** This simply asks if a behavior goes against the rule that the class made up (see Chapter 5). If the student replies that they do not feel that the behavior causes a problem, this presents an even better opportunity not only to avoid hoarding control but to share that control more fully. In this case, thoughtfully say the following to the student:

> *You know, you may be right. Let's talk later about this. I want*
> *to hear your thoughts. For now, just do me a favor and stop,*
> *and we'll figure it out later together.*

Later, you can ask about the logic behind the student's thought process and render a decision. This shouldn't lead to a Delayed Learning Opportunity. If you feel that the student is, in fact, correct that the behavior does not cause a problem, you should agree and even announce the decision to the class, emphasizing that you were wrong and the student was right. You can also open the entire discussion up to the class and have them decide. This will build the relationship whether you agree or disagree with the student. At the very least, you respected them enough to think that they might be right, and you took the time to hear them out.

36. **"Are you OK?"** These should often be the first words by any human who sees another human being who appears to be suffering. This is very helpful with students who are in tears, appear to be agitated, have their heads down on a desk, or walk into a room with a frown.

37. **Change the Student's Location.** This is another GGI that has been used by teachers for years. You can ask a student who is causing a problem to move or ask a student who is being bothered by the other student's negative behaviors to move. You can also have a student move for no reason at all, just to remove any possible punitive feeling from this GGI. It is best to assume cooperation in this case by asking, "Could you move over here? Thanks," and immediately moving away as you say the words. Note that these changes in location are merely temporary until the next transition.

38. **Contraband Removal.** This can be done as a follow-up to Contraband Tap if the contraband is not removed. It can also be done as the first intervention when contraband is present. Simply take the contraband. Whether and when you use this GGI will depend on you: how important is it to you that all

students are trained to not bring all or certain contraband into the classroom? It may also be affected by your school's rules for how strict you must be with cell phones, makeup, electronics, fidget spinners, food, and so on.

Use your Calm Signal as contraband is removed. The object(s) should be put away. For GGIs #39–43, if the removal of student possessions is likely to cause an explosion of negative behaviors, it may be wiser to simply use your DLO Delaying Script (see Chapter 11) and change the behavior later by using a DLO, because if you are reasonably sure that explosive behaviors will occur after the use of an intervention, you will have to do a DLO anyway. In this case, this student will still have to learn some important behaviors, and you can avoid an explosion of negative behaviors. Similarly, if a student physically attempts to stop you from removing an item, simply delay the learning opportunity.

39. **Contraband Removal (as a Gateway to a DLO).** This is exactly the same as 38–42, but you will note (figuratively or literally) that you will be giving a DLO at a later time regarding the improper classroom importation of contraband. Of course, contraband such as weapons, drugs, and alcohol may have to be dealt with in a manner dictated by school policies, but try to use DLOs whenever possible to deal with even these kinds of rule infractions.

40. **Problem Stimuli Removal.** While contraband is, by definition, not allowed to be present in a classroom, any object can be used in such a way that it causes a problem. Anything that can be played with can become a distracting toy, and when it does, GGIs are necessary. Take the item exactly as you do when executing Contraband Removal.

41. **Problem Stimuli Removal (as a Gateway to a DLO).** See #39.

42. **Plan a Meeting.** This GGI is usually one that is used for behaviors that almost need a DLO. Sometimes students just need to be told honestly that their behavior is causing a real problem. This helps the student see you as a real person who is trying to do a difficult job. Of course, you should never do this at the moment of the negative behavior. Instead, whisper to the student:

    Oh, man. We need to have a meeting. Please meet me here at
    __:__.

    Then, at that time, briefly let the student know that their behavior is causing a real problem for you, perhaps communicating that the behavior is making it difficult or impossible for you to do your job. Depending upon the nature of the behavior, you may want to make an honest statement about the fact that other students are becoming very frustrated with them and that this continued behavior may cause the student to lose friends. This is not to be a discussion; just make the statement, warmly thank the student for coming, and dismiss them.

10

Mindfulness Breaks

Mindfulness Breaks are a special intervention that require extensive explanation in order to do them correctly. They can be done at any time and can be initiated by the students themselves. They are done as needed, without anxiety or haste.

Traditional discipline uses something somewhat similar called "time-out," and other common programs use comparable methods. None of these methods is a true Mindfulness Break and all will come up short, especially when used with difficult students.

Not every student can learn and function as a prosocial member of a classroom during every second of every day. Past and current traumas, lack of sleep, lack of nutrition, mental or physical illness, or current agitation that is exacerbated by these other underlying issues can make it impossible for students to learn. Students must be able to retreat to a minimally stimulating environment so that they can feel a healthy kind of control and change their own brain chemistry in order to again be able to be part of the learning environment in a prosocial way. In addition, teachers need to be able to maintain a functional learning environment by making sure that students who are not in the right frame of mind for school are not affecting that learning environment.

Mindfulness Breaks offer all of this to all students. The use of these breaks allows students to understand that it is OK not to be in the right frame of mind for school and that they have a safe, calm place where they must be until they are able to be a part of the learning environment. The learning environment is set up for people who are ready to be prosocial learners and teachers; others must take Mindfulness Breaks until the moment they are able to become prosocial learners and teachers. (Yes, as a teacher, you can use Mindfulness Breaks as well.)

Mindfulness Breaks: What They Are Not

Mindfulness Breaks are not desperate, last-ditch attempts to remove the student after they have become belligerent and angry. They are not punishments that attempt to inflict pain on students to get them to "behave." They are not a way of rejecting students. They are not a means of embarrassing students. They are not a way of hurting students' feelings. *They are not time-outs.*

A Necessary Alternative to Catastrophic Tactics

Mindfulness Breaks are a desperately needed alternative to two of the most hurtful tactics of traditional discipline: sending disruptive students to the principal, and using a sensory room when students use disruptive behaviors. These tactics are often employed with the best of intentions by people who care about students. Unfortunately, sending students to the principal or using a sensory room in this capacity can destroy entire schools—and has done so over and over again.

At first glance, these two tactics seems to make logical sense. They both accomplish their primary goal: they remove disruptive students from the learning environment so students can learn and teachers can teach. In addition, a sensory room is designed to give students a chance to return to a functional state of mind and return to class after someone has engaged the student in sensory activities.

Unfortunately, as any experienced teacher can tell you, the negative outcomes from these tactics far outweigh the supposed benefits, and those benefits are only immediate in that the student is removed from a negative situation. However, both tactics *make negative behaviors far more likely in the future.* To be clear, the catastrophic effects of a sensory room refer to using a sensory room to house students who have been disruptive. *Scheduled* trips to a sensory room managed by staff (usually occupational therapy professionals) are a functional and appropriate use of effective interventions.

Negative Effects of Sending Students to the Principal's Office

Any teacher can tell you that sending a student to the principal does not make negative behaviors any less likely. Sending students to the office often encourages negative behaviors, which leads to suspensions, which leads to expulsions, which leads to dropping out, which leads to mass incarceration. Specifically, sending students to the principal's office creates this and other types of dysfunction for the following reasons:

- It takes away the teacher's power and implies that the teacher should not be seen as an authority figure.
- It can diminish the amount of respect that parents have for the teacher as an authority figure.
- It can create tension between the principal and teacher if the parties disagree on how disciplinary situations are handled in the office or in the classroom.
- It is usually prefaced with warnings and threats, which condition students to think that they will always be warned or threatened before any action is taken.
- It doesn't take into account that the principal is often not immediately available to address the problem.
- It makes the school office a chaotic place to work.
- It creates a threatening situation that activates the student's brain stem.
- It creates (or continues) an unwinnable power struggle.
- It makes the student feel rejected.
- It makes the student feel that they are not as good as the other students.
- It implies that the teacher feels that the student cannot handle the challenges of life.
- It is punitive.
- It takes an undue amount of control from the student.
- It allows the student to avoid work.
- It creates logistical problems regarding the student going to or being "picked up" by the principal.
- It rewards students who use negative behaviors to get what they want, as some combination of attention, control, and avoidance is achieved every time a student is sent to the office.
- It creates a "negative ripple effect": other students who want some combination of attention, control, and avoidance will see that one student has gotten these things, so they will use negative behaviors to get these things for themselves.

Negative Effects of Sending Students to a Sensory Room

There is no research that shows that sending a student to a sensory room makes future negative behaviors less likely, and there is significant research that the opposite is true. Specifically, sending students to a sensory room in response to negative behaviors creates dysfunction for the following reasons:

- It makes regularly scheduled (and extremely positive) sensory room activities dysfunctional.
- It implies that the teacher feels that the student cannot handle the challenges of life.
- It allows the student to avoid work.
- It creates logistical problems regarding the student going to or being "picked up" by a school staff member.
- It takes an undue amount of control away from the student.
- It makes the student feel rejected.
- It makes the student feel that they are not as good as the other students.
- It rewards students who use negative behaviors to get what they want, as some combination of attention, control, and avoidance is achieved every time a student is sent to the sensory room. This effect can be greatly magnified depending on the amount of attention given in the sensory room and the amount of fun to be had when participating in sensory activities.
- It creates a "negative ripple effect": other students who want some combination of attention, control, and avoidance will see that one student has gotten these things, so they will use negative behaviors to get these things for themselves.

The Alternative and Solution

When done properly, Mindfulness Breaks offer all the positives of these two dysfunctional tactics without any of the negatives. In addition, every time they are used, it gives students a feeling of healthy control instead of reinforcing negative behaviors.

Teaching Mindfulness

Sometime during the first day of class, you should teach some sort of mindfulness activity. Feel free to use any quality instruction, such as teaching deep breathing (in through the nose, out through the mouth) or basic yoga positions (Sun Salutation, Warrior 1, Warrior 2, and Warrior 3 are favorites). Find or create whatever you want, and demonstrate and practice with students. It's probably a good idea to do some type of mindfulness activity every morning, or every class, for middle and high school students.

Introduce the concept of mindfulness in whatever way you like or in whatever way a program that you like suggests. Give students the option to use certain mindfulness activities whenever they wish (make sure that you only allow activities that won't cause a problem for you; if a student doing Sun Salutation at their desk during your instructions will bother you or others, don't allow it!). Many teachers allow students to close their eyes at their desks and deep breathe whenever they want.

The other important element in teaching your students about mindfulness is to make sure that your introduction is not in any way connected to Mindfulness Breaks. The emphasis of the introduction needs to be on using mindfulness to prevent your brain from being hijacked by difficult situations. If you connect the concept primarily to using it to cope once you are so upset that you can no longer function as a member of the group, students will tend to wait too long to try it. You will also see in the directions for using the Mindfulness Breaks intervention below that you should only briefly mention mindfulness activities as a part of the intervention. Emphasize that students should use Mindfulness Breaks when they need to calm their minds, but emphasize that they should do so preventively and before they get too frustrated!

Introduction to Students

The introduction of the Mindfulness Breaks procedure should occur on the first day, after the first yoga/breathing instruction, but not immediately after this instruction. You do not want students to primarily associate mindfulness and breathing with Mindfulness Breaks. It is best for people to think of and practice mindfulness and yoga primarily as something preventive for good health and self-care.

The following is how I introduced Mindfulness Breaks in my class. Make this script your own, but be sure to project a casual, kind, relaxed manner.

> OK, folks, I want to talk with you all about something important. I want to explain a problem that I have and a way that I deal with my problem. Sometimes I get frustrated. Sometimes I get upset. This is especially true here at work. It may be easy for you all to forget, but I am at work right now, and work can be frustrating. Sometimes, because I have too many things to do, or because I didn't get enough sleep, or because something bad is going on in my life, I get so frustrated that I feel like I can't even be part of the class. Raise your hand if this has ever happened to you. [Look

for a show of hands.] OK, because of this problem I have, I have placed Mindfulness Centers in the room. One is here [point] and one is there [point]. From time to time, you may see me walk over to a Mindfulness Center and sit and breathe. Or you may see me stand right in front of the chair and do yoga. Mostly, I am telling you this so you don't think that your teacher has gone crazy. When I do this, it just means that my brain isn't quite working right and that I need to take a break from my job, calm my brain down, and relax.

I want to apologize in advance, because when I am really frustrated, or tired, or overwhelmed, or sad, or whatever, I may stay over there for a long time, if that's how long it takes to get my brain working right. I won't talk to you all when I am taking one of these breaks, and I just ask that you ignore me when I'm back there. My being back there is telling you that I can't handle teaching right then, so I'll ask you to please leave me alone and just keep working. I'll try not to, but if I have to go take a break when I'm in the middle of teaching, I will just ask that, if I don't come back after around one minute, you start on your Nows and Laters. I thank you in advance for not causing problems while I'm getting myself back together. I promise that I will come back as soon as I am able. Just know that, if I take a break, it doesn't mean I'm angry at you or that I am not OK. I'm just needing a break.

Here's the deal: a lot of hands went up when I asked if you have ever been so mad or sad or hurt or frustrated that you couldn't handle being part of the class. I get it, believe me. I'm going to let you also use these spots if you ever feel like I feel sometimes. Some of you will never need them, and that's fine. Some of you will need them, and that's fine, too. Use them whenever you want. You don't have to ask. Just like when I'm in there, please completely ignore whoever is in the Mindfulness Center so they can chill out and come back when they are ready. You can stay as long as you need to; just know though that you are still responsible for all the work that you miss. Please don't bring anything over there, and come back whenever you are ready!

Now, as a kid expert, and as someone who often has to take breaks myself, I am incredibly skilled at telling when a kid might need to take a break. In fact, I may notice that you need to take a break even before you notice that you need to take a break. I may give you a little nudge or ask if you need to take a break. If I ask, don't be offended. You can either go or stay. Either way is fine. If you go, stay there as long as you want, and come back when you are ready.

If you choose to go, great! If you choose to stay, great! If, however, I see that you are not looking like you can be with us because you seem agitated or because you are causing a problem or both, I will actually ask you to go to a Mindfulness Center, but, like always, you can come back as soon as you are able to come back.

Please listen to me: this is not a punishment! I don't punish students. If it were a punishment, I wouldn't let you come back, but I wouldn't do that because I would miss you. I want you to be with us. So if you feel like, "Whoa, Mr. Ervin is right—I need a serious break," just go and stay there until your brain is right. Or, if I ask you to please go to a Mindfulness Center and you think that I am being ridiculous and that you weren't really acting agitated or that you weren't really causing a problem, just go to the center and see how quickly you can tap your butt on the chair and come right back. That's fine. I make mistakes all the time. That's your way of telling me that I was wrong and ridiculous and that you can totally stay in class without causing a problem.

I may need to tell you to go to a certain Mindfulness Center, so we need a name for each one. No time to vote, so first come, first served: we can name these two places to chill the names of any country in the world except for the one in which we are currently living. I will call on silently raised hands! [Get names of two countries.] Sudan and Luxembourg it is! You will notice that Make Mindfulness Center Labels is a Later for today. Feel free to make those if you would like. Turn them in and we can laminate them all together to make cool signs.

In addition, my friends Mr. Hetrick and Mrs. Singer across the hall also have Mindfulness Centers for themselves and their students. I may ask you to use one of those centers, or I may give you a choice of a center in here or over there. All I ask is that you please don't go there on your own, since there's a rule about teachers knowing where their students are. If you do end up in there, look for a chair with the name of a country on it. Just sneak in, use the Mindfulness Center for as long as you need it, and come back as soon as you can. You don't have to talk to anyone. Again, I can't emphasize enough that this is not a punishment! Just take a vacation in your mind, or do some breathing, or do some yoga, or do some

> *combination of those, and come back whenever you are ready. Just make*
> *sure you follow our rules, just like always, when you are there.*
>
> *Any questions?*
>
> [Take questions.]
>
> *OK. I'm never going to talk about this again. Let's move on!*

Then . . . move on, and don't ever talk about it again, unless asked—and then only answer the question during noninstructional time.

Simple, Positive Goals

The only goals involved with the use of the Mindfulness Breaks procedure are that the learning environment will be maintained and that students will be able to use an environment change to regain their neurological ability to act as a positive, prosocial member of the learning environment—and that they can stay there if they are unable to do so. Mindfulness Breaks systematically share healthy control with students who are struggling to use the necessary behaviors in the learning environment. This is in contrast to the chaos-inducing tactics through which students use negative behaviors to "make it to" the principal's office and sensory room, respectively—places where they get what they want (attention, control, avoidance, fun squishy objects) through their negative behaviors, making those behaviors more likely.

Mindfulness Breaks avoid giving unhealthy control to students and simultaneously give healthy control under the following conditions:

- They are used *before* negative behaviors have become too heightened.
- They are used in context of the control-sharing and relationship-building methods in this manual.
- Where Mindfulness Centers are located and how they are utilized does not reinforce negative behaviors by giving students attention, control, avoidance, or squishy fun things.
- Students can use them whenever they need to do so.
- They allow students to return to the learning environment whenever they feel ready.
- They are not punitive and are even used by teachers and staff.

All of this is happening at a time when students are teetering between being able to be prosocial and not being able to be prosocial. It is at this time when students, especially ones who have experienced or are experiencing trauma, are in desperate need of control. If you don't share some healthy control with students by using Mindfulness Breaks, they will take that control in an unhealthy way that is likely to cause chaos.

Explicit Instructions for Creating, Implementing, and Maintaining Mindfulness Breaks

As with many things that are difficult and important, exactly how you create, implement, and maintain Mindfulness Centers is the difference between success and failure. Simply designating a spot in the room where you send students once they use particularly bad behaviors, or once they exhaust or anger you, is not a Mindfulness Break, and the two should not be conflated. Keep reading for details on optimizing the Mindfulness Breaks GGI.

Mindfulness Centers: What They Are

From the perspective of the educator, a Mindfulness Center is neutral in every possible way. It is simply a chair placed somewhere that is not a focal point for anyone, where a student can be at least minimally monitored and totally ignored. It is neither comfortable nor uncomfortable. It is a place that has fewer stimuli than the learning environment. This means that the center includes nothing to play with, work on, or do. Students who visit a Mindfulness Center need less stimulation, not more. It is acceptable, healthy, and helpful for students to be permitted to bring sensory objects that they already have to the Mindfulness Center, but they won't be able to get a new one there. Schoolwork is not permitted in the center.

It is helpful, whenever possible, to have a chair situated in the Mindfulness Center so that to the seated student's left or right (good) or both left and right (best, though not usually possible) there is a solidly colored surface that obstructs the student's view of visual stimuli and slightly muffles auditory stimuli. Having the chair back against a solid wall or surface is also helpful. This is usually facilitated by having a wall on one or two sides of the student, and sometimes using a bookshelf to create a third wall. The chair should never be positioned facing a wall, since this has a punitive connotation, though if a student moves the chair to face a wall, allow it. It can sometimes help to use a chair that is slightly shorter than a normal classroom chair, as the lowered seat position can further minimize visual stimuli. The chair size should not, however, be so small that the student will be significantly uncomfortable or embarrassed.

The area immediately around the Mindfulness Center should, of course, be as safe as the rest of the classroom, and there should be an attempt made to not have objects nearby that are overly stimulating, tempting to touch, or easily available. However, it is not necessary to make sure that the area is "mischief proof." Students who need training to be prosocial while in the Mindfulness Center will be trained through a specific DLO (see Chapter 11) to do so.

Mindfulness Centers: Where They Are

In-Room Mindfulness Centers

An In-Room Mindfulness Center should be as removed as possible from any focal points in the room. The center should not be at the front of a forward-facing classroom. It should not be next to or facing a reading table in an elementary room. It should also be positioned so that you are able to casually monitor students in at least a minimal way (while ignoring them). Mindfulness Centers should never be in or next to the classroom door and should *never* be in the hallway. It is rare for a Mindfulness Center to not utilize a classroom wall.

In a typical preK–12 classroom, there should almost always be room for two different Mindfulness Centers, though you may need or want to have only one. Larger rooms typically used for PE, music, or career-based instruction may even have room for more than two Mindfulness Centers. Multiple centers can exist under the following guidelines. In-room centers should not be near each other, for obvious reasons. Mindfulness Center chairs should not face each other, even from across the room. Though a specific DLO will be used to make sure all students are trained to not cause problems while taking a Mindfulness Break, it is very difficult for any two people not to get the giggles when made to face each other. In addition, having to look directly at another person works against the goal of decreased stimuli for a Mindfulness Center.

Reciprocal Room Mindfulness Centers

If another school staff member has a room near yours, has read this manual, and wishes to coordinate with you, their In-Room Mindfulness Centers can be your Reciprocal Room Mindfulness Centers (and vice versa). Discuss with reciprocating teachers exactly how student(s) will travel between rooms and how you and the reciprocating teacher will make sure that they arrive at the reciprocal room while receiving minimal or no attention. Mindfulness Breaks must follow the procedures exactly as described in this manual; *do not* attempt to use Reciprocal Mindfulness

Centers with a person who has not absorbed these lessons. Attempting this may cause more problems than it solves.

Mindfulness Center Alcove

Due to space constraints, it may not be possible to find a suitable location for a Mindfulness Center Alcove. However, if using one is possible, here are the ideal parameters. A Mindfulness Center Alcove must be a place in a common area or back office that is constantly supervised by a person who has read this manual and can simultaneously monitor and completely ignore the student. This, in and of itself, is a rarity to have in a school. This cannot be in the principal's office (which can be the most stimulating place in the school), and it can't be in a hallway. If it just so happens that there is a convenient spot in the far reaches of the back end of a business office staffed by someone with their associate's degree in Being Boring and Not Really Enjoying Children, this could be a perfect Mindfulness Center Alcove spot, if it can fulfill the parameters previously described.

Mindfulness Room

A Mindfulness Room is *not* an in-school suspension room. This is simply a room with multiple Mindfulness Centers staffed by a person whose only job is to monitor and *completely ignore* students. The staff member must have read this manual and should acquire some kind of reading material, because there should be no interaction with the students who visit the room. Students should be able to come and go as they please. Logistics of how students will come and go from this room must be worked out by the Mindfulness Room monitor and teachers. It is usually unnecessary to have a Mindfulness Room, but it can be useful and effective for schools that need and can provide such a room.

How to Use Mindfulness Centers Correctly

Now that you understand the importance of Mindfulness Breaks as an alternative to other chaos-inducing options, you understand what Mindfulness Centers are, you have created your Mindfulness Centers, you have your new Mindfulness Breaks paradigm, and you are ready to use Mindfulness Breaks in the context of the other parts of this book, you are ready to learn how to use Mindfulness Centers to create an excellent GGI!

Again, it is important to recognize the use of Mindfulness Breaks as a gentle intervention, not as a punishment and not as something to do when all other hope is lost. It is important to recommit yourself to the idea that not all students can be in the learning environment at all times and that this is not their fault. When they are unable to be in the learning environment, they must be able to take control in a healthy way by being able to go to a low-stimulation location and take as much time as they need to regulate themselves so they can re-enter the learning environment. Keep in mind that Mindfulness Breaks are to be used in the context of the rest of this manual. The Real-World Workshop procedure, for example, makes using Mindfulness Breaks to avoid work a nonfunctional behavior for students. This knowledge will help you to make the necessary paradigm shift, because it further helps you convince students that negative behaviors are nonfunctional.

The Mindfulness Break Interventions (MBIs) below are once again in menu form—this time, a menu within a menu. Just as with the greater GGI menu, they go from least intrusive to most intrusive, and from least time-consuming to most time-consuming. Again, ignore the ones you don't like. Use your favorites over and over. Experiment.

Keep in mind that you should usually use multiple other GGIs from the GGI menu in Chapter 9 before you use Mindfulness Breaks. After all, most agitation builds relatively slowly over time. However, students may sometimes show up to your fourth period calculus class, or your 3rd grade room in the morning, or your kindergarten room after recess in a mental state that immediately requires a Mindfulness Break. Or something particularly upsetting may happen, all of a sudden, in your classroom. A fantastic "gateway intervention" to a Mindfulness Break for a student who has become locked into their brain stem is GGI #36: simply asking, "Are you OK?" After all, what else would a nice person say to someone in distress?

The Interventions

There are six Mindfulness Break Interventions (MBIs). The first four are Choice Interventions, and the final two are Directive Interventions, though one of the Directive Interventions also involves a choice. All verbal parts of these interventions should be whispered whenever possible.

Choice MBIs

1. **Confused Eye/Point/Mindfulness Break.** The first, and therefore least intrusive, intervention is perhaps the most effective, in that it builds relationships

every time it is used. However, it may not be optimal for students, especially younger ones, until they are comfortable with Mindfulness Breaks as a concept. This MBI is a combination of GGI #2 and GGI #11, with the only difference being that you will point toward a Mindfulness Center. When done correctly, this says to the student, "Are you OK? Do you need a break? I respect and like you, and I'm trying to give you a little prompt without embarrassing you."

In one way, this is a bit more intrusive than MBIs #2–4 because it usually requires some kind of response—often nonverbal—from the student. Usually it will garner a quick "no" head shake. This is fantastic: it's a healthy form of rejection of a suggestion from a teacher. Your response should be a quick, discreet head nod, as if to say, "Cool. Good. Just checking." The most effective use of Mindfulness Breaks involves teachers implementing this MBI almost exclusively.

2. **Ask MBI.** Simply whisper, "Do you need a break?" Wait for a response without eye contact and without squaring your shoulders to the student. "No" is a great answer. "Yes" is a great answer. No answer is a great answer. Walk away if you don't get one.

3. **Rule-Choice MBI.** Ask, "Can you follow our rules, or do you need to go to [name of Mindfulness Center]"? Say it and walk away. Notice that the question stimulates thinking and the choice gives the student preventive, healthy control. An answer is not required. You can—but don't have to—come back soon after and whisper, "You stayin'?" The colloquial writing is purposeful and important. Language here should be overtly comfortable and familiar. It should be spoken in a register that is close to the student's own. Of course, you don't want to force anything that feels inauthentic, but crisply asking, "Are you staying?" is less effective at keeping students out of their brain stem.

4. **Rule-Statement MBI.** Say to the student, "Feel free to stay with us as long as you are following our rules," and walk away. If the student chooses to take a Mindfulness Break, great. If the student chooses not to take a Mindfulness Break, great. Either way, the student is taking control and advocating for themselves through their actions. They are choosing the best way to regulate their own behavior. Having choices about how they regulate themselves helps students to regulate themselves!

If students choose to take a Mindfulness Break, you need to *always* invite the student back using the following script, and nothing else:

Come back as soon as you are ready. We want you to be with us.

Directive MBIs

Every effort to use Choice MBIs should be made before resorting to a Directive MBI. If you have to jump directly to a Directive MBI, it usually (not always) means that one or more parts of the strategies or procedures in this book has broken down. Often, there's not enough Strategic Noticing taking place. Perhaps not enough procedures are being employed. Perhaps not enough GGIs are being used. Perhaps, though, a behavior may reveal itself immediately and without warning, even when sufficient strategies and procedures have been in place.

As their respective names suggest, Choice MBIs allow agitated students a choice about whether they need to take a Mindfulness Break; Directive MBIs require them to. From a practical perspective, notice that Choice MBIs do not give students a chance to refuse to go to a Mindfulness Center, since they aren't required to go. This is why you should always try to use a Choice MBI before a Directive MBI. If a student refuses to go to a Mindfulness Center, you're forced to follow the procedure on page 218.

5. **Directive-Choice MBI.** Say to the student, "Feel free to go to [name of Mindfulness Center #1] or [name of Mindfulness Center #2]. Come back as soon as you are ready. We want you to be with us." Notice that even though this directs the student to do something, it still involves a choice. Notice also that this and the next MBI both include the mandatory invitation to rejoin the class.

6. **Directive MBI.** Say to the student, "There's a spot for you in [name of Mindfulness Center]. Come back as soon as you are ready. We want you to be with us."

Whenever possible, use MBI #5 instead of MBI #6. Only go straight to #6 when either all other centers are full or you are frustrated enough with a student that it is wise for all involved that you do not see the student for a bit. In this case, direct the student to go to a Mindfulness Center outside your classroom.

Which Mindfulness Center(s) you offer to students in MBIs #5–6 to go to is up to you. It is optimal to give a choice of two centers, one that is in your room and one that is out of your room. This gives the student more control than offering only in-room choices. Just as you may not want to look at a student's face, the student may choose to go to another room's center because they're tired of you as well! (Note: Keep in mind that if you are continually getting so frustrated with students that you often need them to leave the room, some or many other parts of the procedures or strategies may be breaking down, or you are simply waiting too long to prompt them to take Mindfulness Breaks. Or you may need to take a Mindfulness Break yourself!)

What If They Don't Go?

Take a moment to look back at the number of Control-Sharing and Relationship-Building Strategies and Procedures that you are now able to put in place in your classroom. From ESPN Greetings, to Strategic Noticing, to all of the prevention woven into the procedures, to the GGIs, consider for a moment how different and more cooperative your students will be once you put these methods in place.

Now consider the MBI menu and pay specific attention to how rare it should be to actually *direct* a student to take a Mindfulness Break. In the context of so much effective prevention and efforts to use Choice MBIs first, the use of Directive MBIs should be infrequent. If you do use a Directive MBI, there is a chance that a student might refuse. If you are faithfully using all of the preventive and other mitigative methods of this manual, the chances of this happening are low, but still, it may happen. Below is a list of DLOs for students who refuse to take a Mindfulness Break when directed to. These interventions are *not* designed to make it less likely to refuse to take a Mindfulness Break the next time this situation arises; they are only designed to enable you to continue teaching with a minimum of disruption to student learning and a minimum of disruption to school staff. What will teach the student to go to a Mindfulness Center when requested is a specific, simple, and very serious DLO that will put much or all of the student's social time on pause until they learn to go to the Mindfulness Center when asked.

For the rest of the elements of this manual to work perfectly, it is essential that students are able to use Mindfulness Breaks effectively. As you may recall, Mindfulness Breaks are the alternative to two destructive tactics of traditional discipline: sending students to the principal, and using sensory rooms as an escape for students who cannot regulate their behavior—both practices that can envelop students in chaos and possibly enter them into the school-to-prison pipeline. Therefore, students must be trained, with serious DLOs, to use these breaks effectively. For many of them, it could be a matter of life and death.

While you can feel confident that you will be able to train your students to use Mindfulness Breaks over the course of the school year, that confidence does you no good in the moment when a student is refusing, sometimes loudly, to take one. Here is another menu for what to do when a student refuses to take a Mindfulness Break when requested to. Remember the guidelines:

- Use only your favorite interventions.

- Ignore the ones you don't like.

- Give a significant DLO later that will teach students proper behavior of taking a Mindfulness Break when asked.

- You can't *make* a student take a Mindfulness Break—not in the moment, anyway!

Tactics for Dealing with Mindfulness Break Refusal

1. **Delay the DLO Verbally.** Simply use your personal DLO Delaying Script, as described in Chapter 11. Concentrate on using your Calm Signal. Move on. This will likely have the effect of the student calming down enough to remain in the learning environment, especially if the inevitability of DLOs has been established.

2. **Delay the DLO with Only a Calm Signal.** For students you know to be more explosive, meet their refusal with only your Calm Signal. Move on. Keep teaching as if nothing happened.

3. **Delay the DLO Mentally.** Simply meet the refusal by walking away. Use this with only your most explosive and savvy students.

Mindfulness Break Refusal DLOs #1–3 should be your primary tools in refusal situations. However, if the student was sent into a belligerent rage either when asked to take the break or in response to these DLOs, the following two interventions can be used:

4. **Coach's Gambit.** In professional basketball, coaches of the most poorly performing teams are often fired in the middle of the season. The average winning percentage for bad teams after the coach is replaced is about .900 in the five games immediately after the coach was fired, though the teams inevitably go back to their losing ways. What is the explanation for the brief fantastic performance of these terrible teams? The players' effort greatly increases when a coach is fired because they are trying to show the world that the coach was the reason they were losing previously: they want to "show the coach up."

This intervention uses the same dynamics. It takes a bit of planning. You will need two student volunteers. Ask one student, when you give a code word, to be in charge of lining up the class and taking them to a predetermined place where they can be monitored for only a few minutes—for example, another classroom (a PE class is often optimal, because 25 students sitting on bleachers usually isn't disruptive).

The other student should be trained to get an adult (preferably not an administrator) who is able to leave their responsibilities for just a few minutes, when you give the code word.

The teacher should sit or stand in a position in the doorway where they can be seen by people in the hallway and where the teacher can see the refusing student. This is important for legal reasons (whenever you can avoid being alone in a room with an angry student, you should). When the alternate adult comes to the room, they should simply use their Calm Signal and then say, "OK, let's get out of here." In all my years, I have never seen the student not go with the other adult, and I have only heard about it not working once. Just like with the coach, the student is angry with you, wants to get away from you, and wants to show you up. How does the student accomplish all those things? By going with the other adult! The audience who saw the refusal has gone, so the student does not lose face, and being able to go with the new, "better than my stupid teacher" adult gives the student a sense of control.

That adult can simply take the student to any Reciprocal Mindfulness Center and follow a slightly modified Rejoin Invitation script: "Go back as soon as you can. They want you to be in there!"

5. **Reverse Mindfulness Break.** This works when you have a student who has had a recent history of being completely out of control—so much so that you know that preventive methods will have no effect, that they have not yet been trained successfully by the more intensive DLOs, and that they will refuse to take a Mindfulness Break. It requires some planning as well as an alternative learning space at the ready. That learning space could be an empty classroom or an outdoor area, depending upon the current learning activity. It also requires another staff member (preferably not a principal). If no alternative learning area can be arranged and no staff member can give up time, you cannot use this intervention. Having to use a Reverse Mindfulness Break is most typical at the beginning of the year with younger students, but it can be necessary at any time with any students, preK–12.

When the student refuses the Mindfulness Break, simply have the previously assigned helper student lead the class to the alternate learning area and have the other student get the helpful adult. This time, stay with your class and ask students to bring any necessary learning materials with them. Make sure you don't leave until the adult shows up at your class. Once you leave to continue teaching, the other adult will simply ignore and monitor the belligerent student in what is now their private Mindfulness Center! For added convenience, a class can begin in the alternative location and plan on going to the home classroom once the predictable belligerence begins.

It may go without saying, but when students need to have other adults involved in the Mindfulness Break Refusal Intervention, that means that the DLOs need to become even more targeted and intensified.

11

Delayed Learning Opportunities

When I received Michael into my classroom unexpectedly, he suffered from a tremendous and life-threatening deficit: he did not know how to use positive behaviors to get what he wanted in life. *There is no more destructive deficit for human beings.* Students who continue to have this deficit into adulthood will live lives of pain and misery. When this deficit is not addressed by parents, it must be addressed by educators.

Delayed Learning Opportunities (DLOs) are an essential part of this endeavor. DLOs are opportunities for students to learn to use positive behaviors that help to create a positive environment in the classroom. DLOs teach students to use positive behaviors and be responsible for their behaviors, giving them the opportunity to become happy, productive, and successful members of society.

DLOs do *not* incorporate warnings, lectures, threats, or punishments. These hurtful strategies, which are all too often part of traditional discipline, are not effective at altering behaviors and are therefore not included in this manual. DLOs are the only way to effectively teach all students, with kindness and empathy, how to use positive, prosocial behaviors. This chapter will systematically and explicitly teach you exactly how to use Gentle Guidance Interventions and Delayed Learning Opportunities with your students.

The Terminal Destination for Negative Behaviors

The terminal destination for negative behaviors that are not prevented by procedures or mitigated by GGIs is that students will need to learn positive behaviors through Learning Opportunities. You know how to use the Procedural Learning Opportunities that are integrated into Control-Sharing Procedures; for example, students who are not silent in response to a Prompt for Silence know that, in the end, they will need to practice being silent. Likewise, teachers must make sure that the terminal destination of all negative behaviors not prevented or mitigated through GGIs is a DLO. When a teacher sees students using negative behaviors, it is necessary for the mental health of the teacher to know that if the behavior does not stop, the students will learn a lesson about not using that behavior in the future. Giving students these two choices is calming for teachers. The third possibility, in which students do whatever they want, their bad behaviors becoming bad habits that become bad personalities that the world has to deal with forevermore, is too stressful of a thought to have while also teaching high school chemistry. Through the use of DLOs, we take away that option from students.

A Sense of the Inevitable: An Essential Piece of the Puzzle

All parties must be aware that a learning opportunity—whether procedural (PLO), natural (NLO), or delayed (DLO)—is the inevitable terminal destination of all unprevented and unmitigated negative behaviors. While this understanding is important for the mental health of teachers, as noted above, it is also important for the mental health of students. Understanding that if they don't use positive behaviors, they will have to learn to do so in a way that may be less convenient than using positive behaviors, is essential if students are to be able to use positive behaviors without Learning Opportunities and even without GGIs. When students accept this inevitability, they are on the road to becoming calm, self-regulated, and able to spend their days learning instead of trying to figure out what they can get away with.

DLOs offer students a logical, realistic opportunity to learn a behavior or solve a problem that they have caused through a negative behavior. These opportunities are delayed, rather than performed in the moment when the negative behaviors occur, for two reasons. First, at the moment of a negative behavior that requires a DLO, it is likely that both teacher and student may be experiencing too much stress to teach or learn, respectively, anything about behavior. Second, class time is for the teaching of lessons. DLOs take place during noninstructional time.

DLOs Versus Punishment

A DLO is *not* punishment.

Punishment is as simple as it is ineffective. Punishment simply prescribes that when a student uses a negative behavior, the teacher makes that student's life arbitrarily painful so that the student learns to not use that behavior again. There need not be any learning or logical connection between the negative behavior and the punishment. The punishment just needs to cause some kind of pain. The pain is the point. Consider these examples of punishment:

- A 6th grade student uses sassy language with her teacher, so the teacher makes her eat lunch by herself in the classroom.
- A 3rd grade student does not finish an assignment, so he is made to "stand on the fence" silently at recess.
- A high school junior amasses a significant number of tardy slips, so he is not allowed to attend a school dance.

Punishments miss opportunities to teach important lessons about the world and how to live successfully in it. These examples illustrate attempts at teaching students nothing besides the idea that teachers will make students' lives more painful if the students are not cooperative. This is not a useful life lesson; it teaches nothing but blind obedience for the sake of obedience itself.

Delayed Learning Opportunities teach important lessons about life and also build skills so that students are prepared for the challenges posed by the real world. Students who struggle using important life skills need to get better at them so that they are sufficiently equipped to be successful in the future.

Delayed Learning Opportunities: Being Able to Think and Learn

While punishment involves fear, pain, and thoughtless obedience, Delayed Learning Opportunities involve learning important life lessons. If students are to learn, they must be able to think. Therefore, all of the tactics typically used with punishment need to be abandoned. The use of DLOs never involves warnings, threats, or lectures. It never involves anger. It never involves "breaking" students in order to make them cry. It never involves intimidation.

Perhaps most important, DLOs never involve students being asked to learn the important life lesson immediately. These are *Delayed* Learning Opportunities. From both a neurological and logistical standpoint, this is the only way this kind of learning can take place.

From a neurological perspective, if a student's behavior has not been prevented by the use of Relationship-Building Procedures, Control-Sharing Procedures, and Relationship-Building Strategies and has not been successfully mitigated by Gentle Guidance Interventions, that student will surely not be in a thinking state once the teacher has determined that the student has reached the terminal destination: a DLO. In this state, the student's brain stem is activated, and the prefrontal cortex is effectively turned off. At that moment, the student cannot learn; indeed, the student is literally incapable of thinking. Even if a perfect learning opportunity could be created at that moment, the student would be noncompliant and incapable of learning the life lesson. And even if the student could learn the lesson, conversely, the teacher in this scenario is also very likely in *their* brain stem and *also* unable to think, so it would be impossible to come up with the correct learning opportunity in the first place!

Furthermore, even if the teacher *could* think, attempting to create the learning opportunity in that moment is a diversion from teaching the other students in the class who deserve an education! Stopping the learning of perhaps 30 other students to try to teach a lesson that can't be taught and can't be learned is not a good use of the educator's time.

One final logistical concern is that attending to the student's negative behaviors by stopping instruction and dealing with a behavior in the moment gives the student attention, control, and work avoidance—the "holy trinity" of student behavioral goals. Even just attending to it immediately reinforces the negative behavior.

Suffering Is Incidental

Just as DLOs are not punishments, they also do not consist of the repeated reteaching of skills. For very young children, minimal reteaching may be performed (once), but DLOs do not make the assumption that students who use a negative behavior simply "forgot" how to use a positive behavior. While this may be true, and DLOs attend to the possibility, it is not assumed.

Students almost always know what positive behaviors they should be exhibiting, but they continue to use negative behaviors because those behaviors get them what they want (attention, control, or avoidance). Instead of repeatedly teaching what the student already knows, you will ask the student to do one of two learning activities:

1. Solving a problem that they caused.

2. Practicing the positive behavior with which they are struggling.

These will be explored in detail later in this chapter.

Being engaged in these learning opportunities may be unpleasant. In life, learning difficult lessons about how to act can involve suffering. The suffering, though, is not the intention, as it is when using punishment. Any suffering that might be incurred by students during DLOs is incidental. While this incidental suffering may reinforce the lesson, it is not the point of the lesson. Learning is the point of the lesson.

Picture a high school basketball coach who is having guards practice coming across a screen and catching the ball in triple threat position while squared to the basket. Everyone does a proficient job except for one player, who does it all wrong. In response, the coach blows the whistle and loudly informs the player that they did the drill wrong and that the player needs to run from baseline to baseline 50 times immediately, while everyone else continues with the drill.

This is an example of a punishment. The coach's intent is to arbitrarily cause pain for the player after a mistake in order to stop the player from making the mistake again. There is no learning involved; this is simply an attempt to get blind obedience through the use of pain—in this case, the pain of lactic acid buildup in the muscles due to a physically demanding activity.

By contrast, using a DLO in the same situation looks like this: When the player makes the mistake, the coach lets the player know that they will be working on that skill later. When others are taking a break or once practice is over, that player practices coming across a screen and catching the ball in triple threat position while squared to the basket over and over again until the skill is perfected. The intention is for the player to *learn how to do this effectively*. In addition to developing the required muscle memory from repeated practice, the player may experience muscle pain, but that is not the point of the exercise: the point is the learning. While physical pain in classrooms shouldn't be a part of learning, there can be other kinds of suffering. Students will often be bored while they are practicing positive behaviors. Sometimes students will have to solve problems that they caused in ways that involve some form of suffering, such as experiencing monotony or not being able to do something that they would rather do. This kind of suffering is only incidental to DLOs, for which the learning is the point, not the suffering.

Safe and Uncomfortable: Two Parts to the DLO

Calming tactics such as the repeated use of a Calm Signal and delaying scripts help students feel safe: unthreatened, respected, and loved. Through every moment of the DLO process, you will make it clear that the student's negative behaviors, no matter how severe, have not triggered anger from you and that these behaviors have not caused you to dislike the student. But while the student will feel as safe as is possible given the situation and the student's own arousal level, it is not your goal to make them comfortable. On the contrary—learning something new involves at least a minimal level of discomfort.

There are two parts to using DLOs. The first involves how to effectively let a student know that there will be a DLO coming in the future. The second section is about how to create and deliver an appropriate DLO. You will see that there is specific instruction about exactly how to make sure your students feel appropriately uncomfortable within the context of a safe, loving environment.

Getting to Later

Here is a logistical truth: *Students own now; teachers own later.*

Savvy students who are seeking attention, control, and/or work avoidance know that, if they are brave enough, they can always achieve one or more of these goals if the teacher attempts to deal with their behaviors in the present. It's inherently true: even if the teacher understands that a learning opportunity needs to be the terminal destination of serious negative behaviors, the student is guaranteed to get some combination of attention, control, and/or work avoidance if the teacher does not know how to delay the learning opportunity.

If you give a student a learning opportunity immediately, you will draw your attention, and the attention of other students, to the student using the negative behavior; you will be allowing the student to control your actions, and perhaps emotions; and you will be allowing the student to avoid work, since they cannot participate in a learning opportunity and do work at the same time.

The fact is that trying to give a student a learning opportunity in the moment only makes the serious negative behavior more likely in the future. Just by responding immediately, you reinforce the negative behavior.

Here is an emotional truth: *When you don't know what to do, it's a good idea not to do it.*

Savvy students know that if a teacher does not have the skills to delay a DLO, the teacher also won't be able to intellectually and emotionally handle behavioral problems while trying to teach perhaps 30 other students. Truly appropriate DLOs are hard to create and implement while you are teaching. Many students find profound enjoyment in forcing teachers to deal with behavioral situations in the moment, knowing that the worse their behaviors get, the more frazzled, upset, and entertaining the teacher will become. This also has a reinforcing effect.

The first goal of the DLO process is to notify students that there will be an opportunity for them to learn about positive behaviors later. There are three subgoals to be accomplished while you are giving students this notification:

1. *Lower or at least maintain the arousal levels of both student and teacher so as to avoid outbursts.* (This refers to outbursts from both student and teacher.) Of course, merely delaying the learning opportunity takes care of most of this by avoiding the immediate power struggle that would take place in front of the student's peers. Exactly what we say and how we say it is important in this endeavor.

2. *Keep teaching.* This allows you to deny the student the work avoidance they are perhaps seeking (and perhaps trying to provide for their friends).

3. *Stop the behavior.* Traditional discipline tells teachers to attempt to overpower students with immediate punishments to stop their negative behavior. This will not work with difficult and brave students who are aware of their strategic advantage in the moment (see above). However, once students see a pattern in the teacher's behavior, and know that a DLO is always inevitable, and if the DLO process is correctly followed, the mere delaying of the learning opportunity will stop the behavior.

Creating Your Own DLO Delaying Script

You will be delaying learning opportunities over and over throughout the rest of your career. The words that you use to do this should be ones that you are comfortable with, and they should be exactly the same every time: a predetermined script. Once memorized, the script will be one less thing to think about, making your life easier. In addition, using the exact same words every time will give you and your students a feeling of consistency that can maintain and even decrease arousal levels.

There are three parts to a DLO Delaying Script:

1. Calm Signal
2. Expression of regret
3. Notification of the DLO

You will choose each part, and then put them all together to create your own personal script that is perfect for you.

While you will be choosing the words for each element, you must not deviate from the order above. The Calm Signal needs to do its magic of changing the student's brain chemistry, and then you will double down on the calm sadness by expressing regret. Only then will you notify the student that a DLO will be coming sometime in the future.

Part 1: Calm Signal

Of course, you have already decided upon your personal Calm Signal. For review, here are some choices:

Oh, man.	*Huh.*
Oh, boy.	*Oh.*
Yikes.	*Whoa.*
Yeesh.	*Blerg.*
Ugh.	*(The sound of a slow exhale)*

To begin to create your DLO Delaying Script, first write your Calm Signal down on a piece of paper.

Part 2: Expression of Regret

Now you can choose an expression of regret. The purpose of the expression of regret is to double down on the sadness expressed in the Calm Signal and to communicate that you are not upset or angry with the student. This shows the student that you are on the same team and that together, you and the student will be working to defeat the behavior itself. Here are some suggestions:

This is a tough one.
This is rough.
This is less than ideal.
This is a difficult situation.
This is unfortunate.

Once you choose one, write it after your Calm Signal.

Part 3: Notification of the DLO

Once you have a Calm Signal and an expression of regret, you are ready to add the notification of the DLO. This is simply informing the student that they will be learning about their behavior through a DLO at some point in the future. Choose one of the following and complete your script by writing it next to your expression of regret:

> I'm going to help you learn about this later.
>
> You can learn about this sometime in the future.
>
> You can do some learning later.

Now you have a completed personalized DLO Delaying Script with a Calm Signal, expression of regret, and notification of the DLO. It should look similar to these:

> Oh, man. This is a difficult situation. You can do some learning later.
>
> Yeesh. This is rough. I'm going to help you learn about this later.
>
> (Sound of a slow exhale.) This is a tough one. You can learn about this sometime in the future.

Delivering Your DLO Delaying Script

Once you have decided that a DLO is necessary for a student to learn about a behavior, it may help you to think of your Calm Signal as something separate. Perhaps by now you have trained yourself to use the Calm Signal even when frustrated. Once you say your Calm Signal, you should be safe from getting angry. Remember to inhale, and then say your Calm Signal on the exhale. If you are far away from the student, feel free to use the Calm Signal as soon as you see the behavior that makes you think that the student will need a DLO. This one is for you; this Calm Signal is used so you don't swear. It's used so you don't say or do something you'll regret. At this point, any calming effect that it has on the student is of secondary importance.

Now you should slowly walk toward the culprit. Avoid squaring your shoulders to the student. Look sad. You can keep your palms up with your hands open. This is your nonthreatening stance. Whenever possible, quietly whisper your script into the student's ear, then walk away.

In certain situations, it may be difficult or impossible to move next to a student and whisper in a way that doesn't draw more attention to the situation (for instance, during a read-aloud with young students). In these situations, you can say the script while fixing your gaze on the middle distance, never looking directly at any student.

This offers the added benefit of stopping other behaviors that you did not even notice and allowing the student in question to save face. At all costs, avoid bringing attention to the student who needs a DLO.

Meet any attempts at argument with your Calm Signal and nothing else. This includes any attempts by the student to find out what the DLO will entail. If you would like, you can answer these questions with a simple "I don't know yet."

And then, *keep teaching*.

Do not make any reference to the negative behavior or the upcoming DLO. It's over. Move on. Any more attention than what is described here reinforces the negative behavior, takes time that you don't have, and tells your students that behavior is more important than learning.

Differentiating for Extremely Explosive Students

Your explosive students are almost always students who have often gotten what they wanted with explosive, belligerent behavior. Some may have a biological or pathological propensity toward being explosive. Even though you will minimize the potential for explosions by using this process as instructed, and maximize the chances that the mere use of your DLO Delaying Script will stop the behavior once students know that the DLO is inevitable, some students will try the same belligerent behaviors. This means that being trained not to use these behaviors is even more important. For the most explosive students, some differentiation may be necessary.

When a particularly difficult student needs a DLO, take a long, slow inhale. Next, the use of an extra and immediate Calm Signal is mandatory when working with extremely difficult students. Once you've used the inhale and Calm Signal, move away from the student. Attend to something else. Help another student. Keep teaching. Then, very, very, slowly, walk toward the student. Inhale deeply. Reapply your whispered Calm Signal with sadness and empathy in your voice. Whisper the rest of your script. Follow the rest of the suggested protocols, including walking away and moving on.

Differentiating for the *Most* Explosive Students

For the most belligerent and out-of-control students, there are two additional strategies to implement. After the first use of your Calm Signal and before the second, whisper the following while smiling broadly or while looking calm, sad, or even silly:

Psst. [*Student name/nickname here.*] Look at my face. Do I look mad?

Be ready for the student to say yes. If so, use your Calm Signal and respond, "I'm not." A silly look can be helpful. Then, whether or not the student becomes explosive, use your Calm Signal and walk away. That's it. Do not use the rest of your script. You will still give a DLO later.

Remember that the DLO procedure is to be done in the context of the previously described highly preventive procedures and strategies. In addition, GGIs will be used to guide students away from needing most DLOs and create a classroom without the yelling and bossing around of students. Furthermore, if you follow this part of the DLO procedure, you will be minimizing the amount of explosive behaviors from students. If you are concerned that you may forget that you have delayed a DLO, write it down. You may even want to have a clipboard that you can use to jot down notes about DLOs.

Finally, once all students understand that the application of the DLO is inevitable, just the continued use of the DLO Delaying Script will stop negative behaviors. This will become even more true once students comprehend that continuing to use negative behaviors after the DLO Delaying Script will intensify the DLO, since the student is communicating to the teacher that the student needs to learn more. The importance of these lessons cannot be understated for a teacher trying to manage behaviors while teaching. Eventually, the students will be so well-conditioned that the mere use of the Calm Signal will stop the negative behaviors, even from the most (now formerly) belligerent students. How quickly this happens will depend on how well you follow these instructions.

The difference between having a chance to live a happy, productive life and not getting cooperation from students through any means at all is the difference between life and death for teachers and their students. For teachers, the inability to act with certainty will create cortisol secretion that will age you, kill brain cells, and may lead to premature death. For students, learning to use positive, prosocial behaviors is the difference between living a happy, productive life or facing a lifetime of being beaten down by a world that does not take kindly to the repeated use of antisocial behaviors.

The only effective way for learning to take place is for teacher and student to be able to teach and learn in a calm environment.

What If They Just Go Berserk?

By using the procedures and strategies in this book, you are doing everything you can do to build relationships and share control to effectively prevent explosive behaviors from students. In addition, using the DLO process and differentiating for the most explosive students will further reduce the instances whereby students will use totally out-of-control and belligerent behavior.

While traditional discipline yields far more of these types of outbursts, they may still happen even if you use every single procedure and strategy in this book perfectly. After all, a student may have been beaten or neglected or assaulted immediately before school. In some of these cases, an outburst may be completely inevitable and, of course, not the student's fault. It is also possible that belligerent behavior has "gotten that student out of trouble" in the past, reinforcing its use.

In these cases, offer students a chance to compose themselves in a Mindfulness Center. If that fails to resolve the problem, remember the importance of keeping your students safe. Once you have given the DLO Delaying Script, you have successfully initiated the process. Do not proceed with any more of the process until later, when everyone is calm. If the student becomes belligerent, you can send them to a Mindfulness Center, use the Coach's Gambit, or create a Reverse Mindfulness Break.

If these interventions fail to keep you and your students safe, you can rely on emergency procedures that have already been established by your school to respond to emergencies. When students pose an immediate physical danger to themselves or others, restraint by a trained staff member may be appropriate and necessary. If students run out of the room, someone from outside your classroom must be dispatched to provide nonresponsive monitoring (NRM), in which they completely ignore the student while staying physically present to keep them safe.

While these tactics in keeping students safe may be necessary, *they are not DLOs!* They are merely the necessary means of keeping students safe. When another person has to be dispatched to restrain, follow, ignore, or use nonresponsive monitoring on your student, this should trigger, at a time in the future, *massive, overwhelming* DLOs (see below). Behaviors that cause other people besides the classroom teacher to have to deal with behaviors must be crushed as quickly as possible, because a school is not structured to have other adults having to "put out fires" for teachers. This simply cannot happen, or the school will descend into chaos.

Again for clarity and emphasis: behaviors that require adults from outside the classroom to react in order to keep students safe must be crushed through *massive, overwhelming* DLOs.

Three Kinds of Learning Opportunities

There are only three kinds of learning opportunities for humans in this Universe:

1. Natural Learning Opportunities (NLOs)

2. Problem-Solving DLOs

3. Practice DLOs

Fortunately for you, only two of them, Problem-Solving and Practice DLOs, are under your control. Before these two kinds of DLOs are described and taught in depth, though, it is necessary to learn how to best interact with NLOs.

Natural Learning Opportunities

NLOs are not taught by humans. NLOs are taught by the Universe or God, depending upon your religious orientation. Let's use the Universe for our purposes in this book.

The Universe is set up to deliver Natural Learning Opportunities to humans when they step out of the bounds of what is naturally good for them to do:

- A human grabs a snake. The snake bites the human, causing pain or death.
- A human runs into a lake without being able to swim. The human drowns.
- A human runs into the woods at night to explore with no weapons or tools. The human is eaten by a bear.

The Universe has organized itself to teach humans lessons. One of two things will happen: humans learn the lesson and change their behavior to make choices that will allow them to survive and have a chance to thrive, or they never learn the lesson, they die, and the genes that may have led them to making such bad choices die out, leading to humans as a species being more able to make good choices that will allow them to survive and thrive. The fact that all of the examples above could have happened today or 10,000 years ago illustrates how they are all Natural Learning Opportunities inherent to being human.

There are also Natural Learning Opportunities in schools:

- A 2nd grade student eats too many cupcakes at a birthday celebration. The student throws up.
- A middle school basketball player forgets her basketball shoes at home and cannot participate in basketball practice.
- A 5th grade student does not study for a test and gets a failing grade.
- A high school freshman runs in the hallway, fails to notice a door opening in front of him, runs into the door, and hits his head on the floor.

In every one of these examples, the Universe has already given the students the opportunity to learn from their mistakes. NLOs are gifts to teachers, because the lesson has already been taught for them. Teachers should pray for nonlethal, non-permanently damaging NLOs to befall their students. Allow the Universe to be your coteacher: allow it to educate when it can. When NLOs befall students, your responsibility as the teacher is to not destroy the lesson already taught by the Universe. There are, however, three things you must do in this case.

1. *Use your Calm Signal and empathize.* Use your Calm Signal immediately; this will help you to avoid doing hurtful actions of #2. Feel free to empathize in any way that does not contradict #3. Make sure the student who fell in the hallway is not injured and, if necessary, refer him to the nurse. For the student with the failing grade, whisper, "Let me know if you need help," as you hand back the quiz with the F. Give the student who just threw up five cupcakes a pat on the back when she returns from the bathroom.

2. *Refrain from using anger and lectures to say, "I told you so."* Students who have just been taught a lesson by the Universe may not be in a thinking state. One of the best parts of an NLO is that the student has no one to blame but themselves. Many students will be looking for someone besides themselves to be mad at. *Don't volunteer yourself for this job by attempting to reteach the lesson that was just taught by the Universe.* The Universe is a better teacher than you. The lesson is done. Stay out of it. Don't yell at the injured student about what he already learned about running in the hallway. Don't lecture the student who got the failing grade about working hard. Don't lecture a basketball player about how she can't participate in basketball practice without shoes, as the player is already not participating. Students will actively unlearn a lesson taught by the Universe just to spite the teacher who lectured them immediately after their lesson provided by the Universe.

3. *Don't save your students from the lesson.* Unless you are preventing death or serious injury, never save a student from an NLO. You should never allow a parent to bring the shoes or the missing permission form. You should never give an extra chance to earn a passing grade. Doing this breeds irresponsibility and the unrealistic expectation that someone will always be there to shield students from the Universe and its lessons. Saving students from their own actions hurts them in the long run.

Allow the Universe to be your coteacher. Allow the Universe to teach life lessons. There are only two remaining lessons that you will have to teach and only two kinds of DLOs that you will use to teach them.

The Creation and Implementation of DLOs

Unfortunately, Natural Learning Opportunities and Procedural Learning Opportunities will not present themselves every time students use a serious negative behavior. When they don't, it is time to create a Delayed Learning Opportunity and deliver it when it is convenient for you. Remember, teachers own "later." Later is when you are in the driver's seat. Once you have avoided trying to implement a learning opportunity immediately, you have the freedom to choose when and how to administer it.

This section is split into two parts: how to create DLOs and exactly how to implement them with students. While you are learning how to create DLOs, you will probably develop some burning questions about exactly how to implement them; these questions will be answered during the implementation part.

Two Lessons, Two DLOs

There are only two lessons that students need to learn about using positive behaviors:

1.   To solve problems that are caused by their negative behaviors
2.   To become proficient at using positive behaviors

The DLOs used to teach these lessons, accordingly, are called Problem-Solving DLOs and Practice DLOs.

Both lessons involve requiring students to strive to become people who do not cause problems for others and who solve the problems that they do cause. When DLOs are executed correctly, students will learn that these lessons are *inevitable*. Students know that their nonacademic lives will stop or be severely limited until they have solved all problems caused and achieved mastery of all the behaviors with which they have previously struggled. Reminder: This section covers how to create and give DLOs. The next section will show exactly how and when to implement the DLOs, keeping in mind every possible eventuality—including student refusal.

When students cause a problem for another person in the school (not themselves), they are required to solve that problem. Put another way, they have a *responsibility* to solve the problem.

Look at the word "responsibility" for a moment. The two words that are at the root of the word "responsibility" are "response" and "ability": the true definition of the word "responsibility" is to have the *ability* to control one's own *response* to stimuli.

The world is full of constant stimuli. The world is stimuli. The goal of this book is to train students to be *able* to control their *responses* to the world so that they are *able* to *respond* in ways that make the world better instead of worse.

The word "discipline," after all, means "to become one's own disciple": to lead one's self. The effective definition of the word "discipline" can be construed as "to be able to control one's own responses to stimuli so that those responses do not cause problems for others." Therefore, responsibility is not *part of* discipline—it is discipline. To be responsible is to be disciplined.

Students must have the *ability* to *respond* to the world in ways that don't cause problems. If they are unable to do this, it is the job of the educator to train them to do so. Thus far, this manual has shown how to prevent negative behaviors and how to gently mitigate the use of slightly negative behaviors through the use of GGIs. The Procedural Learning Opportunities within the procedures will do much of this training and will become part of the daily fabric of your classroom. You have also learned how to not destroy the lessons of the Universe and its Natural Learning Opportunities. These PLOs and NLOs create a healthy terminal destination for negative behaviors, in that the negative behaviors do not get the student what they want. The final piece of the puzzle to address negative behaviors that cannot be dealt with through any of these means is through Delayed Learning Opportunities.

Problem-Solving DLOs

There are two kinds of Problem-Solving DLOs: Situational and Destressing. Situational Problem-Solving DLOs are used when students cause problems for other people and there is a realistic way that the student can solve the problem by taking action. These are DLOs that seem more or less obvious to most. It is likely that experienced teachers will have already used many of these, though without proper instruction, most teachers use them ineffectively. Remember that these should never happen immediately after the negative behavior: They are *Delayed* Learning Opportunities. You must "get to later" the proper way before giving the DLO. Some examples follow:

- DLO-*worthy behavior*: A 2nd grade student has a temper tantrum in art class and knocks over her table's art supplies.

  Problem-Solving DLO: The student must pick up the art supplies that she knocked over.

- DLO-*worthy behavior*: A high school junior threatens to beat up a classmate.

Problem-Solving DLO: The student must create a comprehensive, written plan for how he is going to make that student feel safe while on school property, including, if applicable, the bus. The student is held back from being in close proximity of the threatened student until this plan is completed. He will be excluded from all situations where the two students would be able to cross paths. This could include proximity in a classroom, changing classes, lunch, recess (for younger students), the bus, or participation in activities or sports where the students may be near each other. The threatening student should be fully restricted from these situations until the plan is completed.

The plan could involve self-imposed rules for avoiding the student while in the same room or area, such as staying at a lunch table away from the threatened student, being restricted to a certain bus seat, or taking a certain route between classes. There might be an agreement that threatening the student while at, for example, basketball practice, would result in a five-game suspension. The threatener should not be forced to write an apology into the plan, though this can be included.

Once the plan is completed, the threatener should present it to the threat-enee by reading it to them. If the threatenee says that the plan makes them feel safe, the threatener may come back into the mainstream of the school under the conditions of the plan. If not, the threatenee can request through a conversation, moderated by you, that certain requirements be added or taken away. If all parties (threatener, threatenee, and teacher) agree to the appropriateness of terms, the threatener may return to the mainstream of the school. If the threatener does anything even mildly threatening to the threatened student, he should be immediately isolated, just as he was before.

At a time that is appropriate and convenient, the threatenee and the teacher can meet and revisit the terms of the plan. The threatenee can be asked if any of the terms of the plan can be relaxed or eliminated. The teacher can notify the threatener of any changes to the plan.

- *DLO-worthy behavior*: A 5th grade student destroys school property.

    Problem-Solving DLO: Destroyer and teacher do research together regarding the cost of destroyed property. The price should be the current cost for replacing whatever was destroyed.

    Destroyer should be introduced to the concept of minimum wage and can even do research on what minimum wage is in their state. The student could do work for the school until the destroyed item has been paid off. Duties can be anything that can be safely done that benefits the school. Custodial duties, often monitored by a school custodian, are appropriate in this case.

This can also be done when a student destroys the property of another student. These jobs can be even more targeted: carrying books for a student or cleaning out lockers or desks for a student during recess could be part of the DLO.

- DLO-*worthy behavior*: An 8th grade student has a tantrum and destroys a classroom. She refuses to clean up the mess, and since class must go on immediately, the teacher and other students are forced to clean the room so that class can continue.

  Problem-Solving DLO: Tantrumer must come back during noninstructional time and be in charge of cleaning the classroom for a certain number of days. Students and teachers, during this time, are allowed to *not* clean and tidy up their areas, as they know that the tantrumer will be tending to it.

You will be able to create many other Situational Problem-Solving DLOs. As you do so, use these four as a guide and remember that pain is not the point. Though the DLO may incidentally cause suffering by being boring/monotonous/annoying, the learning is the point.

Destressing Problem-Solving DLOs

While untrained teachers often have no trouble coming up with Problem-Solving Situational DLOs, they are usually at a loss when a student uses a DLO-worthy negative behavior but there doesn't seem to be an authentic Situational Problem-Solving DLO that logically corresponds with the behavior in question. For example, there is an obvious Situational Problem-Solving DLO when a student makes a mess during a tantrum (they have to clean up the mess they made). But what if a student constantly interrupts you? What if a student is whining habitually in such a way that it makes you want to choose another profession? What if they are always invading the personal space of other students? In every one of those cases, the problem that the student is causing is that they are *totally stressing people out!*

Make no mistake, this is a major problem. You cannot teach when you are stressed out, which means that your students cannot learn. They also can't learn if they are stressed out. Therefore, students cannot be allowed to stress out people at school. These behaviors need DLOs. But what does that look like?

The simple answer is that the student in question will solve the problem of stressing people out by taking away their stress or "destressing" them. All Problem-Solving

DLOs that are not Situational are Destressing. While each Situational Problem-Solving DLO has its own unique characteristics, all Destressing Problem-Solving DLOs have the same description: the student is required to do things for the person or people whose lives were made more stressful because of their behavior. What that student does for the stressed-out person or people will depend on what would best improve the lives of the stressed-out party.

- *DLO-worthy behavior:* A student constantly interrupts the teacher.

  Destressing Problem-Solving DLO: The student is required to enter data and grade papers for the teacher, thus lowering the teacher's stress level back to normal after it was raised by the behavior of the student.

- *DLO-worthy behavior:* A student whines habitually at the PE teacher.

  Destressing Problem-Solving DLO: The PE teacher requires the student to deep-clean the equipment closet (because cleaning the closet is stressful).

While the person who most often needs to be destressed is the teacher, students are also often stressed out by repeated or major negative behaviors. For example:

- *DLO-worthy behavior:* A student habitually does not respect the personal space of another student.

  Destressing Problem-Solving DLO: The close-talking student cleans the other student's desk, turns in their work for them, and delivers work materials to them.

When you have both Situational Problem-Solving DLOs and Destressing Problem-Solving DLOs at your disposal, *any* behavior can be given a DLO to allow students to learn that they must solve the problems that they cause.

Practice DLOs

The concept behind this final type of DLO is as simple as it is logical: if students are not experts at using particular positive behaviors, they will be required to practice using these positive behaviors until they *are* experts. This can be a great equalizer for students who have not used many positive behaviors at home throughout their lives when compared to their peers who have been trained at home to only use positive behaviors. This DLO gives these students the opportunity to catch up to their peers in terms of positive conduct.

Just like the Destressing Problem-Solving DLOs, the Practice DLOs can be used for *any* behavior, because if a student needs a DLO, it means that they are presently struggling to use a positive behavior, so they need to practice that behavior. To illustrate this, let's look at every DLO-worthy behavior mentioned in this chapter in terms of a corresponding Practice DLO.

Reminders: These learning opportunities are delayed to a noninstructional time of day. All logistics and details of how to deliver these DLOs will be described later in this chapter.

- *DLO-worthy behavior:* A 2nd grade student has a temper tantrum in art class and knocks over her table's art supplies.

  Practice DLO: The student is required to sit next to neatly arranged art materials for 45 minutes without knocking them to the floor.

- *DLO-worthy behavior:* A high school junior threatens to beat up a classmate.

  Practice DLO: The student is required to sit next to a teacher, pretending that he is the threatenee, while he practices not threatening the threatenee.

- *DLO-worthy behavior:* A 5th grade student destroys school property.

  Practice DLO: The student is required to sit next to said school property and not destroy it.

- *DLO-worthy behavior:* An 8th grade student has a tantrum and destroys a classroom. She refuses to clean up the mess, and since class must go on immediately, the teacher and other students are forced to clean the room so that class can continue.

  Practice DLO: The student practices doing things that the teacher asks her to do: clean paintbrushes, wash tables, stack chairs, and so on.

- *DLO-worthy behavior:* A student constantly interrupts the teacher.

  Practice DLO: The student sits and practices not interrupting the teacher.

- *DLO-worthy behavior:* A student whines habitually.

  Practice DLO: The student practices not whining. This can be done by simply sitting at a desk and doing anything besides not whining, or practicing having a conversation with the teacher without whining.

- *DLO-worthy behavior:* A student habitually invades the personal space of other students.

Practice DLO: The student is required to stay out of the personal space of the teacher, while pretending that the teacher is the student who has been habitually physically crowded by the student who is practicing.*

Remember, the Practice DLO is a DLO, not a punishment. Students can read books or do activities while practicing. They can enjoy themselves. Pain is not the point. Learning is the point! Students can learn and enjoy themselves at the same time. *Any* behaviors that students struggle with can be practiced until students attain proficiency.

DLOs for Failure to Use Mindfulness Centers Correctly

As the alternative to highly destructive tactics that contribute to the school-to-prison pipeline, it is essential that students are able to effectively use Mindfulness Centers. Without them, schools will revert to the catastrophic countermeasures detailed earlier. Therefore, students' behaviors cannot be allowed to interfere with the effective, efficient, and faithful use of Mindfulness Breaks. Common negative behaviors that occur related to the use of Mindfulness Breaks include students refusing to go to a Mindfulness Center and talking or being disruptive while in the center. Now that you have learned about the two kinds of DLOs, simple DLOs that would be appropriate for these behaviors may be obvious to you. Just in case they are not, the following are the possible Problem-Solving and Practice DLOs for students using negative behaviors instead of properly utilizing Mindfulness Breaks.

Problem-Solving DLO

Simply use a Destressing Problem-Solving DLO for any and all DLO-worthy negative behaviors that are related to Mindfulness Breaks.

Practice DLOs

Students who cause problems while in a Mindfulness Center should get extensive practice sitting, standing, or doing mindfulness activities nearby a Mindfulness Center. The student should not be made to sit or do yoga, or med-

---

* Note that when one student needs to practice a behavior that caused a problem for an innocent student, the innocent student should never be called upon to be the "dummy" to be practiced on. Instead, the teacher can stand in, getting work done while ignoring the practicing student. For younger students, a large stuffed animal or cardboard cutout can be a stand-in for a wronged student. When two students need to practice a behavior around each other, both students can practice not causing a problem for the other by being in close proximity successfully.

itate (forced mindfulness misses the point!). They should be, as always, given the choice to use the center in any way that does not cause a problem.

Students who refuse to go to a Mindfulness Center should practice going to a center over and over again. After that, they should practice sitting at the Mindfulness Center for an extensive period of time. Similarly, students who attempt to talk to or bother students in the Mindfulness Center should practice not bothering others in the center.

The amount of time and/or effort required for these DLOs should be substantial, because taking away from the effectiveness of Mindfulness Breaks can create a catastrophic environment and chaos.

Delivering DLOs

Here is where the rubber meets the road!

You should have a tremendous number of questions about DLOs. Thus far you have only seen instructions on how to delay learning opportunities and what the learning opportunities should be. Exactly *how* to deliver these DLOs and make it inevitable that your students learn these essential lessons will be the focus of the remainder of this chapter. We will go into detail about how long to delay the learning opportunity, how to decide upon the amount of practice or problem solving needed, how to give the DLO, how to handle student attempts at argument, how to give away healthy control while giving DLOs, how to monitor and scaffold while present for DLOs, when and how to schedule the DLO session, and how to create and use inevitability logistics for when students experiment with refusing to take part in a DLO.

The central goal in the delivery of DLOs is that you are able to create a feeling of inevitability within your students. They need to understand that from the moment you utter your Calm Signal and DLO Delaying Script, the fact that they will be experiencing a DLO sometime in the future is 100 percent inevitable.

How Long Should I Delay Learning Opportunities?

There are three considerations when determining how long to delay the DLO. They are listed here in order of importance:

1. *Developmental appropriateness.* It is best to deliver the DLO while the student is able to remember their DLO-worthy behavior (keep in mind that the vast majority of the time that students say they forgot it, they are merely attempting to get out of the DLO). To decide whether it is likely that a student has forgotten the DLO-worthy behavior, use the ice cream test: if you think the

students would remember you saying you would get them ice cream ___ days ago, they can remember their past behavior for at least that long. And if students do forget, you can remind them!

Still, it is optimal for students to be able to recall the behavior. The following statements are given with the understanding that the age of students is in reference to regular education students. Special education teachers know best what is appropriate for their students. These are also very generalized guidelines.

Students above 1st grade can have DLOs delayed for several days; students in middle and high school can have DLOs delayed for weeks. Kindergarten and 1st grade students should usually have DLOs delivered within 48 hours of the behavior. It can be slightly longer for more advanced students or for students near the end of 1st grade. PreK students should usually not have DLOs delayed for more than 24 hours—in other words, not longer than when the behavior happened the previous day. Remember that a learning opportunity delayed for five minutes (perhaps just long enough to transition from painting to discovery play) is still a *Delayed* Learning Opportunity.

2. *Honeymoon period generation.* As a principal, I once delayed a middle school student's DLO for two weeks just because his teachers reported that this exceedingly difficult student had been perfect since I had informed him of the DLO. Often the mere introduction of the DLO will stop not only the triggering behavior but also other negative behaviors, as the student is concerned with what the DLO might entail. The delay can cause a "honeymoon period" that you should not be in a hurry to end.

3. *Whether inevitability has been achieved.* Students who have come from classrooms taught by teachers who have not read this book, either the previous year or during the same year after transferring schools, will likely not understand that it is inevitable that the terminal destination for their repeated or serious negative behaviors will be a DLO. When this is the case, it may be a good idea to not wait too long to give the DLO. Before the DLO delivery, the student may have the mistaken impression that you won't actually give a DLO when you say you will. In this case, it's a good idea to make the DLO a priority. However, don't give it so soon that the student (and you) are still not in a thinking state.

If you are at a school where teachers have all read this manual, DLO inevitability will already be programmed into students. While students may test you at the beginning of the year, the only students who don't understand the inevitability of DLOs will be transfer students.

If you get students each fall from teachers who have not read this book, you are likely to get an entire roster full of students who don't comprehend DLO inevitability. This will cause a bit of stress in that, no matter what grade level you teach, you usually will not want to delay for more than 48 hours for the first several weeks, until your students develop this understanding.

How Do I Decide upon the Amount of Practice or Problem Solving?

There are three issues to consider when deciding upon how much problem solving or practice needs to occur for a DLO:

1. *Developmental appropriateness.* Use your best professional judgment of what constitutes developmentally appropriate problem-solving or practice tasks, but err on the side of the tasks being too challenging. We live in a culture that believes children are weak and incapable. Make the DLOs challenging from the start.

2. *Number of learning failures.* When a student keeps using the same behavior over and over, even after a DLO or multiple DLOs, it does not mean that the DLOs "aren't working." It just means that the student has, thus far, failed to learn the proficient use of the behavior. Each time you give another DLO, turn the knob up on the amount of practice or the amount of problem solving, rather than changing tactics.

3. *Whether the DLO-worthy behavior is a "hot button" for you.* Again, put yourself first. If there are certain behaviors that cause you to lose patience particularly quickly (it's smirking and whining for me), you need to train students to not use those behaviors, and you need to do this quickly. Simply use bigger DLOs for these types of behaviors than you do for your non-hot-button behaviors.

When Do I Schedule the Delivery of a DLO?

The possible times to deliver a DLO are as follows:

- Before school
- Lunch
- Recess
- After school
- On a weekend

- As a behavioral "Now" activity (see Chapter 8 and the Real-World Workshop procedure)

Notice that these are all noninstructional times. Your school rules, your schedule, or your own personal value structure or priorities may prevent you from using all of these options, but you must use some of them if you are going to be able to successfully train students to use positive behaviors. Choose the times that work best for you. A student can, and often will, do DLOs over multiple time periods. If recess is all that is available, it may take 10 recesses to solve a problem or practice a behavior, especially if a student refuses to learn during the first DLO implementation.

Keep in mind that the more outlandish these times appear to be, the more effective they are. For years, I planned on coming into work for one Saturday in August and one Saturday in early September for about three hours each day to deliver DLOs. Even though I donated just six hours for the year, my students "knew" that I lived at school and that I was perfectly happy to spend all my free time helping students solve problems and practice positive behaviors. Similarly, DLO delivery after and before school can let students know that no matter how long it takes for them to solve problems and practice positive behaviors, you will be there to help them do so.

After-school activities may be missed in order to take part in a DLO. This supercharges the lesson that when you use negative behaviors, your life gets worse. Just remember that the pain in this scenario must be incidental, not the point. If it is the point, then it is a punishment, not a DLO. Never couch a DLO in terms of "You backtalked me, and now you're not going to football practice! Hah!" That's a punishment, not a DLO. If the student happens to miss football practice, just let the pain of that reality do the teaching, instead of piling on and pouring lemon juice on the wound.

How Do I Deliver a DLO?

Once you have thought through your DLO, including making sure it follows DLO guidelines (no punishing), chosen a noninstructional time to deliver it, and worked out all of the logistical issues, you can deliver your DLO. During DLO delivery, act as a friendly person who is going to teach something, not an angry dungeon master who is there to inflict pain. Act exactly as you would if you were having a student come in to learn about algebra, division, or keyboarding. Concentrate on being nice.

For now, let's assume that all students will be cooperative (many will not; see below for how to use proper inevitability logistics for students who, at first, refuse to learn lessons). Whether you are picking up a student or they are coming to your room, greet them as though you are going to teach them a lesson (because you are). You can engage in small talk, especially if you are picking them up from another room and have some time to interact before you arrive at the location for the DLO, optimally a place free from the presence of the student's peers or unfamiliar adults.

Sitting down in an assertive position will show the student that you are relaxed and in charge of the situation. It will also tell your brain the same thing. To sit in an assertive position, sit in a chair with your legs extended out in front of you, heels down, toes up. Lean back in the chair. Put your hands behind your head, elbows out, with your fingers interwoven behind your head.

Once you are situated, use your Calm Signal to make sure you are emotionally regulated and to increase the odds that the student is emotionally regulated. Draw the Calm Signal out: start with a very deep inhale and then say the Calm Signal especially slowly as you exhale. It may help to rub your eyes or face or stretch out your arms toward the ceiling the way you might when you wake up in the morning.

You are ready to speak.

For a Practice DLO, you may say something to the effect of the following:

> Hey. You are really struggling with not running out of the room when you get frustrated. I'm not mad at you. It's just important that everyone in the classroom become an expert at staying in the room. Since you presently struggle with this, I'm going to give you the chance to become an expert at staying in the room. I am going to simply have you sit, stand, or lie down somewhere in the room and practice not leaving. You can read or do work, or just stare at the wall and think your thoughts. Whatever you want to do that doesn't cause a problem is fine, just as long as you are in the room.

For a Problem-Solving DLO, you may say something like this:

> All righty, dude. I gotta tell you, you really caused a problem for me last week when you kept interrupting me during algebra class. I'm not angry about it, and I know you get excited to answer questions. While I love that you get excited, it just stresses me out when I can't teach. I have been so stressed out that I have not had it in me to put together the class homework folders for next week. I'm going to ask you to do it in order to destress me.

At this point, it is time to systematically give away control to the student. Do this for every consequence. For the Practice DLO above, you can give the student a choice on how long they need to practice:

> How long will it take you to become an expert at staying in the room: 20 minutes or 45 minutes?

For a Problem-Solving DLO, give a choice on how they will destress you, within the parameters that you already set up:

Feel free to either put the homework papers in the folder one at a time or stack them all up and put them all in a folder at once. Either way is fine.

If the student refuses to choose one way or the other, choose for them. Feel free to give as many choices as you would like; the more, the better. Optimally, it's best to include at least one choice.

If you have time and are in the mood, you can give the student the opportunity to solve a problem in a way that they wish to solve it, or they can decide exactly what behaviors they need to practice and for how long. The more healthy control you give away, the better. Even when allowing for this higher level of control, make sure that you have your own DLO ready to go if, at any point, you feel that the student is beginning to bargain or the discussion is simply taking too much time.

How Do I Avoid Arguing with a Student When I Am Giving a DLO?

A student can't get you to argue with them without your consent. The minimum amount of people it takes to argue is two; just don't be one of those two people. If a student attempts to argue with you in the middle of your instructions, ignore this attempt and "steamroll" through it as you keep delivering the DLO. If the student continues to try to argue, use your Argument Shield (see pages 45–47). If the attempts at argument become a real problem, say your DLO Delaying script and then ignore the student. Students who have achieved the understanding of inevitability will stop the argument attempts. If they have not, keep in mind that the forthcoming DLO will involve more and more practice or problem solving the more they attempt to argue.

How Do I Monitor, Scaffold, and Reinforce Positive Behaviors During the Completion of the DLO?

Your first priority when overseeing completion of a DLO is to take care of yourself. If you are working hard to monitor or scaffold a DLO, you are doing it wrong. Monitor while ignoring the student as much as is appropriate (see below). Get work done or eat your lunch or stare off into space—whatever you want to do. Scaffold by using any GGIs that are appropriate, preferably without looking up from what you are doing. As is always true with scaffolding, give as little help (preferably none) as is necessary for the student to be able to be successful in completing the task.

If a student is able to complete a DLO but, in your professional opinion, is choosing not to, allow that student to suffer by having their noninstructional life placed on pause, perhaps for a very long period of time. This is time well spent for the student. They may be learning that any number of negative behaviors don't work with their teacher. Behaviors like whining, playing dumb, or working slowly all will be revealed to be nonfunctional for the student.

The simplicity of tasks involved with Practice and Problem-Solving DLOs makes both monitoring and scaffolding easier. Situational Problem-Solving DLOs may be slightly more involved. A 6th grade student making a plan for another student to feel safe may take more involved scaffolding, but again, always err on the side of students suffering through work that is difficult instead of offering more support than is needed. Prioritize your work ahead of that being done by the student.

If you feel that a student is causing serious problems for you and your stress level, rub your eyes. Perhaps groan about how you are getting stressed out and say your DLO Delaying Script. Then ignore the student. Let the student suffer. In this case, the student is imposing the suffering upon themselves by using negative behaviors. If you stay sad and empathetic enough, the student may be able to connect their use of negative behaviors with their own suffering and realize it is inevitable that continued negative behaviors will not get them what they want. The DLO will occur later.

One highly effective way to scaffold for a Practice DLO is to treat the DLO like a video game, using difficulty levels. This can be especially effective for students who you feel are not yet skilled enough to practice without more intensive scaffolding. For the 1st grade student who has trouble not running out of the room, for instance, you can add onto the script above by saying the following:

> Right now, you are struggling so much that I'm not yet sure if you could stay in the room without some help. This is going to be like a video game. We will begin on "easy," where I will sit and do my work while sitting in the doorway. This will help remind you to stay in the room. Since you picked 30 minutes, "easy" level will be for 10 minutes. Then you can get to "medium" level. On "medium," I will move from the doorway to be next to the doorway for another 10 minutes, and this may still remind you to stay in the room. Then will be "boss" level, when I will go and sit down at my desk and leave the door wide open. If you can stay in the room for the entire 30 minutes, you will have said to me with your actions, "I can stay in the room! I am an expert!" Then you will be all done, and you can move on with your life!

What Do I Do When the Student Is Done Practicing or Solving a Problem?

Act the same way you would if your student just mastered an academic standard. Be happy and excited. For a Problem-Solving DLO, thank them for solving the problem (or perhaps for destressing you or other students). For a Practice DLO, ask if the students are experts at their new positive behavior. In both cases, feel free to use another Strategic Noticing and give a high five, handshake, hug, or class handshake, whatever is appropriate for you. Congratulations, you have built your relationship with your students *through their negative behavior!*

What Are Inevitability Logistics?

The most common anxiety that teachers have when trying to hold students accountable through DLOs (or punishments, for that matter) is the worry that the students will refuse to take part in whatever accountability procedures the teacher creates. They will worry, for example, that a student will refuse to clean up a mess that they created, or practice a behavior, or destress a teacher's aide. What then?

The irony is that, when handled correctly using the methods detailed below, student refusal of DLOs will be the means through which students will learn the most important lesson of their entire lives: *the refusal of a reasonable request from an authority figure will not absolve you from responsibility for your actions and will not get you what you want.*

It is virtually impossible to lead a happy, healthy, positive life without learning this lesson. A person who never learns this is not likely to be able to successfully complete elementary school, let alone high school. A person who never learns this will not be able to become and stay employed. It is common for a person who never learns this to end up in prison or suffer an early death.

Remember that by using the DLO Process within the context of all of the other procedures and strategies, we have systematically removed all obstacles that we possibly can that would stop a student's brain from being able to learn this lesson. If the manual you are holding were a book of fiction, this would be the climax. While the book's other procedures and strategies help to create a positive classroom environment, all roads lead to the inevitability of the DLOs. Either students will *be* cooperative and prosocial, or they will have to *learn* to be cooperative and prosocial. They have no choice in the matter.

DLO inevitability logistics create this essential paradigm for students. Once inevitability is achieved, students will be cooperative when they are asked to solve problems they caused or practice a positive behavior. In addition, creating inevitability will cause the student to stop their negative behavior when you use your DLO Delaying Script. What's more, if DLO inevitability is consistent, the mere use of the Calm Signal will be enough to stop the behavior.

Furthermore, once inevitability is achieved, GGIs will be significantly more effective. The power of each one will be supercharged, allowing you to control behaviors in ways that you could not previously. Inevitable DLOs act as a vaccine that works its way back up the continuum of the procedures and strategies in this manual, making them all more effective. Eventually, students can concentrate on learning while feeling safe and happy at school.

Unfortunately, not establishing DLO inevitability and allowing students' DLO refusals to get them out of responsibility for their actions has the opposite effect. It acts as a cancer that spreads to everything in this manual, making it all less effective in eliciting positive behaviors from students.

How Do I Actually Create DLO Inevitability for Students?

Creating DLO inevitability first involves a teacher paradigm shift. Instead of dreading a student's refusal of a DLO, you should hope that it occurs. When a student refuses, they are saying to you that they have not yet learned that the refusal of a reasonable request from an authority figure will not absolve them from responsibility for their actions and will not get them what they want. This is the most important learning opportunity they will ever have, and you have the honor of being a part of it. This is where you can save a life; they will not be happy or successful in life without learning this lesson.

The essential understanding of DLO inevitability logistics is that, as long as you have the logistics set up correctly, every moment that a student refuses to be cooperative is *a positive learning experience for the student*. During DLO refusal, a student is constantly attempting to get out of responsibility for their actions. As long as the tool of refusal doesn't work, the student is learning that it doesn't work. When they are belligerent or even violent, they are using tools to the same end, with the same result. In this way, the worse the behavior gets, the more they are learning, and the more important the lesson becomes. The purpose of DLO inevitability logistics is to make sure that, no matter how long it takes, the student will continue to learn their most important lesson.

Now to the logistics. If a student refusing to be cooperative with a DLO is learning, nothing needs to be done because the lesson is in progress. This is the optimal scenario. The student is learning while you get work done, eat lunch, check your phone, and so on. The student is learning, and you are taking care of yourself. Ignore and monitor the student simultaneously, but there's no need for teaching or scaffolding—the student is teaching themselves.

Use Strategic Noticing if positive behaviors occur. For instance, imagine a student who is supposed to be practicing staying seated and listening, but is instead choosing to run around the room screaming. When the student takes a break to catch their breath in their seat, notice this positive, although perhaps nearly accidental, behavior: "I noticed you sitting in your seat." Then immediately state, "I am starting the clock on your practice time—30 minutes to go. I'll keep counting as long as you are silently in your seat." Do not praise the student. If the student starts running around again, ignore them. If they continue to sit silently, notice it again, exactly the same way: "I noticed you sitting in your seat." Notice every few minutes. Slightly decrease the noticing as the student gets nearer to the behavioral goal. By ignoring the negative, belligerent behaviors and noticing the positive, you will make positive behaviors more likely and negative behaviors less likely.

Remember that students who are refusing are students who are learning! I once had a student refuse to sit and be kind to me for five recesses in a row. Every other day, he experimented with sitting in his seat, which I noticed. On the sixth recess, he sat from the beginning. He practiced perfectly for 17 minutes that recess and 3 minutes the next recess. He became an official expert at sitting silently and being nice to me and maintained expert status for the rest of the year.

As long as the refusing student remains in the DLO location, the student is learning the lesson we want them to learn. This is even more true if the student is destroying property or yelling, if we deal with it properly (see below). What we want to avoid, if possible, is the student leaving the DLO location. Once the student leaves a DLO location, the mere act of not being in that location anymore reinforces the refusing behavior. If an adult gives attention to the student, that reinforcement is significantly more destructive. Put another way, the student is learning cooperation while in the DLO location.

If you are concerned that the student may leave the DLO location, you should sit in the doorway while working and using the above ignoring, monitoring, and noticing strategies (unless your school has rules that specifically prohibit this). Be nonchalant, and do not warn the student about leaving the room. Only a tiny fraction of the students who would walk out of an unobstructed door will actually push past a teacher in a doorway.

However, some will. If you have school or district rules regarding this eventuality, follow them, but none of those rules should be used to supplant further DLOs. If the student attempts to get past you, do not grab or hold them, and do not get into any type of physical altercation to stop them from leaving. If they do leave the DLO location, use your DLO Delaying Script. Further DLOs can be arranged that involve the parental notification and legal considerations being addressed that would be necessary to close doors and use safety locks to create further inevitability.

Crushing Behaviors with DLOs

If you are reading carefully, you may notice a small gap between the DLOs and the parameters put forward by most schools and districts and what they require for keeping students safe with restraint and seclusion. "What if," you may ask, "a student is belligerent and stopping all learning, and even perhaps destroying school property, but is not posing an immediate physical threat to themselves or others? What then?"

When a student uses behaviors that create this type of chaos—chaos that disrupts the entire grade level or school—the behaviors need to be crushed with DLOs. This does not mean that the *student* should be crushed; it means that the *behavior* must be crushed. Remember, DLOs are the end of the line. They are the dead end whereby even the most extreme negative behaviors must be made nonfunctional: they cannot be used by the student to get what they want. In response to these behaviors, the student's nonacademic life must be put on hold as much as possible until they have learned the lesson that belligerent defiance is an inherently nonfunctional behavior that will not get them what they want. This response might require both Problem-Solving DLOs and Practice DLOs; it might require DLOs being scheduled and staffed by a grade-level team (using such tactics is preferable to giving suspensions, which train students to think that belligerent behaviors get them vacations).

Still, all of this is done later. What about now? Now is the time to prioritize keeping students safe. There are GGIs for this, such as Mindfulness Breaks and Reverse Mindfulness Breaks, that can occur before or after you use your DLO Delaying Script as an intervention for keeping all students both calm and safe. However, even when you have done everything possible to prevent such an outburst by following the content of this manual, there is still the possibility that it may happen.

Keeping students safe is the province of the procedures and policies created by schools and districts, which may be helpful, hurtful, or both. There are ways of keeping students safe that minimize or neutralize making belligerence functional. The less inhibitive the policies are regarding restraint and seclusion (for instance, allowing belligerent students to destroy property), the more significant the DLOs will have to be to counterbalance the functionality of those belligerent behaviors.

Ideally, districts and administrations will use crisis response training to implement policies that keep students safe while minimizing the functionality of negative behaviors.

How Do I Work with Other Teachers and Staff to Share the Burden of DLOs?

Whenever possible, you should give and administer DLOs yourself. From an organizational standpoint, it is advantageous for as many DLOs as possible to be taken care of by the educator directly involved simply to cut down on the need for extra communication. From a teaching and learning perspective, it also shows students that their teacher is the ultimate authority figure in their lives at school. While it is optimal for you to implement the DLO process on your own, you should always feel comfortable getting advice on DLOs from your fellow educators. Oftentimes, one teacher ends up being the "go-to" person for the best and most effective DLOs. The delayed nature of DLOs lends itself to being able to get advice on the best Practice and Problem-Solving DLOs at a time when all is calm in the school (usually when students are not present). Many schools, grade levels, or departments have weekly meetings to talk about appropriate DLOs for students. Again, being able to delay the DLO allows for this.

While it is optimal for educators to completely handle the DLO process on their own, it can also be highly useful for educators to lean on each other when implementing the DLO process, as long as it is done correctly. The educator who implemented the DLO must always take the lead role in the DLO process. This trains all students to understand that the main authority figure in their lives at school is always the adult standing in front of them at any given time.

This means that the adult who gives the DLO Delaying Script must be the person who gives the student the instructions for their DLO. It does not mean that that educator must be with the student while they are solving problems or practicing. Schools, grade levels, teams, or departments can work together to staff noninstructional locations to schedule (perhaps daily) times that can be used for DLOs. Working together, educators can create that all-important feeling of inevitability in students: "I might as well do what is expected, because having to solve the problems that I caused or practicing doing what is expected doesn't work out as well."

Some educator teams make a schedule for noninstructional times (often before or after school or for several hours on the weekend) in which everyone on the team will take a certain period of time every week. For instance, Mr. Colvin may take every Monday afternoon from 3:00 to 4:00, Mr. Sears may take every Tuesday afternoon from 3:00 to 4:00, and so on. Some educators work with only one or two other educators in a rotating schedule to create these consistent DLO sessions.

During these times, educators can bring their students to their rooms to practice or solve problems. The educators who gave the DLO do any and all communication with home if necessary, and they are there at the beginning of all DLO sessions to give students their instructions or to create the instructions with the students. Once the student knows how they will solve the problem that they caused or knows what behavior to practice, the educator can leave the student with the teacher who is monitoring the DLO session.

If you wish to implement DLOs on the same day as the negative behavior, it is usually best to do it during lunch or recess, as these times will not require parent communication. This is fine. Make sure that, if you use a lunch period, the student always gets lunch and enough time to eat said lunch; never withhold food.

Unless you can find a way to make it convenient for you, don't put an emphasis on communicating with parents in order to facilitate doing after-school DLOs on the same day as the behavior. You usually won't have time to arrange it. Besides, implementing the DLO the next day, or even a week later, can create a honeymoon period as the student anticipates the coming consequences.

One final way that educators can coordinate with one another to help with DLOs is by batching them. You will see many of the same negative behaviors from a number of students in your school—for example, being disruptive, repeatedly talking in the hallway, or antagonizing a certain student. When these behaviors occur, it can be helpful for educators to "batch" DLOs. All of the students that antagonized a particular student can go to the same room to destress that student by cleaning and arranging their things for them. All of the hallway talkers can go to a hallway to practice being silent. All of the disruptive students can report to one room to practice sitting silently in class. These DLO sessions can occur on the same day or on successive days, and can happen during any noninstructional time.

It is important to note that when educators put effort into DLOs in the first two months of school, behaviors will become more and more manageable and will result in very few, if any, DLOs once spring rolls around. Do your DLOs in the fall when you have the energy. The goal is to use lots of DLOs early so that you eventually don't need them. Create and enforce limits early so that your students don't spend the entire year trying to figure out where the limits are!

When It Feels Like DLOs Are Not Working

If it seems as though you are repeatedly using DLOs to address the same behaviors over and over again, here is a simple checklist of questions to ask yourself to make sure you are not making some common mistakes:

1. *Am I trying to use DLOs in a vacuum?* If you are trying to use DLOs without using the rest of the procedures and strategies in this book, they won't be very effective, because there won't be enough prevention or mitigation going on. Similarly, if you are using only a few parts of the book, DLOs will tend to pile up. If this is the case, concentrate your efforts on just two or three procedures or strategies (you cannot neglect Strategic Noticing and be successful, for example).

2. *Am I remembering to delay my DLOs?* Remember that students won't be likely to learn anything and may react with explosive behavior if you attempt to institute a learning opportunity immediately after a DLO-worthy negative behavior.

3. *Am I always using my Calm Signal when I delay and when I give a DLO?* If not, the student will not be as calm as they could be, you won't be as calm as you should be, the student probably won't be able to learn anything, and you probably won't be able to teach anything.

4. *Is my DLO a logical learning opportunity that teaches, or is it a punishment that just causes pain?* If you have accidentally created a punishment, a student is likely to dig in and be endlessly resistant because they feel that they have lost what they will perceive as a power struggle.

5. *Has the student learned enough?* This is the most common mistake educators make. Usually, very difficult students will use their old negative behaviors over and over in multiple failed attempts to get what they want. That is who difficult students are: they have gotten what they wanted for a long period of time through repeated negative behaviors, so they will continue to make these attempts for longer than other students would. These students will need to see a *pattern* of behavior from you that shows them (not tells them) that when you say you will hold them accountable, you will. Remember that the

lowest number that denotes a pattern is three. For even relatively difficult students, take for granted that they won't even consider changing their behavior until they receive a DLO three times for that single behavior. For these students, whether or not they see these patterns that are necessary to hold them accountable can be a matter of life or death. And whether or not you can establish this inevitability in the first two months of the school year will determine whether or not you can do and enjoy your job for the rest of the year.

What Is the Role of School Administration in the DLO Process?

In the DLO process, administrators do not initially deal with disciplinary issues in response to the negative behaviors of students. Having an administrator take a primary role with discipline in a school is an inherently dysfunctional arrangement that, by definition, actively encourages negative behaviors. Students who attempt to get what they want through negative behaviors are almost always trying to get some combination of control, attention, or avoidance of a person or a thing, and that "thing" is usually work. What does a student get when a teacher sends them to an administrator as a reaction to their negative behaviors? Some combination of attention, control, and avoidance. The behavior is reinforced. When this dynamic plays out every single day for 180 days per year, the result is some level of chaos accidentally created by well-meaning people who have had no instruction or guidance on changing this dynamic.

Of course, this manual is that instruction and guidance. It doesn't matter if you are the only teacher in your school using this manual. You don't need anyone else. As someone who did not call on help from an administrator even once in a decade of using these procedures and strategies, I can tell you that if you explain to your administrator that you will be handling all of your own discipline, they will tend to love that arrangement, and they may even be very flexible in not asking you to enforce the "systems" that others may be required to use that are far less effective than the contents of this book.

Administrators reading this book should keep reading for ways to support teachers in their efforts to create a positive, prosocial school.

Strategic Noticing

Difficult students, almost by definition, have had great success using negative behaviors to get attention, control, and avoidance. Traditional discipline puts school administrators in the unenviable position of reinforcing those negative behaviors by reacting to them, systematically, giving students attention, control, and avoidance. Instead of reacting to negative behaviors by reinforcing them, administrators can flip the script and use consistent Strategic Noticing to systematically *prevent* negative behaviors.

Therefore, the most important job of an administrator is to move throughout the school and use Strategic Noticing 600 times per day to recondition the school in this regard. Six hundred instances of Strategic Noticing may sound like a lot, but it is not. Most administrators, especially ones that work with at-risk populations, react to negative behaviors with warnings, lectures, and threats far more than 600 times a day. Therefore, the choice is whether the administrator is going to systematically *prevent* negative behaviors or react to and thereby *reinforce* negative behaviors.

Supporting Teachers When Parents Complain

Using the contents of this manual will put teachers in a good position for dealing with parents for obvious reasons. These are best practices that don't involve anger or punishment. Still, there will always be parents who complain about teacher practices, even when they are best practices. The most common complaints will be from parents who do not understand DLOs and view them as punitive. Even after an initial parent communication letter and corresponding conversations about the contents of this book (see Chapter 8), they may not fully understand the instructional and nonpunitive nature of DLOs. Often, parents "fill in the blanks" of their non-understanding with the memories of their own school experiences, which probably involved punitive measures. If a parent has a complaint and is unsatisfied with a teacher's answer, administrators should support the use of DLOs, using the same techniques as the teacher.

Coordinating DLOs

Administrators can help teachers coordinate with colleagues regarding DLOs. Batching DLOs or scheduling times and locations for DLO sessions can be a helpful and very much appreciated service that administrators can manage.

Acting as a DLO Location Substitute

Similarly, teachers should staff DLO locations if possible, so that they have an opportunity to build relationships with students and families and demonstrate that they are the ultimate authority figures in the lives of these students at school. If the logistics of staffing prevents teachers from being able to do so, however, administrators can help by taking on this responsibility.

Delivering Students

As a part of a plan for DLO implementation, administrators can participate by delivering students to a DLO location. This should be done in a friendly way. Remember, DLOs are not punishment; the administrator is just escorting the student to a lesson. The administrator does not need to know anything about the nature of the DLO or the DLO-worthy behavior, nor should they discuss it with the student. The administrator should give a friendly ESPN Greeting and engage in friendly conversation, and an Argument Shield should be used to deal with any student's attempts at argument. The administrator is not in charge of this situation; they are merely acting as a delivery service for the educator receiving the student.

Attending DLO Meetings and *The Classroom Behavior Manual* Book Club Meetings

Administrators should be firmly aligned with staff by attending DLO meetings, but they do not need to lead the meetings. In fact, it is often most helpful for them not to. Having another staff member in charge allows for a leader to arise naturally from the staff. This also makes it less likely that the parties involved—educators, students, and parents—will feel that an administrator is "in charge of discipline" when they should not be.

Doing Their Own DLOs

When DLO-worthy behaviors happen away from teachers and in front of an administrator (typically in a common area), the administrator is now the primary authority figure. It is their responsibility to delay and then give the DLO.

What If Students Seem to Be Enjoying Themselves?

A common sign that you are using the DLO process correctly is that, due to the lack of anger, lectures, and threats, students may remark that they enjoy the solving of a problem or the practicing of a behavior. This is a wonderful outcome! Educators who are used to using anger and punishments may feel uncomfortable about this. They may have, deep in their bones, a feeling—not even a thought, but a feeling—that students should be in pain if they do something they shouldn't do. If this happens to you, let that feeling go! Students may or may not feel that a DLO is painful or boring, or that they would rather be doing something else, or they may not. The pain is not the point: *the learning is the point!*

If students are enjoying themselves, use the circumstances to further build relationships with them. For example, if you have a student who purposely broke pencil leads sharpen 30 pencils for you, and she mentions that she loves sharpening pencils, tell her that you are happy to hear that and that you have hundreds of pencils that she could sharpen during noninstructional time. If she agrees, great! You will get lots of pencils sharpened. Make a huge deal about it when she is done. Shake her hand and go on and on about how helpful she's been! If she declines the offer, it is highly likely that she was just trying to manipulate you by implying that she is not affected by this DLO, and you have called her bluff in a kind, calm way. Either way, you have handled the situation with calm empathy.

How and When Do I Communicate with Parents About DLOs?

Because we are teaching instead of punishing, and because parent communication is an extra thing that takes time and energy, parent communication about DLOs should be kept to a minimum. Treat DLOs as the learning situation that they are. You would not need to tell parents about every single struggle their child is having with trigonometry, and you should not (and could not) tell parents about every struggle their student is having with walking through the hallway silently. For reasons that have already been discussed, students should be able to participate in multiple DLOs without notifying parents.

Parents should be notified about learning regarding their children's behavior for the same reasons that parents should be notified regarding their children's learning of academics: when they are beginning to fall behind the rest of the class in a significant way. This should be done in a way that does not ask the parent for help but is merely informative:

> Hi, Mr. Kiely. It's Mr. Jones from school. I pet your dog two weeks ago in your front yard. I want you to know that I'm not going to make this a problem for you, and I don't need you to do anything, but Charlie has really been stressing me out by talking to his friends while I'm trying to teach. I get stressed out because it's my job to teach my students, and I just can't when he's talking while I'm teaching. As you know, I don't

punish kids, and I don't get angry. He has been spending his recesses off and on for the last two weeks taking away the stress that he created by doing work around the classroom for me. This solves the problem of me being stressed out, which I appreciate. I'm sure he is going to mature into someone who stops causing this problem. I just wanted you to know that he's falling behind the rest of the class in his ability to not cause problems. I would want to know this as a parent, but there's nothing that you need to do about it. I'm sorry to take your time, and I know Charlie's going to get the hang of this!

If it fits in with your or your team's plans, and if it is convenient for you, this may be a time to ask if it is convenient to arrange for before-school or after-school or weekend DLO time. Many teachers complain of parents not being flexible in this regard. In the context of anger and punishment, this is understandable; most parents do not like to inconvenience themselves so that their child can be angrily punished. Look at the suggested script for communicating with parents above. Would you be amenable to work with a teacher who used the DLO process and explained it that way? Probably. Most parents will gladly agree to the calm teaching of positive behaviors by a kind, loving adult—and to getting an hour of free babysitting to boot!

Putting It All Together: A Scenario

The following DLO process was used with two high school students who got into a fistfight during the teacher's fifth period class. They were removed from the school for safety reasons. The DLO took place the next day as an alternative to further out-of-school suspension. This is how the teacher delivered the entire DLO, from start to finish.

Note that such a DLO involves planning, and it should only be done after approval from a principal and all appropriate school administrators, and perhaps even a school lawyer. It may seem like a good deal of work, but implementing this DLO versus punishing students with suspension or expulsion could circumvent the school-to-prison pipeline and be the difference between life and death.

> The teacher is in a seated assertive position as the principal calmly delivers the two high school juniors to the teacher's classroom. It is 30 minutes before school is to begin.
>
> "Hey, fellas," the teacher greets them. "It is good to have you back. I was so sad to see you guys punching each other yesterday. I was sad to

know that you had to leave and go home so we could keep you guys and the other students safe. Right now, you two are really struggling with being peaceful and calm around each other. Since you are in four of each other's classes, as well as a study hall and lunch, this is an important skill for you to master. I don't know what's going on with you guys, and frankly, it's none of my business. All that is my business is that you learn this skill for the sake of everyone's safety. I am going to have you guys practice being safe and peaceful around each other. You will be able to rejoin the school's general population as soon as you have mastered this skill. Feel free to hate and despise each other as much as you would like. All you have to do is not be violent. How long do you need to practice not hurting each other, two days or three days?"

"Two days."

"OK, two days it is. The way that you will practice is that you will sit next to each other for two days. If you can manage to not hurt each other for those two days, you will have shown me that you are experts at not hurting each other, and you can go back to living your lives. The problem is that right now, I'd be crazy to just have you guys sit next to each other, because every indication leads me to believe that you are not experts at being peaceful, and I'd rather you two not hurt each other. So I'm going to have you practice this like you are playing a video game, with levels, starting with "easy" level, then "medium" level, then "difficult" level, and ending with "boss" level.

"Here's how this will go: The easy level will involve you guys sitting next to each other on either side of a brick wall. In a minute, we are going to go over to the elementary wing. I have arranged for you guys to sit on either side of a wall between two 2nd grade classrooms. Please understand that I am not trying to embarrass you or imply that you were acting like 2nd graders or anything like that. Actually, the opposite is true: I'm taking you guys over there because I didn't want to embarrass you by having you do this around your friends. The easy level will take all day today. As long as you can pass the easy level today by not causing any problems or hurting each other or trying to break down the wall to get at each other, you will report here tomorrow for instructions on the medium, difficult, and boss levels. You can do old schoolwork, read, stare off into space, or whatever you want to do that involves silently practicing being nonviolent while seated in the back of a classroom. You can't do any other work that you are missing until you get back to your classes, though. No sleeping, because you can't sleep and practice at the same time. No one will talk to you. You will be left to practice with no distractions. Your lunch will be delivered to you. I'm going to walk you over to 2nd grade now."

The teacher walks the students over to the elementary wing while building relationships by chatting and relaxing with the students. If either student has any issues, he repeats the easy level while the other student temporarily goes back to class, since this DLO is a two-person practice situation. If both students have issues, they both repeat the easy level. If both pass the easy level, they report the next day as planned.

Every 40 minutes or so, an adult should notice the positive target behavior by saying, "I noticed you being peaceful." This should continue throughout the levels.

If the students are successful with the easy level, at the end of the day, the teacher should congratulate the students for passing the level and instruct them to report back the next day. The next day, they will be greeted with the following:

"OK, easy level cleared! Today you have an opportunity to clear the medium, difficult, and boss levels. The medium level involves you both sitting in Mrs. Shaw's office, on opposite sides of the room. You will practice being around each other, this time without a wall between you. The difficult level involves you sitting in her office but next to each other. These levels are completed just like the easy level: do whatever you want without standing, sleeping, napping, or talking. Before I tell you about the boss level, you guys need to decide how long you need to spend on the medium level: three hours or four?"

"Three."

"Three it is. OK, the boss level will be different. The boss level will only be 30 minutes in which you will be sitting next to each other in the assistant principal's office while he completes some work, and you won't be allowed to do work. You can sit silently, or if you want to challenge yourselves, you can talk to each other. You don't have to, though, as long as you can sit silently, talk pleasantly, or both. If you fail at the medium or difficult level, you won't get to the boss level, and you'll redo whichever levels you failed tomorrow. If you succeed, you will be showing me that you are experts at being peaceful with each other, and you can get back to real life tomorrow. It's all up to you guys."

The teacher holds the students accountable by allowing them to fail or succeed at practicing effectively and reapplying practice time if and when needed. Once students have passed the boss level, the teacher says the following:

"It looks like you did it! You've completed the boss level. Are you guys experts at being peaceful with each other?"

"Yes."

"All right. I did notice how peaceful you guys have been over the course of the last two days. [Shake students' hands.] I am glad to have you guys back in school! I'll see you tomorrow."

This DLO and the planning for all of the necessary logistics allows the teacher to build relationships with students through their negative behaviors, instead of instituting a punishment that will inevitably hurt their relationship.

When Do I Use a GGI and When Do I Use a DLO?

The answer to this question might surprise you: it isn't tremendously important, so don't get stressed out about which one you choose in any given situation. The reason for this is that, regardless of whether you choose a GGI or notify a student of a DLO, you have done no harm, and any harm or unfairness that you might cause in the future can still be reversed if necessary. This is by design.

Imagine you are teaching in a 7th grade classroom and, arriving at a Power Position, you see what appears to be two students, seated next to each other, playing tug-of-war with an unidentifiable object. It appears that they are both trying to discreetly pull the object from the other's grip below desk level.

What you do not know is that Student A had been rooting around in Student B's desk while you were at another Power Position, from which you could not observe this activity. Having found a stress ball, Student A started to remove it from the desk of Student B. At that point, Student B realized that he was being robbed, and you are now witnessing the ensuing tug-of-war.

You now have a choice to notify the students of a DLO or use a GGI. Let's say that you use a GGI. You keep teaching while using GGIs #5 and #6: Reactive Movement and Hover. Let's say, just for the sake of the scenario, the tug-of-war stops, and life goes on. Of course, if the behavior continues or starts up again, you can pick another GGI or go to a DLO.

Notice that, if you had all of the information, you would probably use your delaying script in order to inform Student A that there would be a DLO coming in the future. The fact of the matter, however, is that teachers often don't have all of the necessary information, which causes traditional discipline to put teachers in impossible situations (more on that in a moment).

Even though most teachers would want to give a DLO, the use of a GGI stopped the behavior without you having to stop teaching: the GGI accomplished its goal! In addition, later, during noninstructional time, you can always get more information and enact a DLO if necessary. You can also make sure stolen property is returned.

Conversely, if you notify both students of a DLO and move on with teaching, it is likely to stop the behavior, even though you have made what could be called a mistake by notifying an innocent student of a DLO. That student may request due process, or not, and then this can be worked out later during noninstructional time. Either way, the use of a GGI or DLO does not require you to stop teaching and allows you to "fix it later" if your assessment of the situation was incomplete or wrong. This is just another example of how GGIs and DLOs can make your life far less stressful.

Let's use this scenario to compare the GGI/DLO model with the traditional discipline model involving verbal demands and immediate punishments. While both GGIs and DLOs are good options, having to choose between demands or punishments puts educators in an impossible situation. A demand such as "Stop messing with each other!" is almost guaranteed to inspire (understandable) arguments or explosive behaviors and is 100 percent certain to stop instruction. If an immediate punishment is used, like sending one or both students to the principal, it is possible that you could be "convicting" an innocent person! Traditional discipline fails once again.

The second, perhaps more helpful answer to the question of when to use GGIs and when to use DLOs is that GGIs should be used with small behaviors that aren't making it significantly difficult for students to learn and for you to teach. This means that whether you choose to use a DLO or GGI will depend upon you and what you are able to tolerate. It will depend upon what your "hot button" behaviors are. If a certain behavior drives you crazy, it needs to earn that student a one-way ticket to a DLO. A behavior that gets a student a DLO in your class may not get one in mine, simply because that behavior doesn't bother me as much as it does you. For instance, note passing may drive you crazy. It happens to not bother me very much. Therefore, you would use a DLO, while I would use a GGI. This is another example of taking care of your sanity so you can take care of your class. If a behavior makes it too difficult to teach at an optimal level, you need to train it away with a DLO.

While note passing may not be particularly bothersome to me, if I have used four or five interventions over a two-day period for note passing, it is probably a good idea for me also to move to a DLO. Any behavior that you feel is very serious or is causing any type of major problem for other people (including you) should generate a DLO. Remember, though, that the PLOs woven into the Real-World Workshop procedure provide learning opportunities for students refusing to do work, so there is no reason to ever use DLOs for this!

✢ ✢ ✢ ✢ ✢ ✢ ✢ ✢ ✢ ✢ ✢ ✢

Individual students may arrive at school with profoundly different experiences. The Michaels of the world have had profound trauma. The Mykeshas have had none. The Mykeshas of the world have been taught and trained by their parents and caregivers to use positive, prosocial behaviors. The Michaels of the world have not.

While the demands and punishments of traditional discipline perpetuate inequity, the use of Gentle Guidance Interventions and Delayed Learning Opportunities creates equity, making them essential elements of this manual.

Conclusion: It Starts with You

You are the hero of this story.

Heroes are those who know that there is a job to be done and set themselves to do it. The job is not seen as a job at all, but as a higher calling, a responsibility: something that *must* be done. A hero's life will feel incomplete if that calling is left unheeded.

That is why whether it is *possible* to do the job that needs to be done is irrelevant to the hero. Indeed, if someone is called to do something, they will get the job done or die trying. At the start of a teaching career, teachers rarely know how they will be successful. They just know that they are called to help students. They think, "I'll have to figure this out. I have no choice."

This book is for the heroes who just need the right support and the right tools to heed their calling. I wrote it because it is the tool that I needed but did not have at the beginning of my career.

Heroes know that change starts with them. Teachers know that it is their behavior, what they do, that can mold their students into people who can be successful, happy, and healthy. This book is simply a manual for exactly how educators should behave so that they can be the best hero that they can be.

You now have the tool and the power to change your behavior.

Once you change your behavior, you can change the behaviors of your students.

Once your students change their behaviors, they can change the world.

It starts with you . . . right now.

Acknowledgments

There is no possible way that this book would have ever been completed without my wife, Jessica Ervin. Her talents as a teacher of children, an editor, a collaborator, a critic, a mother, a thinker, a problem solver, and a person who always knows where I left my keys made this book what it is. She put at least as much effort into the creation of this manual as I did. I love you, Jess.

We couldn't have written this book without our daughter, Violet Ervin. She was always understanding when we had to work long hours on this book and was patient when conversations at the dinner table would drift to work, to editing, or to the book's content. I love you, Vi, and I am inspired by who you are and who you will become.

Bob Sornson, your wisdom knows no bounds. Your mentorship guided me before, during, and, hopefully, after publishing this book. Our conversations led me to greater understandings of what it is that I am working toward and what this book should be.

To my mentor, Jim Fay. All I ever wanted to be was a teacher and a dad. Without you, I wouldn't have been very good at either. This book could never have been written without you because, without you, I would not have survived my third year of teaching. When they write about the most important people in the history of education, anything without your name will be incomplete.

Bill Pflaum, your singular genius enabled you to see an actual book within my original "angry manifesto." Your insight, advice, selfless hard work, brilliant ideas, and wisdom transformed this manual from something barely readable into something a publisher would be interested in.

Chris Dendy is a fantastic editor and author who understood our work and made it so much better. Thank you, Chris.

To Genny Ostertag, Allison Scott, Megan Doyle, and the entire team at ASCD for seeing the value in the book, for your expertise, for your know-how, your hard work, and your enthusiasm. I value our partnership, and I know that we will change the world together!

To my mother, Anice Ervin. Mom, you told me once that I had to be great. I heard what you said and understood what you meant. You inspire me to be a better person, which made this book possible.

To all K–12 educators. This book was not just written *for* you—it was written *by* you. I created these strategies and procedures from watching other teachers' best practices that worked but were not written down anywhere. I improved them, systematized them, and created something new and comprehensive in scope. Teachers are the experts. Behavioral leadership is a trade: something that you *do*, not something that you merely *know about*. This is a trade manual, created by and for educators.

References

American Academy of Pediatrics. (2014). *Adverse childhood experiences and the lifelong consequences of trauma*. Retrieved from https://www.aap.org/en-us/Documents/ttb_aces_consequences.pdf

Balfanz, R., Byrnes, V., & Fox, J. (2014). Sent home and put off-track: The antecedents, disproportionalities, and consequences of being suspended in the ninth grade. *Journal of Applied Research on Children: Informing Policy for Children at Risk, 5*(2), article 13. Retrieved from https://digitalcommons.library.tmc.edu/childrenatrisk/vol5/iss2/13

Brehm, S. S., & Brehm, J. W. (1981). *Psychological reactance: A theory of freedom and control.* New York: Academic Press.

Eley, T. (2009, October 13). One in ten US high school dropouts incarcerated. World Socialist Web Site. Retrieved from https://www.wsws.org/en/articles/2009/10/drop-o13.html

McCombs, B. (2010). Developing responsible and autonomous learners: A key to motivating students. American Psychological Association. Retrieved from https://www.apa.org/education/k12/learners

Public Safety Performance Projects. (2009, March 2). One in 31: The long reach of American corrections. Pew Trusts. Retrieved from https://www.pewtrusts.org/en/research-and-analysis/reports/2009/03/02/one-in-31-the-long-reach-of-american-corrections

Index

The letter *f* following a page number denotes a figure.

About the Author

 Scott Ervin has worked with kids for more than two decades. Most of his experience has been spent working with extremely difficult, at-risk, abused, and neglected kids. For the last 11 years of his teaching career, he requested that all of the most difficult kids in the grade be placed in his classroom as a teacher and in his building as a principal and superintendent. For the last five of those years, he worked at one of the largest primary schools in the United States and requested that all of the most difficult kids out of 400 3rd graders be placed on his class roster. In addition, students in other classrooms whose behavior made it impossible for others to learn in their assigned classrooms throughout the year were all moved to Scott's room.

Scott has served as a principal, superintendent, and discipline specialist. The classrooms in which he has worked had poverty rates between 84 and 98 percent. As a consultant and founder of Ervin Educational Consulting, Scott has traveled the country teaching parents and educators alike how to be calm and assertive with children.

Scott has a Bachelor of Arts in political science and a master's degree in education. He has taught classroom management as an adjunct professor at Antioch University Midwest and as a visiting lecturer at Ohio University, University of Dayton, and Wright State University. He also writes a syndicated newspaper column, "Ask the Kid Whisperer." To hire a behavioral consultant or for more information, go to www.ervineducationalconsulting.com or email support@ervineducationalconsulting.com.

Related ASCD Resources: Classroom Management

At the time of publication, the following resources were available (ASCD stock numbers in parentheses).

Print Products

Better Behavior Practices (Quick Reference Guide) by Dominique Smith, Nancy Frey, Douglas Fisher, and Lee Ann Jung (#QRG120049)

Better Than Carrots or Sticks: Restorative Practices for Positive Classroom Management by Dominique Smith, Douglas Fisher, and Nancy Frey (#116005)

Building a Positive and Supportive Classroom (Quick Reference Guide) by Julie Causton and Kate MacLeod (#QRG120098)

Discipline with Dignity: How to Build Responsibility, Relationships, and Respect in Your Classroom, 4th Edition by Richard L. Curwin, Allen N. Mendler, and Brian Mendler (#118018)

From Behaving to Belonging: The Inclusive Art of Supporting Students Who Challenge Us by Julie Causton and Kate MacLeod (#121011)

Motivating and Managing Student Behavior with Dignity (Quick Reference Guide) by Allen N. Mendler and Brian Mendler (#QRG119048)

So Each May Soar: The Principles and Practices of Learner-Centered Classrooms by Carol Ann Tomlinson (#118006)

We Belong: 50 Strategies to Create Community and Revolutionize Classroom Management by Laurie Barron and Patti Kinney (#122002)

For up-to-date information about ASCD resources, go to **www.ascd.org**. You can search the complete archives of *Educational Leadership* at **www.ascd.org/el**.

ASCD myTeachSource®

Download resources from a professional learning platform with hundreds of research-based best practices and tools for your classroom at http://myteachsource .ascd.org

For more information, send an email to member@ascd.org; call 1-800-933-2723 or 703-578-9600; send a fax to 703-575-5400; or write to Information Services, ASCD, 1703 N. Beauregard St., Alexandria, VA 22311-1714 USA.

WHOLE CHILD
TENETS

1 HEALTHY
Each student enters school healthy and learns about and practices a healthy lifestyle.

2 SAFE
Each student learns in an environment that is physically and emotionally safe for students and adults.

3 ENGAGED
Each student is actively engaged in learning and is connected to the school and broader community.

4 SUPPORTED
Each student has access to personalized learning and is supported by qualified, caring adults.

5 CHALLENGED
Each student is challenged academically and prepared for success in college or further study and for employment and participation in a global environment.

ascd whole child

The ASCD Whole Child approach is an effort to transition from a focus on narrowly defined academic achievement to one that promotes the long-term development and success of all children. Through this approach, ASCD supports educators, families, community members, and policymakers as they move from a vision about educating the whole child to sustainable, collaborative actions.

The Classroom Behavior Manual relates to the **safe** and **engaged** tenets.

For more about the ASCD Whole Child approach, visit **www.ascd.org/wholechild.**